10.15.

The Canadian Career of the Fourth Earl of Minto

The Education of a Viceroy

Carman Miller

The Governor-General of Canada was an influential political figure of major significance at the turn of the century. The Fourth Earl of Minto, who held this office from 1898 to 1904, is regarded by some Canadian historians as a romantic hero and by others as a bungling instrument of British imperialist designs. According to the author of this monograph, he was neither. Aided by an examination of Minto's early life and personal character and an analysis of the existing political institutions, the author describes the way in which Minto discharged his duties as Governor-General during this period of political change in Canada and Britain.

Informative and well documented, the study will be useful to students of Canadian history and politics.

Carman Miller is the Chairman and Associate Professor in the History Department at McGill University. He holds the Ph.D. degree from King's College, University of London. His previous publications include articles focusing on the career of Sir Frederick Borden, a Minister of Militia at the time of the Fourth Earl of Minto, and Canada's participation in the South African War during Minto's term of office as Governor-General.

The Canadian Career of the Fourth Earl of Minto

The Education of a Viceroy

Carman Miller

The Canadian Career of the Fourth Earl of Minto

The Education of a Viceroy

Carman Miller

Wilfrid Laurier University Press

Canadian Cataloguing in Publication Data

Miller, Carman, 1940-
    The Canadian career of the Fourth Earl of Minto

Bibliography: p.
ISBN 0-88920-078-5

1. Minto, Gilbert John Elliot-Murray-Kynynmound, 4th Earl of, 1845-
1914. 2. Governors general — Canada — Biography.* 3. Canada — Politics and government — 1896-1911.* I. Title.

FC551.M55M55   971.05'6'0924   C79-094907-5
F1033.M55M55

27,747

Copyright © 1980
WILFRID LAURIER UNIVERSITY PRESS
Waterloo, Ontario, Canada   N2L 3C5
79 80 81 82 4 3 2 1

Table of Contents

List of Photographs ix

Introduction 1

Chapter One   The Aristocratic Vision 7

Chapter Two   The Canadian Apprenticeship 24

Chapter Three   The Search for Place 39

Chapter Four   The Office 51

Chapter Five   The Wooden Governor 60

Chapter Six   The Heavy Dragoon 80

Chapter Seven   The Imperial Pro-Consul 96

Chapter Eight   The Defence of Empire 119

Chapter Nine   The Defence of Canada 131

Chapter Ten   The Pursuit of Continental Concord 156

Chapter Eleven   The Shadow of Monarchy 172

viii / *Table of Contents*

Conclusion 192

Bibliography 197

Index 213

List of Photographs

Plate 1. Lord Minto in civilian attire x

Plate 2. Photograph of a painting of Minto by L. Galarneau
which formerly hung in the Montreal Hunt Club xi

Plate 3. Lady Minto, considered by *Vanity Fair* among Britain's best-dressed women xii

Plate 4. Lady Minto and her two eldest daughters, Eileen (born
in Canada) and Ruby xiii

Plate 5. Publication of photos picturing the Mintos in furs
aroused the ire of Canadians wishing to erase the
country's nordic image xiv

Plate 1. Lord Minto in civilian attire

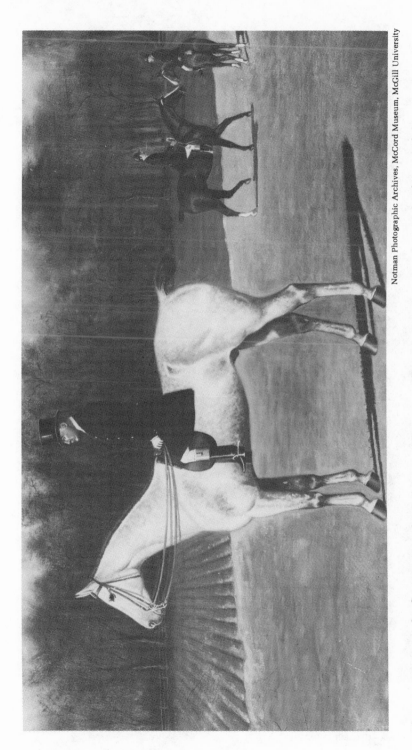

Plate 2.   Photograph of a painting of Minto by L. Galarneau which formerly hung in the Montreal Hunt Club

Plate 3. Lady Minto, considered by *Vanity Fair* among Britain's best-dressed women

Plate 4.   Lady Minto and her two eldest daughters, Eileen (born in Canada) and Ruby

Plate 5. Publication of photos picturing the Mintos in furs aroused the ire of
Canadians wishing to erase the country's nordic image

Introduction

Except for his noble birth, there was little in the early career of the fourth Earl of Minto to suggest the making of an imperial statesman. A poor scholar, distrustful of politicians and impatient with democratic institutions, Minto seemed to prefer horses and soldiers to studying constitutions or laying cornerstones. Ambitious but undistinguished in British public life, he sought and received two important imperial appointments, the Governor-Generalship of Canada (1898-1904) and the Viceroyalty of India (1905-10). These two important positions finally provided him with the prestige and responsibility he craved.

Historical circumstances have made Minto's Canadian administration one of unusual interest. The rising tide of imperial sentiment, the South African war, the Alaskan boundary settlement, Joseph Chamberlain's campaign for an imperial tariff preference, the controversial firing of two British General Officers commanding the Canadian militia, and the British government's abandonment of the naval defence of British North America all combined to make the subject of Canada's imperial relations one of primary public importance during Minto's term as Governor-General. By virtue of his office, in all of these issues Minto occupied a very conspicuous position. Despite his lack of training or experience, his character guaranteed that he would try to become something more than an idle but interested observer.

Historians' assessments of Minto's Canadian career have followed two quite different lines of argument. His defenders base their case on an interpretation first outlined by John Buchan in his book, Lord Minto: A Memoir, published in 1924 and written at the request of the late Earl's family.[1] According to Buchan, Minto was a romantic adventurer and hero, not unlike the characters who peopled Buchan's novels. In Buchan's mind Minto was a type of Tory-democrat, whose common sense and broad humanity enabled him to "read more clearly the hearts of the plain man than the plain man's official exponents."[2] He saw Minto as a correct constitutional ruler, familiar with the precepts of Alpheus Todd's Parliamentary Government in the British Colonies, a viceroy who fearlessly defended imperial and Canadian interests against a dictatorial Prime Minister and his corrupt Cabinet colleagues.

On the other hand, the members of the "Liberal-Nationalist" school of Canadian history, particularly J. W. Dafoe, O. D. Skelton, and L.-O. David, have described Minto as a country squire and "heavy dragoon," untrained in constitutional law and practice. They have seen Minto as a man chosen by an aggressive Colonial Secretary, Joseph Chamberlain, to be the instrument of the Colonial Secretary's policy to entangle Canada in an expensive network of imperial obligations against which Laurier struggled heroically for six years in defence of Canadian autonomy. According to this school, Minto was the villain rather than the hero; he was the incompetent, bungling imperial pro-Consul, not Buchan's wise, sensible colonial administrator saving Canadians from themselves.

Minto's Canadian career is neither the success story of a born leader of men nor the tale of an imperial conspirator. When Minto became Governor-General in 1898, despite his brief apprenticeship as Lord Lansdowne's Military Secretary (1883-85), "he was absolutely untrained in constitutional practice."[3] His undistinguished early career, as a jockey and occasional military adventurer, his distrust of politics and politicians, and his impatience with democratic institutions scarcely suggest the making of an imperial statesman. Minto's initial blunders, particularly his partisan and ill-advised defence of Major-General E. T. H. Hutton's contentious conduct, were the result of his lack of knowledge, experience, and judgment, coupled with his desire to make a reputation in Canadian public life which he had failed to achieve in Britain, not the execution of a well-laid imperial conspiracy.

In spite of the assumptions of the Canadian Liberal-Nationalist historians, Minto was not a Chamberlain appointee and he frequently disapproved of the Colonial Secretary's policies. When Minto quarrelled with the Canadian government, the Colonial Office often deplored his actions and supported the Canadian government's position. Minto belonged to neither the Imperial Federation League nor its

[1] Janet Adam Smith, John Buchan (Toronto, 1965), 231.
[2] John Buchan, Lord Minto: A Memoir (London, 1924), 121.
[3] O. D. Skelton, Life and Letters of Sir Wilfrid Laurier, vol. 2 (Toronto, 1965), 207.

successor, the Imperial Federation (Defence) Committee, and he only joined the Royal Colonial Institute in 1898, the year he became Governor-General. Except for a brief period during the South African war, he distrusted formal schemes of imperial reorganization. Minto believed that Canada's survival in the North American context depended upon British military, economic, and cultural assistance as a solid guarantee against continental absorption. He also felt that self-interest and sentiment, not constitutions and legal obligations, were the Empire's strongest ties, and cooperation, not integration, the best means to achieve imperial unity.

Although this study is not a biography it does attempt to see Minto in a biographical perspective. To a certain extent this course has been dictated by Minto, his friends, and his critics. Minto's forceful intervention in public affairs has evoked both praise and abuse but no general agreement on the main lines of his character. Indeed, sometimes it would appear as though two writers were describing two quite different men. Unfortunately, the Buchan biography, which the author himself described as "perfunctory . . . unjust and captious," is an unreliable authority.[4] Consequently this study has re-examined Minto's early years in order to focus more effectively on Minto, the man; and thereby attempt to assess the impact of his personal character upon his Canadian career.

While personal character doubtlessly transforms institutions, it is also true that institutions influence and mould behaviour. An assessment of Minto's Canadian career, therefore, requires an understanding of the institutional framework within which he performed his official functions. Minto occupied a unique position in Canadian political life. For six years he was Canada's Governor-General, and in 1898 the office of Governor-General was considerably more important than it has since become. Moreover, the office itself was in a period of transition.

Given the nature of the office and the times, that is to say the pivotal position of the Governor-General in the network of imperial communications and the crucial period of imperial evolution, an examination of Minto's Canadian career provides considerable insight into the mechanics of imperial administration. As such it helps to dispel many unfounded but firmly entrenched myths surrounding the methods and intentions of British administration as applied to Canada.

This study is based primarily on three collections of manuscript papers: the Laurier Papers, the Minto Papers, and the Colonial Office 42 series. Although Canadian scholars have thoroughly mined the Laurier Papers, this collection still remains an indispensable source of information. The Minto Papers at the National Library of Scotland contain two important sections of material unavailable on microfilm

---

[4] Robert Laird Borden Papers, Public Archives of Canada, John Buchan to Sir Robert Borden, August 25, 1932. In reply to Borden's stinging criticism, Buchan confessed that his Canadian chapters were the weakest in his book and promised to revise them should the book ever be reprinted.

in Ottawa, Minto's Diary and a comprehensive, three-volume scrapbook of newspaper clippings related to his Canadian career. Perhaps the single most useful collection for this study is the Colonial Office 42 series. Past writers have often depended too heavily on the Governor-General's numbered files, which contain the final polished version of Colonial Office deliberations. Consequently, they have failed to appreciate the diversity of departmental and interdepartmental opinions contained in the Colonial Office collection.

One article and several books have contributed a good deal to this study. The first is scarcely a recent work but deserves special mention. In 1952, H. Pearson Gundy read a paper to the Canadian Historical Association's annual meeting entitled, "Sir Wilfrid Laurier and Lord Minto," in which he destroyed the fond Liberal myth that Minto forced the Canadian government to send troops to South Africa in 1899. Carl Berger's The Sense of Power, Desmond Morton's Ministers and Generals, Norman Penlington's Canada and Imperialism, 1896-1899, and Richard A. Preston's Canada and Imperial Defence have all increased my knowledge and influenced my interpretation of this period. In addition to these works, three studies of Minto's Indian administration served to convince me of the need, expressed over twenty-five years ago by C. P. Stacey, for a critical re-assessment of Minto's Canadian years.[5]

Finally, I wish to acknowledge the aid of several people and institutions. Generous financial assistance from the Independent Order of the Daughters of the Empire and the Canada Council enabled me to spend two useful years in the United Kingdom preparing the doctoral thesis upon which this study is based. Subsequently a Canada Council summer research grant gave me the opportunity to examine material in the National Library of Scotland relating to Minto's pre-Canadian career, more particularly the administration of his estates. The courteous and efficient service of the staff of the National Library of Scotland and the Public Archives of Canada made the task of research a very pleasant one indeed. I also wish to acknowledge the assistance of the staff of the Public Record Office and the British Museum. This book has been published with the help of a grant from the Social Science Federation of Canada, using funds provided by the Social Sciences and Humanities Research Council of Canada. The careful criticism, advice, and good humour of my thesis supervisor, Professor G. S. Graham, have improved both the argument and style of this study. Professor George Rawlyk of Queen's University has read this work at various stages of its evolution and has offered many useful criticisms and comments and much encouragement which I acknowledge with appreciation. I wish to thank Mrs. Margaret Blevins for the care and patience with which she typed this manuscript. Paula LaPierre's editorial suggestions have saved me from many

[5] M. N. Das, India Under Morley and Minto (London, 1964); Syed Razi Wasti, Lord Minto and the Indian Nationalist Movement, 1905 to 1910 (Oxford, 1964); Martin Gilbert, Servant of India (London, 1966); C. P. Stacey, "Canada and the Nile Expedition of 1884," Canadian Historical Review (December, 1952), 330.

errors. My wife, Pamela, read, criticized, typed, and endured with me the early drafts of this study. Finally, a very special thanks to Danielle, Marc, and Andrew whose contribution has been more real than apparent.

Moser's River, July, 1978   C. M.

Chapter One

The Aristocratic Vision

In 1845, the year of the future fourth Earl of Minto's birth, the shadow of great houses still fell upon the land. Conspicuously installed in the places of power and influence, the old British landed aristocracy seemed secure in the enjoyment of their ancient rights and privileges. Their habits and assumptions governed the acquisition and exercise of power and influence in the army, church, and state. But appearances were deceptive. An economic transition had already begun which was slowly eroding the bases of their power and prestige. Organized around the exploitation of coal, iron, and steam, the new industrial classes, with their own peculiar habits and assumptions, were challenging the old landed orders, forcing them to share, then concede, their historic claims to control and influence. The changing social and economic relationships created by an emerging industrial economy made accommodation a far from painless process for Britain's landed society, particularly for those who possessed only a precarious claim to rank and standing within that society. The social and economic tensions created by this conflict between the old and new orders helped shape the mind of the fourth Earl of Minto. Like so many men of his class and generation Minto resented the forces of change then radically reshaping the contours of Victorian Britain. Fortunately his death, early in 1914, spared him the spectacle of the Great War which finally destroyed the world of British landed society.[1]

The Minto (Elliot) family itself possessed no claim to ancient nobility, great wealth, or influence. Their relatively small estate of 16,071 acres, situated in Roxburghshire, close to the English border, entitled them to only a modest place in the hierarchy of titled landed society. Nor was their title consecrated by time or outstanding public service. Since the sixteenth century the Elliots, a small border family, had grown slowly but steadily from squirearchy to nobility, richly rewarded by the English during the dark days of border strife. In the United Kingdom their family fortunes continued to prosper as its members fattened themselves on the spoils of Whig patronage, propitious marriages, and hard work. By 1700 the Elliots had obtained a Scottish Barony. But they remained "paper Lords," to borrow John Buchan's phrase, until the fourth Baron became an Earl in 1806.[2] He received this advancement only after a long and distinguished career in law, diplomacy, and the lucrative colonial service, and a year before he won the greatest professional plum of his life, the Viceroyalty of India. Securely possessed of a title, the second Earl, apart from a brief appointment abroad as British ambassador to Berlin, confined his public activities to Britain. There, assisted by his marriage into the powerful Grey family, he gained a modest reputation in British politics. The career of his son, the third Earl, however, was far from illustrious. A shy, affable country gentleman, the third Earl possessed neither the desire nor the ability to achieve national prominence. Instead, he spent his time shepherding the precarious family fortunes which had been largely neglected by his father. The Minto family fortune had never been great, and despite the efforts of the third Earl, continued to be a cause of considerable anxiety to the family. Their own tenuous prosperity served to increase their concern over the erosion of the power and privilege of the landed class throughout the latter half of the nineteenth century.

Despite the truth of the old Arab adage that men resemble their times more than their fathers, there was a striking likeness between the third Earl and his eldest son, Gilbert John Kynynmound, the future fourth Earl of Minto. Small, tough, and competitive, Gilbert shared his father's passion for sports, games, and outdoor life. Both preferred horses, masculine company, manly sports, and adventure to debates, drawing rooms, and polite conversation. Frequently found in the company of his father, Gilbert absorbed much of his father's philosophy or, as his mother complained, "his Tory and old world habits."[3]

[1] F. M. L. Thompson, English Landed Society in the Nineteenth Century (Toronto, 1963), 1.

[2] Buchan, Lord Minto, xv.

[3] Minto Papers, National Library of Scotland, Lady Minto to Arthur Elliot, July 26, 1865.

The third Earl lived in a world governed by a "social settlement," based on rank and subordination, enforced by a code of gentlemanly conduct and a sense of service and responsibility. He considered his first responsibility to be the management of his estates ("lording," as he called it): keeping tenants' buildings in a habitable condition, remitting rents in years of poor harvests, building, supervising, and maintaining local libraries and educational facilities. Above all, he devoted careful attention to the local Whig politics of his shire.

In politics, the third Earl remained an orthodox Whig of the Palmerston vintage, increasingly restless with and often contemptuous of Gladstone's leadership of the Liberal party. Palmerston's "vision of a manly aristocratic country of free men, ready to teach foreigners their duty,"[4] agreed more with Minto's political philosophy than Gladstone's threatening concern with internal social and political reform. A man of parochial perspective, the third Earl confined his interests to local and regional problems. Defence of the Church of Scotland, reform of Scottish education, and changes in the poaching and gaming laws received his closest attention. As a member of the House of Commons and later of the Lords, he served his shire conscientiously, if somewhat unimaginatively.[5]

Gilbert shared his father's social perspective and his political philosophy. While his perception of social reality may have suited the generation of the third Earl, it became increasingly anachronistic during that of the fourth. Gilbert's early difficulties in finding a position suitable to one of his blood, breeding, and ambition only increased his resentment against the emerging new era and the men in places of power who failed to recognize his claims. In later years, in the company of soldiers and friends whose ambitions seemed similarly blocked, Gilbert's disdain was to develop into a more pointed critique of the emerging liberal, democratic age. Yet, even as a child at home he did not escape a broader, more liberal perspective.

His mother, Nina Elliot, a grand-niece of the first Earl, was a sensitive, articulate, and intelligent woman, a friend of literary men and statesmen. She was also an author of several good family histories, including an edition of the first Earl's correspondence, and a devoted Liberal.[6] Although physically weak and often ill, she possessed a strong, determined character and a consummate ambition for her four sons, particularly the eldest. She impressed him with the importance of success, duty, family, and place and never let him

---

[4] Keith Feiling, *A History of England* (London, 1952), 914. In G. W. T. Ormond, *The Lord Advocates of Scotland*, 2nd Series, 1834-80 (London, 1914), 192, Lord Minto is described as a "second Palmerston."

[5] The third Earl (1814-91) was Liberal Member of Parliament for Hyth (1837-41), Greenock (1847-52), Clockmannanshire (1857-59); and a Member of the Lords (1859-91). He was also Deputy Lieutenant of Roxburghshire and Chairman of the Board of Lunacy Commissioners for Scotland.

[6] Her publications included *Notes from Minto MSS* (1862); *A Memoir of the Right Honourable Hugh Elliot* (1868); *The Life and Letters of Sir Gilbert Elliot, 1st Earl of Minto* (1874).

forget the career of his illustrious great-grandfather, the first Earl. She also twitted Gilbert and his father about their antiquarian political views and attempted to give her son a broad, liberal education. Despite initial appearances, some of her admonitions were not entirely misplaced. For Gilbert had inherited his mother's ambition, restlessness, and interest in the wider world around him.

With what the St. James' Gazette much later described as one of "the finest libraries in the Northern Kingdom," Lady Minto took command of her four sons' pre-public school education.[7] She established a well-balanced curriculum of history, geography, biology, geology, languages, theatre, painting, and a form of ancestor worship consisting of the adventurous border tales popularized by Sir Walter Scott. Under her careful tutelage Minto Castle became a comprehensive and exacting academy. But from the start Gilbert's intellectual capacity proved disappointing. His interest and concentration were limited. He was, Lady Minto complained, "a little slower to quicken than the others," a child who displayed "a certain placidity and contentment which lived happily in the day and might foretell a lack of mental enterprise." She soon realized that his "learning will never be deep nor his energy great, nor is he remarkable either for originality or quickness." Yet he was "sensible, easily interested ... and will ... learn more when his learning is of a kind to his mind."[8] Gilbert never did meet his mother's exacting standards of academic excellence.

Lady Minto's second son, Arthur, the philosopher, as his family affectionately called him, displayed much greater intellectual promise. Handicapped by the loss of a leg in his early youth, Arthur spent a good deal of his time indoors with his mother. He shared her opinions, interests, and activities and absorbed much of her attention and ambition. Debate, writing, and public speaking, the essential tools of an aspiring public servant, became the foundation of his early education. Arthur had both the desire and capacity to fulfill his mother's ambitions but, unfortunately for her, he was not the eldest son.

In the autumn of 1859 Lady Minto relinquished the education of her two eldest sons to Eton. Sending Gilbert to Eton was not so much a decision as an assumption. Eton had been the alma mater of both his father and grandfather. Since then its reputation had not waned. Fired by the reforming zeal which had swept British public schools since the 1830s, Eton had considerably enhanced its renown as a training ground for the British ruling classes. Lady Minto hoped it would work its spell on Gilbert.

But Gilbert's first year at Eton was neither happy nor rewarding. Eton's regimented routine, order, and discipline proved a stark contrast to the freedom he had known at Minto Castle. Moreover, the death of his grandfather considerably disrupted life at home for a time; and academic studies provided little satisfaction since Arthur's superior performance always overshadowed Gilbert's best efforts. Nor

[7] St. James' Gazette, December 1, 1904.
[8] Buchan, Lord Minto, 6-7.

had Melgund (the title he assumed following his grandfather's death) yet attained an athletic reputation. In his first tub sculling race, he placed seventy-second. Painfully shy and self-conscious of his small stature, he developed a slight slouch, which his masters tried to correct. The long hours of tedious routine were filled by studying, stamp collecting, and writing long, illustrated letters home in which he humourously described the oddities of his masters. Even at fifteen, he possessed an eye for the amusing and the unusual, a quality which he retained throughout his life.

Within a year, however, Melgund preferred Eton to vacation. It was probably his new tutor at Eton, Edward Warre, who was responsible for this transformation. A future Eton headmaster, Warre epitomized the cult of athleticism which permeated British public school education at mid-century. According to the new doctrine, sports and games were the instruments for building the well-mannered, able-bodied English gentleman.[9] A staunch Protestant, Warre deplored "unbalanced intellect" and preached the virtues of military training and patriotism together with its vaunted attributes of loyalty, discipline, courage, and fair play.[10] Warre lived by Lord Rosebery's definition of an Eton education: "not the education of the brain, but the education of the character."[11] He had a profound influence upon Melgund's early development, and became and remained a trusted counsellor, friend, and something of a hero to Melgund.

Warre encouraged Melgund to develop his natural physical aptitude for sports and games. Soon racing, rowing, football, and cricket left little time for letters home. Melgund's stamina, determination and single-minded devotion inspired the admiration of his fellow students and tutors, and he soon possessed a host of friends. His sporting endeavours brought success and popularity, although they also brought increasingly poorer grades.

Melgund's mastery of sports and Eton's rules helped him to endure and then enjoy school life. Essentially hierarchical, the government of public schools constituted a model of English society. In the style of a strong constitutional monarch the Headmaster reigned supreme, advised by his masters who ruled through the sixth form. In the course of his school days, a student learned both how to give and to take orders. In short, the system taught him the habit of authority, which was structured, deferential, and orderly. As seniority gave Melgund the right and duty to enforce Eton's edicts, they soon seemed to him correct, natural, and indeed necessary.

However, academic failure terminated Melgund's happy school days somewhat prematurely. Although athletic prowess seemed to have pleased his indulgent father, Melgund's mother remained singularly unimpressed, and more than a little disturbed by his lack of academic progress. She had hoped that Eton would lead her son to a

[9] R. H. Tawney, *The Radical Tradition* (London, 1964), 60.

[10] Christopher Hollis, *Eton: A History* (London, 1960), 285, 288, 294 and 295.

[11] *The Times*, October 29, 1898.

public career. Now she feared that repeated failure might make this impossible. When Melgund was not promoted in 1861 and had an equally poor term in 1862, his mother withdrew him from Eton and placed him in the care of a German tutor for the autumn and winter of 1863. The tutor was a Hanoverian living in Dresden with his British-born wife. Under his strict supervision Melgund studied languages, history, mathematics, drawing, surveying, military tactics, and army organization. Obviously the family had abandoned all hope that Eton would work upon him its spell. They had other plans. In the summer of 1864 they brought Melgund back to Scotland and then placed him in the care of a crammer on the Isle of Wight to prepare him for entrance to Cambridge.

Melgund and Arthur entered Trinity College, Cambridge, as fellow commoners, in the autumn of 1864. Cambridge differed little from Eton except perhaps that its academic obligations were fewer and its freedom more ample. Although serious students—like Melgund's classmate, Lord Lorne—complained that the only useful things learned at Cambridge occurred after hours, Cambridge's academic shortcomings bothered Melgund little.[12] While there he led an academically undistinguished but happy social existence.

Riding constituted Melgund's chief Cambridge passion. During his initial year at Trinity he shared living quarters with his brother, Arthur. Later, drawn more closely to his riding companions, especially John "Cat" Richardson, his lifelong friend and racing mentor, Melgund moved to a famous set of apartments called French's. Here Cat presided, the reigning Cambridge racing king. "A visitor to his Cambridge rooms once asked for a book to pass the time of waiting, and was told by his servant that Mr. Richardson did not possess a book of any sort."[13] While Melgund remained in Cat's company, Lady Minto complained bitterly of her son's lack of intellectual development.

Melgund left university in 1867. At Cambridge his only real achievements had been in riding. He had won the Cambridge trophy, the gold whip, and the third Trinity mile race. He also held the singular distinction of having been the "only man who has ever taken his bachelor's degree in racing kit."[14] It was typical of his academic career. He had a race that afternoon and had no time to change his attire between obligations. Therefore he cloaked his riding breeches in an academic gown.

However, the purpose of his Cambridge career had never been academic. Long before he left Cambridge his future career had been decided. Lack of interest precluded an ecclesiastical position, if indeed it would have been suitable. Similarly, the traditional family vocations of law and diplomacy failed to appeal to him. He refused resolutely to consider a political career, which his mother would have

[12] The Duke of Argyll, *Passages from the Past*, vol. 1 (London, 1907), 97.
[13] Buchan, *Lord Minto*, 24.
[14] *The Times*, March 2, 1914.

preferred, because he regarded Parliament as a "disreputable coffee shop" and politicians as "the noisiest set of old covies I have ever seen."[15] On the other hand, army regulations allowed students of Oxford and Cambridge who passed the examinations for an arts degree to purchase commissions. His parents agreed, therefore, to an army career. After all, the army provided a respectable refuge for sons of gentlemen who possessed sufficient private income.

Confident that they had made the correct decision, in April 1867 his parents bought him an ensign's rank in the fashionable Scots Fusilier Guards. A Palace regiment open to men of good blood and breeding, the Guards was an elite corps dating back to 1662, and seemed a particularly appropriate regiment for the eldest son of a Scottish noble. Its duties were not onerous; they were chiefly decorative, social, and ceremonial. Melgund, however, remained in the Guards only three years. In March 1870 he sold his commission. The reasons for this decision are difficult to determine precisely.

John Buchan suggests that Melgund left the Guards because of the monotony and boredom of barracks life, physical restlessness, and its inordinately expensive social life.[16] While it is true that the sedentary routine of barracks life was dull, Melgund did not remain long in barracks. Soon after he joined the Guards he moved to his Uncle George's apartments.[17] Moreover, it is clear that Melgund's social life suffered little from his military service. He spent a good part of the year away from London pursuing the seasonal sporting ritual of his class—rowing, racing, and hunting. For example, in 1868 his diary records the following itinerary. He spent the entire month of September on sick leave in Brighton with his family. Then he returned in early October to do a fortnight's duty before leaving again for four month's leave on call. Much to his annoyance, he was recalled once by mistake in December, and once for cause in mid-January. He then served a week on piquet and left again for an additional three weeks which extended into seven. In the twilight days of the gentleman's army just before the introduction of the Cardwell reforms, officers could easily make arrangements to allow for the maximum amount of personal freedom, an arrangement which Melgund exploited fully. Guard duty might be monotonous but it was scarcely onerous. Sometimes it consisted of little more than shooting pigeons on the palace roofs. In the absence of some alternate plan it hardly constituted sufficient cause to abandon a career.

Buchan's suggestion that it was the prohibitive cost of social life, entertainment, mess balls, and dress which led Melgund to quit is no more convincing. At this time, Melgund worried little about money. He had an annual allowance of £900 from his family which he supplemented by horse trading, and he never hesitated to ask his

[15] Minto Papers, Melgund to Hugh Elliot, March 9, 1884.
[16] Buchan, Lord Minto, 22.
[17] Minto Papers, Lady Minto to Arthur Elliot, June 13, 1867.

father for more money. More to the point, Melgund seems to have grown tired of military life and careless in carrying out its minimal obligations. For example, his diary records his failure to make the routine military rounds while on duty. Twice during the first two weeks of November 1869 he appeared before his commanding officer to explain his unaccountable absence from parade.[18] Each time he contrived an adequate excuse. Obviously he had become bored and indifferent. Yet neither boredom nor cost provide a satisfactory explanation for the haste with which Melgund left the service.

Melgund's brother, Fitzwilliam, himself an officer, had another explanation. He believed that Melgund's military career had terminated by some unfortunate personal incident.[19] This opinion is supported by some circumstantial evidence. In late November 1869 Melgund had an unseemly altercation over a woman with Major Hope Johnstone, a senior officer and racing rival. Melgund and Johnstone had met at a ball at the Wellington, the sort of thing which cost ten shillings admission. Impetuous by nature, Melgund claimed he saw Johnstone "shamefully maltreating a woman" known to them both as Baby Ashton. He interfered and Johnstone hit him on the face. The rest he records in his diary: "Of course I had no chance with him, as he is about six times bigger than me & was only too glad, when the row was stopped by the lookers on, though not before my coat had been torn off my back."[20] Both men later apologized, Melgund for having interfered and used "certain words" and Johnstone for having hit him. It was not the last time Melgund would fight over a woman. Nevertheless he must have realized that a public rumpus with a senior officer would do nothing for his military career. Therefore, bored and disgruntled, Melgund sold his commission and quit the regular army to become a "gentleman jockey."

Again, it appears that Buchan makes far too much of Melgund's racing career. In Buchan's view it consisted of six years of unstudied success and serene simplicity, where in this schoolyard of life Melgund lived a blameless, healthy existence. This rather happy image does not bear careful examination. At the time Melgund himself regarded his racing career as neither a successful nor satisfactory occupation but as a temporary diversion. And so it was. Soon after Melgund left the army he joined Cat Richardson at the Machell stables in Limber Magna, Lincolnshire. Here he raced under his old Cambridge title of Mr. Rolly. But until Richardson retired in 1874, after twice winning the Grand National, Melgund remained very much in his shadow. Consigned to the northern circuit, Melgund rode "wherever he could get a mount."[21] Moreover he failed to win a Grand National, although he ran four times. His only significant victory,

[18] Minto Papers, Diary, November 7 and 14, 1869.

[19] Minto Papers, Fitzwilliam to Arthur Elliot, April 4, 1870.

[20] Minto Papers, Diary, November 26, 1869.

[21] Moreton Frewen, "Memoires of Melton Mowbray," Nineteenth Century and After (December, 1915), 1426.

therefore, was the French Grand National which he won at Auteuil in 1874.

His racing career also strained family ties. His parents, particularly his mother, were perplexed and not a little disappointed by their son's decision to quit the army for what they saw as a frivolous and dangerous racing career. Above all, they feared that he would gain the reputation of an idler. Although prodded by his mother to seek more serious employment, Melgund resisted family attempts to redeem or reform him. He refused to be forced into some predetermined mould, and to avoid painful family encounters he rarely visited home even when he rode in the vicinity. His letters also became scarce, sketchy, and short. If he required money, he borrowed, gambled, or traded horses rather than appeal directly to his family. In despair, Lady Minto followed his career through the racing journals, sombrely predicting imminent disaster.

Melgund's self-imposed absences from home, however, did not rid him of unwelcomed, gratuitous advice. Friends and relations plied him with similar admonitions. When he visited Limber Magna, Cat Richardson's stepfather, the Reverend H. Southwell, never ceased to lecture Melgund on the need to abandon horses and the steeplechase and to seek employment more appropriate to the eldest son of a noble family. "Life is short," Southwell warned him in September 1877, "and you will fritter it away and will have nothing to do as you grow older but eat and sleep and be weary of life."[22] Southwell found Melgund shortsighted, materialistic, and shallow, and although Melgund was only thirty-two, Southwell's assessment of him is shrewd and perceptive though bristling with moral judgment. He advised Melgund to read and reflect more deeply and to move beyond his political prejudices which Southwell considered to be largely phantoms of Melgund's lively imagination. Southwell even drew up a reading list for his young friend which consisted of books by Charles Kingsley, Thomas Carlyle, Edward Freeman, Edward Gibbon, and the Bible, but there is no evidence that Melgund followed this prescription for self-improvement.

Many of Melgund's friends shared Southwell's concern as well as his analysis. But there was another side to Melgund. He was not deaf to the call of ambition. His difficulty was that his ambition often outran his talent and training. Nor had he entirely deluded himself. He realized all too well that racing was not a "thing to make a career of" and he made several efforts to break out of its confines.[23]

In 1872 he returned home briefly to raise and to lead a volunteer corps of mounted infantry. Obviously the Guards had not killed Melgund's love of soldiering. Its security, order, discipline, and comradeship continued to attract him, as well as its pageantry and display. He also loved great causes, almost as much as he loved great

[22] Minto Papers, H. Southwell to Melgund, September 26, 1877.
[23] Buchan, *Lord Minto*, 25.

men, and in the early 1870s the concept of a mounted infantry became a cause, hotly debated among military men of the day. Developed out of a need to add mobility to the power and range of the new rifle, the idea of a mounted infantry, that is to say a sort of hybrid infantry/cavalry regiment, roused the wrath of traditionalists. Cavalrymen, seeing its creation as a threat to their raison d'etre, tried to block it at every turn. Melgund became an early convert to the virtues of mounted infantry and, under the approving eye of Sir Garnet Wolseley, the ambitious assistant Adjutant-General at the War Office, determined to prove its utility by example. He returned to Roxburgh to recruit and lead the 1st Roxburgh Mounted Rifles, a regional body drawn largely from the professional classes of society. He trained this unit until it became a model corps, considered to be one of the best volunteer corps in the country. His devotion to the cause won him the admiration of the Wolseley gang, a coterie of military careerists, as well as the personal friendship of the great man himself.[24] This was a valuable if not indispensable asset to an ambitious young officer, for the reformed post-Cardwell army was far from free of favouritism.

War experience, too, even that of an observer, enhanced the reputation, not to mention the table conversation, of a serious soldier. Twice during Melgund's racing days he found time for military adventures. Much to his regret he missed the Franco-Prussian war. At the time he had been asked to accompany his friend, Kit Pemberton, a *Times* correspondent with the Prussians, but he abandoned the idea because he was "hard up" and could not speak German. However, a year later when the Paris commune uprising began, Melgund could not be restrained. He left London on May 22, accompanied by his two youngest brothers, Hugh and Fitzwilliam, and armed with letters of introduction to French officers and officials of the British Embassy in Paris. A letter from Lord Lyons, the British ambassador, got them into Paris and lodged in a small hotel, the St. Honoré, situated near the embassy. Although the Elliot brothers remained in Paris only three days, their stay was not uneventful. Once they were on the rue de Rivoli and forced to help put out a fire nearby. When they fled after only a half-hour, they were chased and caught at Place de la Concorde and forced back to work. This experience taught them that it might be difficult to leave the city. The embassy, however, rescued them by writing a dummy dispatch to Lord Grenville and charging them with its delivery. Even so, it took a Breton soldier who spoke little English but who despised the French to get them past all the sentries.[25] Originally, Melgund had gone to Paris with the reputed purpose of reporting for *The Scotsman*. Whatever its original purpose this visit produced little more than a highly coloured tourist report, laced with military jargon.

[24] Twenty years later Melgund wrote an article entitled "The Best Mounted Arm for the Volunteers, the Mounted Rifleman," *United Service Magazine* (September, 1890), in defence of mounted infantry.

[25] Minto Papers, Diary, May 25 and 27, 1871.

Melgund's second continental escapade, a sojourn with the Carlists in the spring of 1874, was more than a schoolboy's frolic through a burning city. The Carlist cause appealed deeply to his romantic, conservative nature. While he served as the *Morning Post's* Carlist correspondent he worked assiduously to stir British sympathy and support for Don Carlos. From the vantage of General Dorregaray's camp at Estella, Navarre, he despatched passionate reports to the *Morning Post* repudiating the popular Republican charges of Carlist religious bigotry, atrocities, disorganization, and starvation. Privately, Melgund's low church feelings were often offended by the secular power of the clergy in Don Carlos' Spain. Nonetheless, he threw his loyal support behind the Carlist cause, naïvely confident that his prose and political acumen would be sufficient to move British public opinion.

But these adventures led nowhere. Obviously, military promotion required more serious service than reporting for a fashionable London journal. And so he returned somewhat reluctantly to racing in 1874. Not until 1876 did he abandon the turf; then in the autumn of that year his mother's worst fears were realized. During a race in Liverpool his mount tripped over a drain and Melgund fell from his horse. The fall caused a severe neck injury which the doctors at the time diagnosed as a broken neck. More likely he suffered a cracked neck bone and muscle damage, an injury which would plague him for the rest of his life.[26] He returned home immediately to recuperate. There, his family persuaded him to abandon his racing career. Their success constituted only a partial family victory, however, since he still possessed no reputable fixed employment. Yet his family seemed to think that it was better for a well-bred gentleman to be idle and available than to be unsuitably employed.

In the 1870s civilian opportunities in Britain were limited for a man of Melgund's qualifications. To him the age seemed increasingly indifferent to the qualities of a landed gentleman. Moreover, his father's political insignificance did nothing to enhance his chances. There were just too many candidates for too few positions and most required some form of political apprenticeship or token of party loyalty. Twice the Liberals had offered him constituencies, once in Lincolnshire, where he had been racing, and once in Roxburghshire, his home riding, but he had declined both, perhaps because he detected in the offer the fine hand of his friends and family and he refused to be tamed so easily. Still unwilling to pay the price of public office, Melgund turned once again to the army, not as a professional soldier this time but as a sort of military adventurer or occasional handyman of Empire.

Melgund embarked on his first serious military adventure, the Russo-Turkish war, in April 1877. All during his earlier convalescence he had watched the foreign news, earnestly hoping for trouble, preferably in the Balkans. When war broke out he volunteered to serve

[26] *The Times*, March 2, 1914.

as war correspondent for the anti-Russian newspaper, the Morning Post, the one he had served in Spain. It was Garnet Wolseley who persuaded Melgund to become a war correspondent. During his last visit to Minto Castle, he had tried to impress Melgund with the military importance of having good, reliable war correspondents. Wolseley understood the potential power of the press which, he felt, a man should "try to manage for himself,"[27] and he tried to convince Melgund to try his hand at war reporting. Not that Melgund possessed all of the qualities Archibald Forbes, a noted contemporary war correspondent, listed as essential to the successful war correspondent. Courage, stamina, and knowledge of warfare Melgund possessed in sufficient quantity. But he could scarcely claim the gift of tongues, and the "sweet angelic temper of a woman . . . affable as . . . a politician canvassing for a vote."[28] Behind his decision to go to Turkey as a war correspondent lay an ulterior motive. He wanted a semi-military posting, something to enhance his chances of promotion, and he was not disappointed. When the War Office, that is to say, his influential friends there, learned of his decision to go to Turkey, he was offered a post as an intelligence officer. The Wolseley connection was beginning to work.

At first Melgund feared he lacked the money to go. Despite his family's constant call for him to economize he had incurred a debt of £5,700, of which his father remained ignorant. Determined to go, he met his immediate difficulty by borrowing another £3,000 from the Standard Life Insurance Company. Cat Richardson had consented to act as surety, and Arthur agreed that he would never see Richardson saddled with the debt.[29] Once Melgund had settled this troublesome detail he left Britain for Venice to catch a boat for Constantinople, dressed in a captain's uniform of the 1st Roxburgh Mounted Rifles.

However, Melgund was no ordinary war correspondent. He had friends and influence. In Constantinople the British Ambassador, Sir Henry Layard, a friend of his family, made Melgund assistant military secretary to the British military attaché, Colonel Sir Wilbraham Lennox, then serving with the Turkish army on the Danube. Much to Melgund's delight, an announcement in The Times that he had been arrested by a Turkish sentry drew attention to his mission and increased his popularity among the men of his home regiment. Then after only two months' service at the front Melgund contracted a fever and returned home.

A year later, in November 1878, he was off again on another military adventure to the Second Afghan war. This time he had neither the promise of a staff appointment nor the pretext of serving as a war correspondent. But he had friends whom he could use. He arrived in Bombay in January 1879 and moved on immediately to Calcutta to visit the Viceroy, Edward Robert Lytton, at Government

[27] Buchan, Lord Minto, 37.
[28] Archibald Forbes, Memories and Studies of War and Peace (London, 1895), 23.
[29] Minto Papers, Arthur Elliot to Melgund, June 24, 1877.

House. There he received permission to go to the front to see his old friend, Major-General Frederick Roberts, the Commanding Officer, who immediately found him employment.

Melgund's military contribution to the Second Afghan war scarcely deserves mention. During his five months in India, he spent only two at the front where he acted as Roberts' aide-de-camp. When he was not touring the countryside, he spent his time "organizing sports, paper-chase, horse shows and speculating on the probable news from Kabul."[30] Once peace returned he declined two other offers of military service. First he refused an opportunity to fight in the Zulu war because he wanted to go home, ostensibly to continue his work with the volunteers. The second offer, a wild mission to Russia via Afghanistan with the British envoy-designate to Kabul, Sir Louis Cavagnari, he considered far too hazardous. What he really wanted was a "good European war," a serious engagement in which he might win rank and honour.

His modest military contribution, however, did nothing to tame his opinions. Under the hot Indian sun his political fears grew to extravagant proportions. Only a few weeks' residence in India, closely closeted with the Anglo-Indian overlords, convinced him that "natives" respected only one thing, and that was power. On the other hand, he saw his Anglo-Indian hosts as a "hard-riding, steeplechasing lot of fellows," whose tough talents, he was certain, would surely go unrecognized in Britain. This was undoubtedly a projection of his own frustrated ambitions. He also explained that British humanitarians, "those goody-goody benevolent people," unlike the born-to-rule Anglo-Indians, would be of no use in India, "except to get their throats cut."[31] A friendly native he defined, with all the authority of a permanent resident, as "a man who only shoots you at night."[32]

In India, too, many of his old prejudices again manifested themselves. Camped with soldiers who were blatantly scornful of ignorant civilians and their attempts during the last quarter of the nineteenth century to bring the military under parliamentary control, Melgund espoused the soldiers' crusade like a convert. Here his tirades against politics and politicians, "those pasty-faced wretches who do nothing but talk," reached new heights. He could not understand a public, he wrote to his mother, who could tolerate such charlatans. He felt that a short stay in India would make men out of many of them. If he could only camp the British public "in a place like Ali Khayl for one night," he explained, "with Gladstone, Chamberlain, Dilke and a few others on out-post duty, I would join the Mongols for the night."[33] Obviously many of his political comments were written for the benefit of his mother, a devoted Liberal.

---

[30] Buchan, Lord Minto, 48.
[31] Buchan, Lord Minto, 47.
[32] Buchan, Lord Minto, 48.
[33] Buchan, Lord Minto, 49.

Blocked ambition may also help to explain some of his attitudes. As the years advanced Melgund craved status and influence in a wider sphere. Frustrated in this search he blamed the system, particularly parliamentary democracy's selfish individualism, corruption, and mediocrity. He also attacked its growing impersonal bureaucracy and its hopeless indecisiveness and chronic procrastinations. An inveterate hero-worshipper, he preferred great men and great issues and would probably have supported a political strong man or chief, democratically chosen or otherwise imposed, rather than tolerate the, to him, tragic flaws of the parliamentary system. As far as he was concerned, good government depended not upon institutions but upon leadership. And leadership was an attribute of birth and breeding; it was a duty of those whose means and social standing placed them above personal temptation and enabled them to devote themselves to the welfare of their communities. In contrast, democracy had put power and responsibility in the hands of the least able and most vulnerable members of society. Under these conditions Melgund could not see how Britain could continue long "under the rule of such an Assembly."[34]

In contrast, Melgund saw the army as a model of a well-run society. It was composed of men of vision who had broken the insular bonds of the British Isles and who had served their country's interests in hardship and often at personal cost on the outposts of Empire. In his opinion, it was these men, not the politicians or the ignorant, self-satisfied, stay-at-home civilian, who understood true patriotism. A soldier's vision was imperial, purged of selfish materialistic motives. While facing common dangers these men had learned the virtues of community, loyalty, and decisiveness. They were the true servants of the state, representing at once all that was best in the old order and a model of what was needed in a rejuvenated new order. Needless to say, he failed to see his ideal realized in the politics of late nineteenth-century Britain.

Melgund's next military venture only confirmed his worst opinions of politicians. When in December 1880 the Transvaal Boers proclaimed a republic which they confirmed by a repulse of British troops at Majuba Hill, the British government, under public pressure, ordered Roberts to South Africa to suppress the revolt. Fond of good company and adulation, Roberts, who had found Melgund an agreeable companion in India, invited him to accompany the contingent as his personal secretary. Melgund agreed immediately, delighted to possess a secure place and the chance for active service. This expedition promised to be Melgund's best opportunity to date. But fortune eluded him once again. Only a few days before they arrived in Cape Town on March 28, Gladstone's ministry recognized the Transvaal's independence and peace was restored. Melgund reacted bitterly to Gladstone's "traitorous" and "cowardly" act which shattered his

[34] Buchan, Lord Minto, 99.

anticipation of recognition and promotion. April 1, he wrote, would have been a more appropriate date for landing! Nevertheless, he refused all offers to remain and serve in Basutoland, since he feared he might "run the risk of gaining the character of a loafer and adventurer."[35] He had suddenly become sensitive of his reputation, though not for long.

In 1882 he was off again, this time to Egypt. This last junket probably contributed most to his military reputation. When Melgund heard that the British government planned to send Wolseley to Egypt to suppress a so-called nationalist revolt led by an army colonel, Arabi-Pasha, he volunteered immediately, confident of employment under Wolseley's command where he was sure to win promotion through active service. Officially, Wolseley declined his offer, owing to Melgund's reserve status. Many other reserve soldiers had similar plans and rules had to be made and maintained, at least for those who lacked influence. But Melgund was not among their ranks. On the reverse side of the official note of refusal Wolseley scrawled a personal message which read, "Meet me in Egypt with a couple of horses, Rolly." Wolseley was as good as his word. When Melgund arrived in Egypt in mid-August Wolseley made him a captain in the mounted infantry, the same rank he held in the reserves.

After two days at the front, while dismounted and talking to a sergeant, Melgund received a slight hand wound and retired to the rear. There he remained until the day following Tel-el-Kebir. Then he returned just in time for the victory march and the Khedive's palace ball. Although his military service had been limited, it was sufficient to press for the promotion he had desired for so long.

As soon as he returned to London he presented his claim to the War Office. His war wound, his record of two days under fire, and his brief command of a corps of mounted infantry gave his claim some credence. Nevertheless, his dossier required careful nursing. In the next few months he interviewed Wolseley frequently, wrote letters to friends, and prodded the Horse Guard relentlessly.[36] Finally the War Office capitulated, but not completely. He received his promotion to major, not in the reserves but in the volunteers. He also received the Khedive's Bronze Star for his service in Egypt. This accomplished, he courted no more military adventures.

Thereafter his life underwent a marked reorganization, although on the surface things went on pretty much as usual. In London, during the autumn and winter of 1882-83, he followed the regular social routine of a man of his class—clubs, teas, hunts, balls, and the theatre. He spent a good deal of his time at his clubs, the Turf, the Travellers, and the Guards, where he talked and reminisced with old soldiers and racing friends. His diary contains tales of teas and balls at the Lansdownes', Rothschilds', Churchills', Barings', Roberts', and Wolseleys'

[35] Buchan, Lord Minto, 60.

[36] Minto Papers, Melgund to Adjutant-General, February 12, 1883; Diary, February 12, 1883.

and it contains little else. He also enjoyed theatre, both the play and the players. His theatrical tastes, however, were scarcely cultivated nor daring. Perhaps the play he liked most was the Royalty's popular production, The Merry Duchess, in which a Duchess falls in love with a jockey. This piece he saw many times. Yet his diary tells only half the tale.

For in May 1883, Melgund suddenly announced his engagement to Mary Caroline Grey, the daughter of General Sir Charles Grey, private secretary first to Prince Albert and later to the Queen herself. The Greys and Mintos had long been political friends and Melgund had first met Mary at Minto Castle seven years before. But since this initial encounter they had met infrequently. Melgund's friends were astounded at the news. For years Wolseley, Roberts, Southwell, and the old family physician, Dr. John Brown, had urged Melgund to marry. Yet he seemed to resist their advice and scoff at the idea of married bliss. Consequently many friends had given up hope. Now their surprise knew no bounds. The suddenness of the announcement was almost as surprising as the news itself. Only a month before his diary records frequent visits to all his old lady friends with only fleeting references to a Miss Grey. Be that as it may, the choice had been made.

Melgund was now thirty-nine. He had waited long, but he had also chosen well. A small attractive woman, Mary possessed the Grey charm, grace, and exuberance. Vanity Fair, London's fashionable social arbiter, doted on her. In its opinion, she was "the best waltzer," "the most beautifully dressed," and the "most graceful lady" in all London. She was also a good athlete, particularly a good figure skater. Her athletic prowess suited Melgund perfectly. She also possessed sound sense, judgment, and, despite her sheltered upbringing, a very practical turn of mind. More important to Melgund's future career, she brought to her marriage court influence. Born and raised at Windsor, she remained a personal friend of the Queen and her family. This friendship proved a valuable asset to Melgund's future career. They were married on July 28, 1883, in St. Margaret's Church, Westminster.

Melgund's mother had not lived long enough to witness his marriage. She had died two years before. But she would undoubtedly have approved. An efficient female force had taken charge of her son's life and brought order and stability where she apparently had failed. She also would have approved of the reformation which seemed to ensue. Melgund immediately abandoned plans for future military adventures. When invited he simply pleaded family responsibilities, for he now resolved to return to Minto Castle, to settle into placid gentility, raise a family, and assist his ailing father with the estates.

However, his resolution faltered only a few weeks before his marriage. Lord Lansdowne, the newly-appointed Governor-General of Canada and an old family friend who had tried for years to find Melgund an administrative post in Britain, asked him to become his

Military Secretary in Ottawa. Melgund could not resist, despite his father's poor health and his wife's reluctance to exchange the Court of St. James for Rideau Hall. A prominent place in the Governor-General's entourage held the enticing prospect of promotion. That is, if he could persuade the War Office to recognize his colonial stint as active military service, a condition which, with the help of Lansdowne and a good deal of correspondence, he wrung from a reluctant War Office. There was also the possibility that this post might lead to something better. Late in September 1883, dressed in full military attire and accompanied by his bride, Melgund left Liverpool bound for Quebec City aboard the *Sarmatian*, a coarse, dirty, re-converted cattle boat. Needless to say, the journey was not pleasant. "If anyone ever advised me to take this vessel again," Melgund wrote to his brother Fitz, "I will have them charged for cruelty to animals."

Whatever the agonies of the trans-Atlantic voyage, Melgund had reached an important point in his search for place. In itself, the Canadian Military Secretaryship was not an important post, since it had lost much of its importance before Confederation by the appointment of a Canadian Minister of Militia. Yet it was an entry into the expanding administrative web of the British Empire and it might be used as a stepping-stone to something better. Despite Melgund's grumblings, the British social system had not been unkind to him. For in the final analysis Melgund owed this position, not to any personal merit, but to the considerations of class and friendship. In other words, he was fortunate to live in a country and at a time when "some deference was still paid to the claims of birth and position."[37]

[37] Paul Ernest Roberts, "Minto," *Dictionary of National Biography, 1912-1921* (London, 1922), 174.

Chapter Two

The Canadian Apprenticeship

Although Melgund had agreed to accept the Canadian post he still had certain reservations and told Lansdowne from the start that he might not be able to stay the full term. He could scarcely have guessed in the autumn of 1883 the large place Canada would eventually occupy in his future public career. Nor could he have appreciated the value of this apprenticeship. Free from heavy administrative responsibilities during these years, he possessed easy access to the people who exercised political power and influence. He also had the opportunity to learn first-hand how the Canadian government worked and to see the country at a formative stage in its development.

The Canada Melgund grew to know during the years 1883-86 was a vast territory stretching from the Atlantic to the Pacific, sparsely settled by only four million people who were drawn together by the promise of steel. When he arrived the Indian peoples still possessed much of the prairie and the chief staple of their economy, the buffalo, still roamed the plains, though in decreasing numbers. Soon all this would change radically. Treaties would confine the Indians to reservations and the buffalo would be driven to the verge of extinction. In Ottawa, the wily Tory Prime Minister, John A. Macdonald, safely

installed in office, pursued his National Policy of securing his trans-
continental Kingdom of Canada from the avarice of its one external
foe, the United States. But behind this busy façade, social, regional,
religious, and cultural tensions were already beginning to appear,
tensions which would challenge the foundations of Confederation
itself. In a short time, Melgund saw much, and as he witnessed the
conflict between the old and new Canadas his sympathies were not
always with the new.

When Melgund reached Ottawa late in 1883, scarcely two weeks
before Lansdowne, he at once set about arranging for the viceregal
transfer of power and preparing for the new Governor-General's safe
arrival. The first month proved a baptism by fire. People, places, and
procedures had to be learned quickly, and decisions had to be taken
without benefit of Lansdowne's direction. To add to these difficulties,
his own house, Rideau Cottage, a three-storey red brick house located
close to Rideau Hall, was far from ready for occupancy. And the
reliable chief clerk who ran the Governor-General's office was on
vacation. Fortunately, Lord Lorne, the departing Governor-General, a
former Cambridge acquaintance, and Princess Louise, a close friend
of Lady Melgund, invited them to remain at Rideau Hall until their
quarters were ready. Meanwhile, Lord Lorne's Military Secretary,
Colonel Francis De Winton, an old soldier friend from the Russo-
Turkish war, quickly initiated Melgund into the mysteries of his
office.

At first the post's activity, challenge, and authority appealed to
Melgund, and his energetic, affable, informal approach created a very
favourable impression. His most important immediate task, which
was to protect Lansdowne from threatened Fenian reprisals, seemed
more than suited to his talents. The rumour that Lansdowne had
received his Canadian appointment as a political payment for opposing Gladstone's Arrears Act of 1882, had aroused the ire of the Irish
Canadian press. They portrayed the Governor-General designate as a
hard, exacting, Anglo-Irish landlord and predicted personal violence
if his appointment was confirmed.[1] To secure the new Governor-
General's safety seemed no easy task. The memory of D'Arcy McGee's
assassination remained sufficiently fresh to frighten many people; the
American border was long and close; the large Irish-Canadian population made detection difficult; and, to make matters worse, Melgund
considered the director of the Dominion police incompetent. Consequently Melgund was forced to assume much of the responsibility for
protecting Lansdowne. He hired two detectives to live among the
Irish at Quebec City and routed Lansdowne's landing parade through
only the safest streets. Although his precautions were out of all proportion to the threat, he could scarcely have known that then.

Throughout Lansdowne's administration, Fenian fact and Fenian fancy mingled with impartial irrationality. Consequently pre-

[1] The Dominion Annual Register for 1883 (Toronto, 1884), 81.

cautions were always necessary. On one occasion a suspicious-looking parcel containing a tin box addressed to Lansdowne turned out to be a real "explosive machine."[2] Again, on October 11, 1884, newspapers claimed that an explosion in the new wing of the Quebec Legislative Assembly was the work of a notorious Irish Fenian, Donovan Rosse.[3] But Melgund shortly learned that the Irish-Canadian population possessed few dangerous men, and his post soon seemed far more placid than he had hoped.

Normally, the duties of a Governor-General's Military Secretary were neither complex, arduous, nor particularly interesting. In fact, by 1883, the title "Military Secretary" had become largely anachronistic. Before Confederation, when the Governor-General had exercised direct and effective authority over the militia by virtue of his title of Commander-in-Chief of the militia, the Governor-General's Military Secretary had played an administrative role in government comparable to a Minister of Militia. Since then all this had changed, and the Military Secretary's duties were now chiefly decorative, social, and ceremonial. More precisely, he was charged with meeting everyone worth knowing, noting their social and political rank and distinction, arranging official tours and visits, identifying local notables, and advising on appropriate subjects for speeches. He was also asked to supervise Government House entertainment, secure information, hear criticisms, and make suggestions. None of these duties required daily attention. Moreover, an experienced chief clerk aided by several assistants performed most of the routine office business, answered begging letters and addressed invitations. Melgund was simply responsible for supervising their work at his two offices, one at Government House and the other in the East Block. Yet much depended upon the character of the incumbent and his superior. Melgund's superior, Lord Lansdowne, was a competent, experienced administrator who seemed to regard his Canadian post as a sort of temporary retirement. Consequently he did most of the paper work himself. To him it was as "child's play compared to the work of an English department."[4] Thus, Melgund's duties were even more limited than they might have been.

Once Melgund had mastered the office routine there seemed little to do, and time lay heavily on his hands. Although Lansdowne had warned him to reconcile himself to idleness under ordinary circumstances, Melgund seemed unprepared for this and during his first summer he decided to break his boredom by touring Canada and the United States. But he did not remain idle and bored for long.

In August 1884, less than a year after his arrival, Lansdowne asked him to recruit and despatch a contingent of Canadian boatmen for service on the Nile.[5] Under strong public pressure, the British had

[2] Minto Papers, Melgund to Minto, November 9, 1883.

[3] Minto Papers, Diary, January 29, 1884.

[4] Minto Papers, Lansdowne to Melgund, July 1, 1883.

[5] For additional information see C. P. Stacey, The Nile Expedition (Toronto, 1959).

agreed to rescue the popular General Charles Gordon who had been besieged at Khartoum by the Madhi's forces, and it had chosen Wolseley to command the relief expedition. Wolseley decided to attack Khartoum via the Nile and, remembering the excellent service of Canadian boatmen during the Red River Expedition, he requested a similar contingent to transport troops and supplies up the Nile. Faced by Wolseley's request, Lansdowne decided to seek the advice of John A. Macdonald and Melgund was sent with a special message to the Prime Minister at Rivière-du-Loup. When Macdonald raised no objection to imperial recruitment in Canada Lansdowne charged Melgund with the task of recruiting, equipping, and despatching the men.

Originally, Wolseley wanted Melgund to command the contingent. Unfortunately, Melgund was forced to decline, owing to his wife's pregnancy. But Melgund's fear of offending the great man caused him much anguish, since he felt Wolseley might misinterpret his refusal. To reassure Melgund, Lansdowne agreed to write to Wolseley explaining Melgund's predicament. Meanwhile, Melgund threw himself into the recruiting mission, determined to justify Wolseley's confidence in him.

This assignment required a diversity of managerial talents, not the least of which were tact and diplomacy. Lansdowne feared that the Militia Department might "be a little huffed," having been short-circuited by the Governor-General's office. Conscious of his Secretary's inexperience, he advised Melgund to be civil and to soothe their ruffled feelings as much as possible.[6] The Militia Department itself and the Minister, A.-P. Caron, created no difficulty whatever, but the British General Officer Commanding, F. D. Middleton, needed careful handling. Middleton, whose respect for Canadians, military or civilian, was never very great, felt the War Office could have procured as good or better men in Britain. Certainly the old voyageur-boatmen of Wolseley's Red River days had long since vanished. On the other hand, Melgund was convinced that experienced and tough lumbermen, inured to hardship, would provide an excellent substitute. To humour Middleton and to neutralize his potential negative influence, Melgund appointed the General to a small supervisory committee consisting of himself, Middleton, Colonel Frederick Charles Denison, the Contingent's Commanding Officer, Captain T. Costain, and J. T. Lambert, an experienced Ottawa lumberman, whose advice and assistance proved essential. Perhaps more than any of the others, Lambert and P. Rice, a Quebec lumberman, were responsible for the success of Melgund's assignment. They faithfully plied him with valuable counsel and advice and saved him from many costly mistakes.

It was Rice and Lambert who pressed Melgund to follow closely the organization and customs of the lumber camp and avoid frightening men unfamiliar with military routine.[7] Recruits were carefully

[6] Minto Papers, Lansdowne to Melgund, August 24, 1884.
[7] Minto Papers, Lansdowne to Melgund, August 24, 1884.

divided into the customary operational gangs of twenty-five men supervised by a boss who received his instructions from the military officers. Officers were drawn from both the French and English communities and a priest accompanied the contingent. Each man received an advance of pay and his family was sent a small monthly allowance during his absence.

Melgund did everything in his power to avoid disrupting the regular routine and customs of the lumber camp. Contrary to British army custom, no limit was placed on the quantity of food consumed and the men's capacity continued to surprise the British military authorities. The recruits also insisted on wearing their long, heavy underwear, despite the heat. War Office officials, accustomed to uniformity and adherence to rules and regulations, were understandably astonished. But Melgund made it clear to them that these concessions were the price that had to be paid for good men.[8]

Eventually, 367 men were recruited and Melgund had to spend several days in Montreal in the late summer negotiating with the Allan Steamship lines for adequate transportation to Britain. Then, little more than a week before the men were to sail from Quebec, the War Office blithely informed him, first through a friend and later officially, that it had made its own shipping arrangements. Both the means and message irritated and embarrassed Melgund. "The way we have been treated is quite abominable," he complained to Lansdowne.[9] To a man accustomed to thinking that politicians possessed a monopoly on stupidity, the War Office's bungling taught its own lesson.

Even before the voyageurs left Canada on War Office transport, Melgund had agreed to a second important special service assignment. Impressed by his efficient and smooth handling of the recruiting of the voyageurs, and aware of his boredom, the Canadian government appointed him to a small committee to examine Canadian defences. This committee owed its existence to imperial prodding as well as the growing Canadian fear of American intrusion following the termination of the fisheries clause in the Washington Treaty, the pelagic sealing rivalry in the Pacific, and the cruiser-torpedo scares of the early 1880s. The committee's original terms of reference were very general. Caron, the Minister of Militia, instructed the committee to consider and to report on all land and sea defences.[10] Middleton, however, insisted that the committee confine itself to coastal defences since he jealously considered land defences his own exclusive domain.

The main burden of work fell upon Melgund and the committee's competent secretary, Colin Campbell, a retired Assistant Paymaster in

[8] War Office 32 (124) 495, Lansdowne to Derby, October 3, 1884.

[9] Minto Papers, Melgund to Lansdowne, September 5, 1884.

[10] Minto Papers, "Memo of the first meeting of the Canadian Defence Committee," December 26, 1884.

the Royal Navy. Together they worked on their report for over one year. Anxious to produce a report acceptable to the penny-conscious Canadian government, they studied files dating back to the Jervois Reports of 1862 and 1865. First they attempted to determine more precisely Canada's defensive obligations following the British withdrawal in 1871. After careful study they decided that apart from imperial naval installations still in British possession, all land and coastal defences fell clearly under Canadian control. Their final report, published early in 1886, contained a catalogue of Canada's potential coastal defence resources which included the number of fishermen and vessels capable of being pressed into service in war, the number and tonnage of merchant steamships capable of conversion into armed cruisers, and an inventory of all transportation and communication links possessing vulnerable coastal points. Then they recommended the creation of a naval militia by utilizing these existing resources.[11]

A thorough report proved only part of the battle. Campbell, a seasoned Ottawa civil servant, warned Melgund that real success meant securing government support, and he assiduously set about to obtain it. To gain the goodwill and confidence of the Militia Department, Melgund and Campbell insisted on making the Deputy Minister, C. L. Panet, a member of the committee, despite Middleton's objections. The report also required a delicate balance between what was possible and what was needed. The committee had been warned that Macdonald would shelve a strong report very quickly. Yet they refused to dilute it too much. "It takes a strong wrench," Campbell wrote Melgund, "to turn the key to the Canadian cash box when money is wanted for the militia service, beyond matters of politics, personal or local interests."[12] Campbell seemed to think of everything. He carefully scattered throughout the report references to the Australian colonies, confident that "you can get more sacrifice out of them through their jealous instincts than in any other way . . . short of war."[13] Yet, despite their best efforts, they failed to stir Canadian politicians from their traditional indifference to military matters. Their printed report, all nine volumes of it, was never even tabled in the House.

Nevertheless, Melgund gained considerable knowledge of the Canadian militia and a valuable glimpse into the inner workings of Canadian politics. He also earned Campbell's sincere respect and gratitude. "You seem," he wrote to Melgund, "to have been the only one to give me any encouragement in this tedious and trying work."[14] Yet Melgund retained the respect and confidence of the Canadian government too, and they readily confided other tasks to his care.

[11] Canada, Committee on the Defences of Canada, *The Defences of Canada* (Ottawa, 1885).

[12] Minto Papers, Colin Campbell to Melgund, January 18, 1885.

[13] Minto Papers, Colin Campbell to Melgund, November 5, 1885.

[14] Minto Papers, Colin Campbell to Melgund, November 3, 1885.

Early in 1885, while Melgund was still labouring over the coastal defence report, the Canadian government asked him to prepare a second report, a plan of defence against a possible Fenian raid on Western Canada. Melgund quickly designed a scheme to repulse an attack on Winnipeg and any area west of the Great Lakes. This assignment was only one token of the government's growing confidence in his military abilities.

Melgund's popularity, it should be pointed out, extended well beyond the borders of official Ottawa. He possessed both the time and freedom from official restraint to entertain widely, and Lady Melgund frankly followed Lady Dufferin's success formula: "I lay it on as thickly as possible here. Nothing is too strong for them."[15] Despite the implied condescension, the method seemed to work. Melgund's title, accessibility, largesse, and his wife's hospitality and charm won him a host of devoted friends. He also travelled extensively outside Ottawa and belonged to the Montreal and Toronto Hunt Clubs, both of which possessed busy social schedules. Perhaps his three most interesting "Canadian" friends were Goldwin Smith, the self-exiled Oxford don, T. C. Patteson, the Toronto Postmaster, sportsman, and horse trader, and George Stephen, the Montreal rail magnate, later Lord Mount Stephen. All these men were British-born. The diversity of interests, backgrounds, and temperaments represented by the three suggest Melgund's range of acquaintances. Yet his wide popularity may have led him into the only serious indiscretion of his secretaryship.

In the spring of 1885, war threatened several parts of Britain's empire. Russian and British troops were preparing to fight along the Afghanistan border and trouble seemed to be brewing in both Burma and the Sudan. As Melgund received letters from excited British officers, describing the military opportunities available in the event of war, he grew restless and anxious to leave Canada. His brother, Fitzwilliam, urged him to organize a Canadian contingent for imperial service. A Canadian contribution, Fitzwilliam insisted, would be well received in Britain. Surprised by the enthusiasm of Canadian officers with whom he spoke, Melgund was tempted by the suggestion. Even public men like Goldwin Smith encouraged him.[16] With the confidence of growing public support, Melgund began drafting a plan for a Canadian contingent. He knew that although Macdonald had no intention of sending Canadian troops abroad, the Prime Minister had no objection to imperial recruitment in Canada. News of Melgund's plan evoked an encouraging response from Canadian officers, and many volunteered to raise and lead a contingent. Meanwhile, Melgund asked his brother to speak to two British Generals, Redvers Buller and Ivor Herbert, and two British politicians, John Morley and the Marquis of Harrington. Unfortunately, the War Office mistook these communications for official offers and wrote directly to the

[15] Minto Papers, Lady Melgund to Arthur Elliot, November 15, 1883.
[16] Minto Papers, Goldwin Smith to Melgund, February 24, 1885.

Canadian government. At this point his plans went awry and threatened to become an acute source of embarrassment. However, Macdonald very quickly punctured War Office illusions by rejecting the notion of an official contingent.[17] He unequivocally informed Melgund that the Militia Act forbade the despatch of Canadian troops abroad and limited them to the single function of self-defence. This lesson remained firmly imprinted on Melgund's mind. Fortunately for Melgund the outbreak of the North West troubles diverted public attention from this indiscretion and provided military employment for other restless Canadian officers.

The history of the North West rebellion has received extensive historical attention elsewhere. Here, it is enough to point out that the Métis people, facing economic destitution owing to the buffalo slaughter and the spectre of drought, had repeatedly demanded government redress of their longstanding grievance before resorting to armed rebellion. After repeated rebuffs they had sought the aid of Louis Riel, the banished Red River hero. Under his nominal leadership the Métis drifted relentlessly toward armed confrontation. Soon they were joined by hundreds of disenchanted Plains Indians.

News of the North West disturbance reached Ottawa on March 24, 1885. That same day, Major-General F. D. Middleton, the Commanding Officer of the Canadian militia, left Ottawa for Qu'Appelle to quell the Métis outbreak. On his way to Qu'Appelle Middleton wired Melgund and invited him to join the campaign. Three days later Melgund left Ottawa, having received his wife's reluctant consent and Lansdowne's ready blessing. Upon his arrival at Qu'Appelle Middleton immediately named him Chief of Staff.

Melgund's appointment was not entirely Middleton's doing, nor was it without design, since the Canadian government, somewhat suspicious of Middleton's military abilities, was also anxious to secure Melgund's appointment. Even though his wife was a French-Canadian, Middleton was obsessed with the notion of French-Canadian disloyalty and was never happy in Canada.[18] He stayed here only because he could not "afford to chuck up."[19] Nevertheless, he resented his exile in this "blackguard country"[20] "of base drunken lying and corrupt men."[21] Even had he been a man of greater military ability, Middleton's contempt for the country and its people would not have inspired the government's confidence in his capacity to lead the Canadian militia in the North West campaign. To reassure themselves and the Canadian people, it would appear (from Caron, Lansdowne, and Melgund correspondence) that the government, par-

[17] C. P. Stacey, "John A. Macdonald on Raising Troops for Imperial Service, 1885," *Canadian Historical Review* (March, 1957), 37-40.

[18] Minto Papers, F. D. Middleton to Melgund, February 18, 1886.

[19] Minto Papers, F. D. Middleton to Melgund, April 27, 1894.

[20] Minto Papers, F. D. Middleton to Melgund, February 4, 1886.

[21] Minto Papers, F. D. Middleton to Melgund, February 18, 1886.

ticularly A.-P. Caron and John A. Macdonald, insisted on Melgund's appointment.

Middleton welcomed Melgund both as a friend and a trusted adviser, despite the Canadian government's insistence on the appointment. Timid, aloof, and almost chronically apprehensive of the military deficiency of the hastily recruited, raw Canadian officers and men of the North West Field Force, Middleton surrounded himself with imperial officers like Melgund, Laurie, Haig, Wise, and Van Straubenzie. During the campaign, Middleton's too close association with these men, and his apparent neglect and distrust of Canadian officers like Otter, Denison, Grassett, and Williams, created serious criticism and dissatisfaction with his command.[22]

After the North West campaign, Middleton's Canadian critics repeatedly attacked his leadership. Their criticism centred around three controversial decisions: the division of the main Qu'Appelle to Batoche column at Clark's Crossing; the alleged command to retreat on the first day of the Batoche battle; and the despatch of Melgund to Ottawa on May 9.

Middleton's Clark's Crossing decision, a self-confessed failure, resulted more from miscalculation than a stubborn retention of his original campaign plan. Middleton's original plan, "simple in the extreme,"[23] consisted of dividing his Field Force into three columns and posting one column each at Qu'Appelle, Swift Current, and Calgary. Major-General T. Bland Strange took the Calgary column, Lieutenant-Colonel William Otter the Swift Current one, and Middleton himself retained the main Qu'Appelle column. According to Middleton's plan, the columns were to march north, thereby cutting in three the Indian-Métis peoples scattered across the prairie from Batoche to Edmonton. For a time Middleton's main column shadowed Otter's men on the west bank of the Saskatchewan River. But the Frog Lake "massacre," the siege of Battleford, and the subsequent fear of Indian reinforcements reaching Batoche changed all this. Otter was forced to remain at Battleford, while Middleton, undaunted by Otter's delay, pressed on, afraid of the conjuncture of western Indian and Métis forces at Batoche. To protect his now defenceless left flank Middleton sent half his own men across to the west bank under the command of Lieutenant-Colonel C. E. Montizambert.

Although Melgund accompanied Montizambert to the left bank he opposed the proposed troop division from the start. The evening before the division Melgund tried to dissuade Middleton by suggesting an alternate plan which might have saved Middleton the humiliating reversal which followed. Melgund wanted Middleton to transport the entire column to the west bank and secure the desired buffer between the Indians and Métis, while retaining intact the full strength of the column. Melgund came very close to persuading

[22] Caron Papers, Public Archives of Canada, F. D. Middleton to A. P. Caron, April 1, 1885.

[23] George Stanley, Louis Riel (Toronto, 1963), 324.

Middleton, but late that night the General received a telegram warning him that a hostile party of Battleford Indians was moving toward Batoche. Determined on immediate action, but without sufficient transport to bring all his men and supplies across the river, Middleton decided to disregard the advice of his Chief of Staff and he divided the force at Clark's Crossing on April 20.[24]

However, it did not take him long to realize the folly of his decision. Four days later, a crack band of Métis riflemen, led by Gabriel Dumont, the able Métis military commander, ambushed the reduced eastern force. Middleton hastily ordered the reunion of his troops but it was too late. The battle left ten dead and forty-three wounded. It also undermined Canadian confidence in their commander. To Middleton the incident proved a rather costly lesson. Some years later, Middleton acknowledged his own error and admitted the validity of Melgund's shrewder judgment.[25]

Over two weeks later, Middleton, still stinging from the Clark's Crossing disaster, approached Batoche, the centre of Métis resistance. The next day, stiffened by reinforcements, fresh supplies, and a Hudson Bay Company steamer, the "Northcote," Middleton launched his first assault on Batoche. Hidden in carefully constructed rifle pits outside the village, the Métis were well prepared. The battle began early in the morning and lasted until late afternoon. But just before the fighting ceased some Canadian officers received a confused order which they interpreted as a command to retreat. Still surrounded by his imperial officers, Middleton offered no explanation to his militia commanders, so they assigned their own, as Middleton soon discovered.

Batoche increased Canadian disaffection, and weakened still further Canadian morale and confidence in Middleton's command. Then after two days of indecisive fighting, Canadian officers, impatient with Middleton's cautious strategy, erupted into open revolt. On the fourth day, the Canadian militia forces, led by Arthur T. H. Williams, the commanding officer of the Midlands Regiment, stormed Batoche. Their actions were contrary to Middleton's command and undertaken without his permission. Prompted by what they considered needless delay, they wanted to pre-empt Middleton's rumoured decision to request the assistance of British regulars. Such a request seemed a galling prospect to the sensitive Canadian militia.

The success of Williams' revolt encouraged others to denounce Middleton's inept leadership. In a lengthy letter to the Toronto Mail on January 28, 1886, a Brigade Surgeon of Middleton's main column, Dr. George T. Orton, M.P.—that "drunken beast,"[26] as Middleton spitefully called him—attributed the prolonging of the campaign,

[24] Carman Miller, "Lord Melgund and the North West Campaign of 1885," Saskatchewan History (Autumn, 1969), 81-108.

[25] F. D. Middleton, "Suppression of Rebellion in the North West Territories of Canada, 1885," United Service Magazine (January, 1894), 376-77.

[26] Minto Papers, F. D. Middleton to Minto, February 20, 1894.

with its attendant casualties and hardships, to Middleton's caution, fear, and indecision. Orton suggested that only a deputation of officers which included Melgund had prevented Middleton from retreating on the first day of the Batoche battle. At the time, Middleton dismissed these charges as the confused, beclouded story of an inveterate crank. But he took somewhat stronger exception when Lieutenant-Colonel Houghton, a more reliable authority (although, according to Middleton, suffering from the same alcoholic weakness), later repeated them in an article published in the *United Service Magazine*.[27] Middleton wrote at once to his old Chief of Staff, Lord Melgund, asking for his version of the story. Melgund had never been blind to Middleton's faults. He regarded him as "a thoroughly incapable old duffer—but a dear old fellow in many ways."[28] According to Melgund, however, Houghton's story lacked any substance. In fact, during the battle, Melgund, on behalf of some senior officers, had urged Middleton to retire to the prairie camps if he met strong Métis resistance, but Middleton had refused. With the aid of his diary, Melgund suggested a plausible alternate explanation for Dr. Orton's rather persistent version of the facts. According to Melgund's recollection, in the early afternoon of the first day, the Métis had set fire to the church which sheltered Middleton's wounded men. Fearing that the Métis might advance under cover of the smoke, Melgund had ordered Orton to remove the wounded to the prairie camp. Then Melgund discovered that the ammunition wagons were also retreating and immediately he ordered that they be stopped. His order, halting both the ammunition and hospital wagons, created the impression that he and others had prevailed upon Middleton to countermand the original order to retreat.[29] In Melgund's opinion, these circumstances may have caused the subsequent confusion which Middleton's critics attributed to his timid, inept leadership.

Whatever the explanation, Middleton had no appreciation of the importance of maintaining good communications with his officers and men, particularly in a militia force. He failed to understand that this force was composed of men unaccustomed to accept unquestioningly the command of a superior officer. His actions therefore created needless mystery and much misunderstanding. For example, Melgund's sudden departure for Ottawa in the late afternoon following the first day of the Batoche battle became a similar source of mystery. Some past writers have dismissed this incident as a meaningless journey for private reasons.[30] Others have suggested that Melgund went to Ottawa to protest the growing insubordination of Middleton's "political" officers.[31] But many Canadians then and since believed

[27] Minto Papers, F. D. Middleton to Minto, February 20, 1894.
[28] Minto Papers, Diary, August 27, 1897.
[29] Minto Papers, Melgund to F. D. Middleton, February 21, 1886.
[30] J. K. Howard, *Strange Empire* (Toronto, 1965), 395.
[31] W. McCartney Davidson, *Riel* (Calgary, 1942), 177.

that Melgund left camp with Middleton's orders requesting British reinforcements. There are elements of truth in all three explanations.

There is no question that Middleton's confidence had been badly shaken by the Clark's Crossing blunder and his subsequent failure to take Batoche during the first days of indecisive fighting. Growing unrest among dissident Canadian officers increased his concern. Obviously something had to be done to reinforce his strength and position. And in his darker moments he considered seriously requesting British troops, but he was afraid to make a formal request since he was all too conscious of the criticism it would create. He decided, therefore, to send a deputy to Ottawa to inform Caron of his difficulties, thereby leaving the unpopular decision to the Minister.

Melgund was an obvious choice for a spokesman. He knew the military situation intimately, he possessed the government's confidence, and he could be trusted to represent accurately Middleton's dilemma. Moreover, ever since the commencement of the campaign, Melgund's wife and ailing father had been urging Lansdowne to secure his early return. Ottawa rumours that he had been shot had only increased their anxiety. Finally, Lansdowne wrote Middleton requesting Melgund's return as soon as his force reached Prince Albert.

But when Melgund left for Ottawa he carried no written instructions. He took a few notes on supplies and other matters, but that was all. Indeed, years later he had forgotten Middleton's desire for British troops until his old commander reminded him. According to his recollection, their employment had been based only on speculation of a long campaign.[32] Before Melgund reached Ottawa, however, Canadian troops had stormed Batoche, the centre of Métis resistance, and their action ended all talk of British assistance.

Melgund did not remain in Canada long after the North West campaign. When he accepted the post of Military Secretary he told Lansdowne he might not retain it for the full six years of Lansdowne's appointment. At the time, Lansdowne had raised no objection to these terms since he himself did not contemplate remaining a full term. Therefore, in January 1885, Melgund, pressed by his wife and father, had no qualms about notifying Lansdowne of his desire to leave. Although he had not made up his mind precisely when he intended to go, he felt that it was sufficient to warn Lansdowne of his intentions. Originally, he thought he might stay until the summer of 1886, but circumstances soon altered that resolve and he left six months earlier.

The news of Melgund's proposed departure annoyed Lansdowne immensely, since he had readily and frequently consented to Melgund's varied requests for leave to undertake special missions—he had hoped to break the boredom of his Secretary's position and thereby retain his services. He had even agreed to grant Melgund a two-month holiday in Britain following his return from the North West. He now

[32] Minto Papers, Minto to F. D. Middleton, December 10, 1893.

feared his benevolence had been misspent and unappreciated and he decided to ask Melgund to explain his future intentions.

Determined to make his own position perfectly clear, Lansdowne reminded Melgund of his frequent absences and explained that owing to Melgund's North West adventures, his holiday in Britain, and his proposed travels with Lansdowne during the late summer and autumn of 1885, he would have been away from Ottawa for no fewer than seven months. Lansdowne felt that it was only fair that Melgund should either leave in July 1885, or stay until the end of his term.[33]

Lansdowne's letter disturbed and upset Melgund. He felt that Lansdowne failed to appreciate his services. After all, he had never promised to remain for the full term. Had Lansdowne forgotten their agreement made simply on the word of a gentleman? Or was Lansdowne trying to dismiss him to make room for another? These were some of the questions he determined to resolve before he relinquished his post.

Melgund immediately consulted his father and his brother Arthur. He also spoke to Sir Garnet Wolseley. They all agreed that Melgund must resign at once but not before confronting Lansdowne and defending his honour. Following their collective counsel, Melgund wrote Lansdowne a cold, curt letter in which he formally submitted his resignation. But Lansdowne refused to accept it until he could talk to Melgund personally.[34]

As soon as Melgund returned to Ottawa in September 1885 he sought an interview with Lansdowne. Lansdowne agreed to see him at Rideau Hall after breakfast on September 7. The row began then and there. Although Lansdowne remained calm and determined and stuck closely to his original argument, Melgund lost his temper and occasionally slipped into profanity. When Lansdowne failed to convince Melgund of his good faith he terminated the argument by promising to speak to Melgund's father, Lord Minto. After dinner they met again but little was accomplished. Each repeated his previous arguments, but more calmly this time.[35] Then at last Melgund agreed to a compromise. He promised to remain until after Christmas to give Lansdowne an opportunity to replace him, an arrangement designed more to soothe Melgund's wounded feelings than to accommodate Lansdowne, for the Governor-General had no difficulty replacing Melgund with his competent aide-de-camp, Henry Anson. Anson had performed most of Melgund's duties during the latter's many absences from Ottawa and knew the work as well, if not better, than the incumbent. On the first day of the New Year, 1886, when Melgund sailed from New York, he was not unhappy leaving the New World for the Old.

Some past writers have suggested that Melgund's early Canadian career, under Lansdowne's close supervision, had altered Melgund's

[33] Minto Papers, Lansdowne to Melgund, July 12, 1885.
[34] Minto Papers, Lansdowne to Melgund, August 13, 1885.
[35] Minto Papers, Diary, September 7, 1885.

naïve political views and had trained him in the strict paths of con-stitutional law and practice.[36] But Melgund never became a close friend and confident of Lansdowne, "the model Governor-General." He found Lansdowne cold, aloof, unsympathetic, small, and unpre-dictable. Moreover, he spent only twenty-seven months in Canada, often far from the daily routine of Rideau Hall. During his last six months in office relations remained strained, despite the formal re-conciliation. In Ottawa, Lansdowne made little real use of Melgund. For example, when Melgund returned from the North West, Lansdowne never once sought his advice on the Riel affair, although the tortuous subject preoccupied much viceregal time and attention. Lansdowne seemed to rely more on the advice of his aide-de-camp, Henry Anson, the man who would replace Melgund as Military Sec-retary. The break between the two men was never really bridged. Melgund felt he never again possessed Lansdowne's respect and confidence. He blamed Lansdowne for his failure to receive "proper" recognition for his North West services, particularly the C.M.G. he desperately wanted and confidently expected.[37] Melgund, it seems clear, learned much less from Lansdowne than some writers have thought.

However, Melgund had learned a great deal about Canada and its people; and he had done so because he had refused to stay too closely tied to his Ottawa desk. During these years he had gained a broad knowledge of Canada's military structure, the practical problems of cultural conflict, and some dimensions of western expansion—all subjects which would dominate his later Canadian career. He had also acquired an affection and respect for Canada and its people which he felt Lansdowne lacked, despite the latter's reputed political sagacity and correct constitutional behaviour. For example, Melgund never forgot Lansdowne's sneering reception of Poundmaker, the great Cree chief, whom they met in captivity, during their North West tour in the autumn of 1885 following the suppression of the Métis uprising. To Melgund, Poundmaker appeared "all dignity, saying through the interpreter that he was so honoured in meeting the representative of the Queen and so regretted the circumstances under which he met him."[38] Much to Melgund's horror, Lansdowne smiled sarcastically throughout, unable to appreciate the tragic situation. More than most, this incident suggests the essential difference between the two men and helps explain the cause of their different historical images. While Melgund later, as Governor-General, may have lacked Lansdowne's political finesse and polish and may have offended many Liberal historians' sense of constitutional propriety, those people who met

[36] H. Pearson Gundy, "Sir Wilfrid Laurier and Lord Minto," *Canadian Historical Association Report* (1952).

[37] Minto Papers, Diary, August 27, 1897; Lady Melgund to Lady Grey, Wednesday, 1886.

[38] Minto Papers, Diary, January 24, 1894. Melgund also opposed the hanging of Riel.

and knew Melgund recognized and appreciated his genial, sympathetic, and human side and were willing to forgive the rest.

None seemed to appreciate Melgund more than the Canadian government, for they did everything to retain his services. Both Sir Charles Tupper, the Canadian High Commissioner to London, and Macdonald, the Prime Minister, tried to persuade him to remain in Canada and accept the Commissionership of the North West Mounted Police. This appointment had aroused a heated Cabinet controversy between those who wanted a Canadian and those who favoured an imperial appointee. Apparently Melgund proved acceptable to both sides, a high tribute given the passion aroused by the debate. Perhaps it was the recognition of Melgund's affection and respect for Canada and Canadians, often lacking in other imperial officials, which led Macdonald to make his perceptive prediction on the eve of Melgund's departure. "I shall not live to see it," he declared, "but some day Canada will welcome you back as Governor-General."[39]

[39] Buchan, Lord Minto, 83.

Chapter Three

The Search for Place

The year 1885 had been an eventful one for Melgund. Apart from his altercation with Lansdowne and his slight indiscretion with regard to the recruitment of Canadian troops for British service, his Canadian career had been an unqualified success. The regrets and compliments showered on him by Canadians during his last days in Ottawa had brought him a deep sense of satisfaction. They had also fired his ambitions and had given him some clearer idea of the position he sought. What he really wanted was to occupy an influential administrative post close to the levers of power or, in his own words, "a larger part in the world of history."[1] But opportunities were few and his qualifications slim, and most positions required a measure of political service, patience, faithful friends, and good fortune. Far from the selfless soul who had greatness thrust on him, the portrait painted by John Buchan, Melgund sought and desired position and influence.[2] Yet the path proved longer and more arduous than he had anticipated, although it did not seem so at first.

[1] Minto Papers, Diary, August 24, 1894.
[2] Buchan, Lord Minto, 114.

For the Irish Home Rule issue had plunged Britain into one of its most serious political crises in years, and soon after Melgund returned from Canada he was invited to contest an election in the interests of the Liberal Unionists. This opportunity held distinct possibilities. A brief political career or even some token gesture might enhance his credit with those who held the gifts of place. No issue provided a more perfect pretext for entry into public life than Ireland. Enlistment in a campaign to preserve national integrity would surely absolve him of charges of hypocrisy or crass ambition. Moreover, his friends knew his longstanding interest in Irish affairs. After all, he had watched the deteriorating Irish situation with apprehension for a number of years and had kept in touch with those who were ready to fight if circumstances required a forceful solution. He had even informed Wolseley of his willingness to fight two years before he had gone to Canada. In Canada his conversations with Lansdowne and Goldwin Smith and his correspondence with Roberts and Wolseley had confirmed many of his worst fears. In his opinion, force might be required to preserve the union, although ballots rather than bayonets might yet achieve that end.

However Melgund perceived the personal benefits of the Irish political crisis, there was really no question of his political opinions. He had long hated Gladstone and considered him a traitor and had voted Conservative despite his family's well-known Liberal affiliations.[3] To him, Home Rule was but another of the Prime Minister's attempts to dismantle the United Kingdom. Consequently, he welcomed this opportunity to join his family's repudiation of the Liberal party for the Liberal Unionist programme. According to Melgund, the failure of other public men to rise to the challenge and renounce Gladstone revealed the depths to which British public life had sunk. Then again, he could not have expected much more from these politicians whom he described as reared on "self-confidence, a smattering of books, impertinence, and the gift of the gab."[4] Given these opinions, he had no difficulty convincing himself that political service was nothing less than a patriotic imperative, a duty transcending petty party lines. Understandably, Melgund welcomed the Unionists' invitation to contest a constituency, the Hexham district of Northumberland.

On June 26, 1886, Melgund outlined his platform to the electors of Hexham. In his appeal he asked his electors to support him for reasons of class, race, and religion. He warned them that a vote for his opponent constituted surrender to "an organized rebellion" which would sell the loyal minority composed of men "of your own north country blood and of your own creed" to a majority of "a different race and a different creed, whose leaders have obtained their positions by dynamite and assassination." These were strong words and there

[3] Minto Papers, Lady Melgund to "My dearest people all," the Greys, February 13, 1886.

[4] Minto Papers, Diary, April 7, 1893.

were more. Aware of the strong Home Rule sympathy among the labouring class, particularly the miners, Melgund predicted economic distress in Ireland. Trading on labourers' fears, he predicted that Irish workers would be driven to England, the nearest labour market, and wages would go "down like a shot." Nor were the tactics of the Clan-na-Gael any secret to him. His Canadian experience with the Fenians had taught him all about them. According to him, their goal was nothing less than an independent Ireland "a few miles from our shores." This being so, no one could deny that Irish independence would prove a standing threat to British national security. This election, Melgund cried, had only one issue—Union—the issue which had forced him on to the public stage.[5]

Melgund's audience, however, seemed unmoved by his rhetoric. They cannily rejected the notion of a one-issue election, a referendum on Home Rule. What they wanted to know was their candidate's opinions on Sunday closing, perpetual pensions, disestablishment, and the abolition of the House of Lords. Except for disestablishment and the abolition of the House of Lords, both of which he repudiated, Melgund informed his audience that he had no opinion whatever on these subjects, owing to his ignorance of the issues caused by his long sojourn in Canada.

For two weeks Melgund canvassed his large constituency and spoke to groups two and three times a day. Several things seemed to favour his election. The president of the Hexham Division Liberal Association, Thomas Tayler, and the Hexham *Herald* joined his cause. His only opponent, Miles McInnis, the Liberal incumbent, had reversed his initial position on Home Rule to return to the orthodoxy of Gladstone's fold. Moreover, the Conservative party nominated no candidate, content to instruct its followers to support Melgund. The Unionists, however, failed to capitalize on their advantages. They possessed no constituency organization and refused to work closely with the Conservative party. Consequently, they failed to bring the Conservative vote to the polls.[6] Furthermore, Melgund's refusal to promise wavering Liberals that he would support Gladstone on all issues other than Home Rule cost him many Liberal votes. Therefore, he lost the constituency by 967 votes.

Melgund accepted his defeat with equanimity, even relief.[7] Although a keen competitor, who had worked hard and would have liked to have won, he was never particularly drawn to a politician's life. Moreover, there were other consolations. The decisive Conservative-Unionist victory more than recompensed for his own defeat, since he knew that a wounded officer of a victorious army rarely went unrewarded.

[5] *The Hexham Herald*, June 26, 1886.

[6] Minto Papers, Lady Melgund to "My dearest people all," the Greys, February 13, 1886.

[7] Minto Papers, Lady Melgund to Lady Grey, July 11, 1886.

Rewards came, but they were meagre at first. In 1886, he became the Deputy Lord Lieutenant of Roxburghshire and in 1892, Deputy Lieutenant of the County of Selkirk. The Board of Agriculture even made him the landlords' representative on a committee to investigate a plague of field voles! Given Melgund's larger ambitions, these gifts were slim fare indeed; yet they were, however small, a form of public recognition. Obviously better fare required more substantial evidence of party loyalty, a price he now seemed more than willing to pay.

Since the years 1892-95 were like one long election campaign, opportunities for political service were ample, and despite Melgund's disparaging comments on party politics he became a faithful party worker. He joined the Central Committee of the Roxburgh Association of Unionists and served as its Vice-President in 1895. Nor were his activities confined to nominal executive positions. In 1893 he tried unsuccessfully to unite the Conservative and Unionist committees of the county. Furthermore, he faithfully attended political meetings and frequently took the chair. He also organized political picnics at the Minto estates and contributed generously toward election expenses. For example, in 1895, he and his brother Arthur, the Unionist candidate in Roxburghshire, shared the entire county electoral expenses between them. He also displayed an astonishingly zealous sense of political partisanship. Despite his later complaints about the petty partisan nature of Canadian politics, he did not hesitate to instruct his estate factor to place advertisements only with Conservative and Unionist journals, unlike his father, who had made no such distinctions. But Melgund himself never again contested a constituency, since just before the next election in 1892, he inherited a seat in the Lords. His father had died on March 17, 1892, and he was now the fourth Earl of Minto.

Unfortunately, Minto's succession coincided with the defeat of the Conservative-Unionist coalition, and this fact temporarily ended all hopes of his preferment. His inheritance, however, entailed new and increased estate and parochial duties. The estates had been somewhat neglected during his father's last years, and they required particularly close attention, for the profit margin began to diminish rapidly during the 1890s. Although Minto, after he returned from Canada, had often tried to assist his father, the third Earl had left management largely to his estate factor and an Edinburgh agent who handled investments and accounting. This was a satisfactory arrangement and the third Earl did not wish to disturb it, despite his son's eagerness to learn. As a result, the fourth Earl remained virtually ignorant of family financial affairs until after his succession.

To a novice the intricate details of estate management demanded considerable application, a prospect which Minto initially welcomed since he was determined to take affairs into his own hands and place them on a more orderly and official basis. It was typical of him that he should begin by insisting that his factor address him in military memo

form and that his estate agent submit a monthly rather than the traditional quarterly statement. At first he displayed unusual diligence and refused to approve his agent's reports, although he knew next to nothing about investments and estate management. He made himself as difficult as possible and played his role to the limit, constantly seeking additional information, questioning, and suggesting ways and means of his own. Handled tactfully, however, he invariably gave way to sounder advice and wisdom.

Yet Minto made little headway in his attempts to establish economic order and to secure the family fortunes against serious erosion. Certainly this was not an easy task. A heavy burden of debt, composed chiefly of mortgages to meet family settlements, rested on the estates. Inheritance duties, amounting to roughly £5,000, a sum equal to the total of Minto's annual free income, ate into revenue.[8] A generous settlement on each of his three brothers increased the problem. The estates also required extensive renovation. Meanwhile, the estate income which came from three main sources—the farm, the mines, and investments (particularly from the latter two)—remained fixed or declined. Low prices, rising wages, foreign competition, increased taxation, and declining rents reduced farm income. Consequently, the annual farm income fell some £2,000 between 1880 and 1894.[9] The Lochgelly collieries, leased to three mining companies, encountered similar difficulties caused by falling prices, strikes, fires, and depleted supplies.[10] Even investments, chiefly in the form of securities, yielded a lower return. Maturing bonds were re-invested at lower interest rates owing to the poorer markets.

Minto desperately attempted to institute financial reforms and reduce costs. But his efforts seemed a discouraging rearguard action. Following his agent's advice, he consolidated his debts and, with some difficulty, persuaded relatives drawing interest on their inheritance to accept a lower rate more in keeping with the current market.[11] He also cut staff, reduced the unprofitable cattle herd, particularly the ornamental highland cattle, and sold paintings as well as one of his two London houses. Still costs continued to outrun income and certain expenses, notably estate renovations which required large outlays of capital, could wait no longer. This fact had become painfully clear the month following the third Earl's death, when an outbreak of typhoid forced the family to vacate Minto Castle. During the investigation which followed, the drains were found to be "in an awful state of filth."[12] Urged on by his wife, Minto, as

[8] Minto Papers, Statement of Debts and Income, 1892-93. The Minto Papers contain an excellent record of the estates' financial affairs.

[9] Minto Papers, Minto to Lady Minto, January 24, 1894.

[10] Minto Papers, James Corwell to J. A. Jamieson, July 28, 1890.

[11] Minto Papers, Sir H. Elliot to Minto, July 19, 1894; Minto to Mrs. K. Childers, July 20, 1894.

[12] Minto Papers, Diary, January-October 1892, summary. Although the contractor, W. Turner, Lord & Co., submitted an initial estimate of £1,342 for repairs and renova-

yet ignorant of family financial affairs, decided, somewhat improvidently, to renovate and redecorate the entire castle. This project took two years to complete and cost far more than Minto had anticipated. To pay for the additional work Minto sold some of his securities. Consequently, at the end of Minto's first three years of management, his assets had been reduced and the estate debt had climbed from £65,000 to £81,844, £15,000 of which represented debt incurred to meet the terms of his father's will.[13] On one occasion things looked so bleak that Minto seriously considered selling the entire Melgund estate. In these circumstances the future seemed dark indeed. The tedious details of estate management seemed endless and the struggle against rising costs and declining income appeared to be a losing battle. It is not surprising, then, that Minto began to seek release, but release had become more difficult.

His succession had increased his parochial duties and bound him more closely to the estate. County and parish council meetings, quarter sessions, school, church, library, hunt, and agricultural society meetings were all part of the regular duties of the resident titular head of a landed family, and occupied a good many hours of tedious labour. Other problems were of his own creation. Resisting the trend of the times, Minto decided to attempt to reassert the influence of the landed interests in local affairs. He was convinced that his father had let things slip too far out of control in his later years. Minto's intrusion into matters his father would have ignored created endless local quarrels and petty political intrigues which were wasteful of time and effort. His first and worst feud, with the local parish minister, the Reverend A. Galloway, began over a question of money when Minto, the church's chief contributor, refused to approve Galloway's modest plans for renovation. The quarrel continued for years and soon spread into school meetings, library committees, sports events, and the parish council. Everywhere, a Minto party representing the conservative property interests confronted the Galloway faction, trading on every conceivable cause of popular discontent. Galloway even supported a tenants' protest movement directed against Minto.[14] Although Minto soon mastered the mechanics of parochial politics, he never learned the art of conciliation and he soon grew weary of the endless strife which plagued his every initiative.

Increased army responsibilities provided some relief. In 1888, when the War Office brigaded all the volunteer regiments, Minto received command of the Scottish Lowland Brigade, a command which included all the county corps in the south of Scotland, and carried the rank of Brigadier-General. Drawn largely from the class of

tions to Minto Castle, their final bill came to £3,926, plus an additional £3,027 for renovations to a London house Minto wanted to sell.

[13] Minto Papers, J. Craik to Minto, May 6, 1895.

[14] Minto Papers, D. Rogers to Minto, April 4 and 12, 1895, January 5, 1896, April 3, 1897.

local country gentlemen and professionals, these corps met as a brigade only once a year. Consequently the Brigadier's duties were largely nominal. But again, Minto refused to play the part of a mere figurehead and insisted on a more active supervisory role. He spared neither his time nor money to advance his cause. He opened the full facilities of his estates to the brigade; he used his estates for camp training, met annual deficits out of his own pocket, granted shooting rights to the officers, donated a sports ground, and provided a challenge cup, the Minto Cup, to encourage drill and marksmanship. One of the most conscientious of brigadiers, Minto did everything to improve the competence and status of the volunteers and to win the respect of the British regulars.

As usual, Minto's enthusiasm carried him beyond the bounds of his powers. His attempts to control the routine affairs of the brigade, normally left to the company commanders, encountered stiff opposition from the General at Scottish Headquarters in Edinburgh, who refused to give Minto the extraordinary powers he requested. Convinced of a conspiracy against him at Scottish Headquarters, Minto appealed to the War Office, confident his friends there would overrule the General.[15] But the War Office refused and had to remind Minto of the rules and insist that they be obeyed. Undaunted by this rebuff, Minto campaigned vigorously to have the rules altered. He wanted brigadiers to have larger powers, particularly control over money, promotion, and inspection, all the elements of real influence. Although he continued to enjoy the confidence and support of the War Office, Minto's campaign eventually ended in failure.

His brigade duties also brought him wider, more diversified associations. He belonged to the Institute of Commanding Officers of Volunteers, the East of Scotland Tactical Society, the Scottish Rifle Association, and the Field Practice Association and occasionally held executive positions in each. Determined to keep informed, and abreast of military intelligence, he regularly attended military manoeuvres in Britain and abroad, particularly France. He also pleaded the cause of volunteers in the press, in Parliament, or on the public platform, always careful to obtain the advance approval of Wolseley, his friend and patron.

Throughout these years, his credit with the War Office climbed steadily. In the Lords he asked the War Office's planted questions, defended their conduct, and tested parliamentary opinion.[16] Twice he wrote full-length articles in journals, once in the *United Service Magazine* in which he argued the virtues of a mounted infantry, and once in the *Edinburgh Review*, in which he upheld the subordination of news correspondents to the direction and control of military com-

---

[15] Minto Papers, Diary, December 4 and 6, 1897; Minto to Wolseley, November 22, 1896, to F. Grenfell, July 30, 1897, to General Chapman, December 18, 1897; Chapman to Minto, August 19, 1897, General Kelly Kenny to Minto, August 19, 1897.

[16] *The Times*, December 11, 1891; Minto Papers, Diary, May 27, 1891; February 13, 1897; Britain, House of Lords, *Debates*, May 18, 1893, 1220.

manders in the field.[17] In this second article, which followed closely the lines he had already laid down in an earlier but similar essay for the *Nineteenth Century*, Minto spoke with all the authority of a veteran news correspondent.[18] In turn, the War Office provided rewards. It sought his advice and placed him on committees of investigation.[19] But until the government changed, it could do little to advance his larger interests.

Then in 1895 a Conservative-Unionist government returned to power. Naturally, Minto's hopes for preferment rose. All through the dark night of Liberal rule Minto's political phantoms had haunted him. He had often wondered if Gladstone's rule would ever end short of rebellion of "all that is loyal & reasonable & prosperous & Patriotic against the visionary proposals & tyranny of a member of Parliament who as Prime Minister apparently aspires to be a dictator."[20] The Conservative-Unionist's return to office changed all this, for the new Cabinet contained many personal and family friends who supported Minto's bid for position. But he left nothing to chance. Encouraged by Wolseley, Minto first sought the Parliamentary Under-Secretaryship for War. Although Salisbury, the Prime Minister, seriously considered his candidacy, which was strongly supported by Lansdowne, the Secretary of State for War, in the end the Prime Minister, needing a man in the Commons, chose Sir John Brodrick. While unsuccessful, Minto's bid for a position reminded friends of his ambitions and won him several loyal promises of future support. The successful candidate, Brodrick, offered to do all in his power to help Minto, a promise which he redeemed when Minto, again following Wolseley's suggestion, sought the Governor-Generalship of Canada.

In his *Memoir*, John Buchan has made a needless mystery of the circumstances surrounding Minto's appointment to Canada. According to Buchan, the request came as a surprise, as a sudden recognition of the worth of "one who had never canvassed or schemed for preferment, and who had been content to perform his duties far from the limelight."[21] Although flattering to Minto, Buchan's assertion does some violence to the facts.

Minto had never made any secret of his desire for preferment. Almost any position would help to free him from the cramped, insignificant position he occupied in British public life. In the decade preceding his Canadian appointment, his diary makes this perfectly clear. On several occasions he considered soliciting colonial appointments in Australia and South Africa.[22] Yet he preferred the

[17] Melgund, "The Best Mounted Arm,"; Gilbert Elliot [Minto, 4th Earl], "War Correspondents," *Edinburgh Review* (January, 1896).

[18] Viscount Melgund, "Newspaper Correspondents in the Field," *Nineteenth Century* (March, 1880).

[19] Minto Papers, Diary, June 12 and March 7, 1897.

[20] Minto Papers, Diary, April 1, 1893.

[21] Buchan, *Lord Minto*, 113-14.

[22] Minto Papers, Diary, April 12, 1891; March 1, 1895; June 18, 1895; March 9, 1896.

prospect of the Canadian position suggested by Macdonald several years earlier. Quite apart from the fact that it was a better post, he felt a certain affinity to Canada, a country he knew and liked. After he left he had continued to keep a close eye on its development and to do everything to promote its interests. In 1886, for example, soon after his return from Canada, he wrote an article on the North West Rebellion for the Nineteenth Century to still fears of prospective British immigrants.[23] At the same time, he tried, unsuccessfully, to persuade The Times to appoint an Ottawa correspondent, to improve the quantity and quality of Canadian news in Britain, and to avoid the dangerous dependence on biased American sources.[24] He also instructed his Edinburgh agent, all things being equal, to invest in Canadian securities,[25] and even considered revisiting Canada in the early 1890s. His correspondence with Canadians—Macdonald, Smith, Costain, and Patteson—and calls from Canadian friends visiting Britain kept him abreast of Canadian affairs. On social occasions he frequently found himself defending the Canadian case on any subject from the cattle embargo to the Bering Sea dispute, a subtle reminder to his friends of his Canadian knowledge and experience. Therefore, when Lord Napier told Minto in 1895, "I feel sure you will one day be Governor-General of Canada," he displayed no particular prescience.[26] As Buchan suggests, he simply told Minto what he wanted to hear.

But Minto's interest in the Canadian position went well beyond wishful thinking; he actively solicited the post of Governor-General. It was in March 1898 that Minto first learned of Lord Aberdeen's impending retirement as Governor-General of Canada. The next day, without telling his wife, he went to see his old friend Wolseley to remind him of his earlier promise of support. Wolseley agreed to write immediately to their mutual close friend, Lord Mount Stephen, who still retained considerable influence in Canada and whose advice on Aberdeen's replacement would undoubtedly be sought. Meanwhile, Wolseley advised Minto to approach all of his influential friends, beginning with Lord Lansdowne.[27] Minto accepted Wolseley's counsel and postponed his plans to go abroad the following week in order to solicit support for his candidacy.

At first Minto hesitated to seek Lansdowne's favour, afraid of compromising their friendship. He was still uncertain of Lansdowne's good offices. Most of all he feared a rebuff, but when Mount Stephen insisted, Minto's reluctance melted. Still his approach remained somewhat oblique. Three days after talking to Wolseley, Minto visited Lansdowne's house to speak to Lady

[23] Lord Melgund, "The Recent Rebellion in North West Canada," Nineteenth Century (August, 1885).

[24] The Quebec Mercury, August 5, 1901.

[25] Minto Papers, J. Craik to Minto, April 12, 1892.

[26] Mary Minto, India, Minto and Morley 1905-1910 (London, 1934), 5.

[27] Minto Papers, Diary, March 25 and 26, 1898; Wolseley to Minto, March 26, 1898.

Lansdowne, whom he always found sympathetic, warm, and charming. While there he confided to her his desire to succeed Aberdeen in Canada. She readily agreed to speak to her husband. During the next few days Minto visited Lady Lansdowne regularly to learn the latest news.[28] Lord Lansdowne himself refused to feed Minto's dreams, and reminded him there were other strong candidates; nevertheless, he promised to place his name formally before his Cabinet colleagues. Lansdowne was as good as his word, and Minto's subsequent success probably owed more to Lansdowne's intervention than Minto ever cared to admit.

Once his candidacy received official recognition he wisely left the rest to friends who possessed more influence and claims to party patronage than he did; and these friends were more than generous. He spoke directly to only one other person, Lord George Curzon.[29] But Brodrick, Curzon, Lansdowne, Wolseley, Mount Stephen, Portland, Lonsdale, and John Baring all spoke or wrote to Salisbury, Chamberlain, Devonshire, and Arthur Balfour, to endorse his candidacy. Minto's brother Arthur and his brother-in-law Albert Grey, both members in good standing with the Unionists, also did their utmost.[30] The news of Minto's desire to go to Canada spread quickly. "At Ascot I was constantly being asked if I was going," he noted optimistically in his diary. But when his spirits lagged he consoled himself on how the amount of "money spent for party causes enhances the chances of promotion of mere mediocrities."[31] He was evidently preparing himself for defeat. At times like this Minto seemed to forget that his own success depended upon much more than the simple recognition of merit.

The Court, too, supported Minto's candidacy, a support he owed more to his wife than to any personal claim. Although the court no longer nominated its representative directly, it still retained some control over important imperial appointments. Sometimes its influence consisted of no more than a royal veto. However, Queen Victoria had not been amused by Lady Aberdeen's Canadian capers. Although often exaggerated considerably in the telling, the affairs at Rideau Hall under the Aberdeens remained a standing court joke. The old Queen's disapproval of the Aberdeens' indifference to "distinctions of birth and occupation, political views, public speaking and support of trade unions and co-operatives" was no secret.[32] Victoria was resolved that these things should not be repeated under their successors. Lady Minto's easy familiarity with court customs offered sufficient assurance that order and decorum would return to Rideau Hall with a vengeance, should her husband replace Aberdeen in Ottawa.

[28] Minto Papers, Diary, March 28 and 29, 1898.

[29] Minto Papers, Diary, June 26, 1898.

[30] Minto Papers, Chamberlain to Minto, July 19, 1898, gives Albert Grey full credit.

[31] Minto Papers, Diary, July 17, 1898.

[32] John T. Saywell, ed., "Introduction," The Canadian Journal of Lady Aberdeen, 1893-1898 (Toronto, 1960), xxv.

Both the Queen and Princess Louise went out of their way to make clear their personal satisfaction with Minto's selection.[33] This point was not entirely lost on Chamberlain.

Still, the ultimate decision rested with the Colonial Secretary, and contrary to what many historians have written, Minto was not the hand-picked choice of Chamberlain, nor did he become the pliant instrument of Chamberlain's so-called grander imperial design.[34] The Colonial Secretary had his own candidates. First, he asked the Duke of Connaught to consider the Canadian post. The Queen, however, refused to let him go on personal grounds. She explained that "of her three youngest sons one was dead—another had become a German sovereign—this was the only one left to her."[35] Next, Chamberlain approached the Duke of Sutherland, but he refused.[36] According to Chamberlain's biographer, there were "other distinguished persons" as well who refused.[37] In other words, Minto's name, although on the list, was nearer the bottom than the top.

Minto knew that he possessed no personal or political claim to Chamberlain's favour. It is true that they had met socially and Minto had been impressed by Chamberlain's decisiveness and breadth of knowledge. He had also found him intriguing, not the insular little Englander he had expected. Still, he did not fully trust him. Henry Labouchère's assessment of Chamberlain, "He is clever but a gentleman he will never be," captured Minto's sentiments precisely.[38] On the other hand, there is no evidence to suggest that Chamberlain had any opinion whatsoever of his future viceregal colleague. They both belonged to the same politial formation but opinions within that party were far from homogeneous or harmonious. In the past, Minto and his father had often deplored Chamberlain's anti-military bias and "almost communistic sentiments."[39]

Chamberlain's imperial policy elicited no more positive a reaction from Minto. Chamberlain's association with Rhodes—that "d--- blackguard"[40]—and the Chartered Company disgusted Minto. Indeed, he felt so strongly about the Jameson Raid, "one of the most disreputable stories in the history of this country," that he refused to be introduced to Rhodes at a dinner party at the Rothchilds.[41] In

[33] Minto Papers, Louisa to Lady Minto, November 8 and December 30, 1898. *Salisbury Papers*, Queen to Salisbury, August 18, 1898.

[34] Skelton, *Life and Letters*, vol. 2, 34-35; J. W. Dafoe, *Laurier: A Study in Canadian Politics* (Toronto, 1963), 56-57; Mason Wade, *The French Canadians 1760-1945* (Toronto, 1956), 475-78; Joseph Schull, *Laurier: The First Canadian* (Toronto, 1965), 377.

[35] Joseph Chamberlain Papers, University of Birmingham, Salisbury to Chamberlain, July 1, 1898.

[36] Austin Chamberlain Papers, University of Birmingham, Sutherland to Mrs. Chamberlain, July 10, 1911.

[37] J. L. Garvin, *The Life of Joseph Chamberlain*, vol. 3 (London, 1934), 490.

[38] Curzon Papers, India Office, London, H. Labouchère to G. Curzon, April 6, 1898.

[39] Minto Papers, Minto to Melgund, February 4, 1885.

[40] Minto Papers, Diary, May 17, 1896.

[41] Minto Papers, Diary, July 27, 1897.

Minto's mind, Rhodes was "not at all the right sort" and as for Chamberlain, he was guilty by association. Together they represented all that Minto disliked in the new imperialism, that is to say, yellow journalism parading under the pretence of patriotism to produce a form of vulgar middle-class diplomacy.

Had Chamberlain wanted a pliant instrument in Ottawa he would scarcely have chosen Minto as Governor-General. He would almost certainly have appointed a safer candidate, a more malleable man who possessed political experience and subtlety. He would not have chosen a novice whose sole claim was his past military service, and whose chief source of support had been Wolseley and the War Office—Chamberlain's distrust of the Horse Guard was all too well known for that. Although Minto belonged to the British Empire League, he suspected, or so he said, all schemes of formal federation, and he only joined the Royal Colonial Institute in 1898, the year he became Governor-General. Chamberlain's preoccupation with larger imperial problems and his understanding of the relative impotence of the viceregal post in Ottawa may explain Minto's appointment more accurately than a conspiracy theory based largely on speculation.

All through the spring and early summer of 1898 Minto waited patiently for the Cabinet decision. Several days before he received official notification, friends in the Cabinet's confidence sent their congratulations. But Minto refused to believe his good fortune until Chamberlain wrote officially on July 19. Then he enjoyed his trophy, piously confiding in his diary that "my appointment as Governor-General of Canada . . . is a position to be proud of—but I can't help . . . feeling that it has not been the path which has usually led to great appointments."[42] There is no doubt that few men who held the office of Governor-General of Canada since Confederation possessed less political and administrative experience, but the prize had not come as a surprise to him. Supported by influential friends and relations, Minto had sought and obtained this high office through the usual political channels. It was a post he had long coveted and had worked assiduously to obtain, although one for which he was not particularly well qualified.

[42] Minto Papers, Diary, July 26, 1898.

Chapter Four

The Office

Minto saw the position of Governor-General as one of great potential power and influence. In his opinion it was a position which possessed a certain elasticity, "one which can be made much or little of," depending upon the strength and character of the incumbent.[1] Minto wanted to be a strong Governor-General. He wanted to be a conscientious, exacting officer of the Crown, no mere figurehead or rubber stamp. He was obviously unaware of the fact that those of his predecessors who had tried to carve out a larger place for themselves in the Canadian government had often known disappointment. As one of Minto's stronger predecessors, Lord Dufferin, noted sardonically in a moment of discouragement, there remained "little scope in the administration of Canada for an ambitious Governor-General."[2] This was particularly true when the man lacked the necessary knowledge, experience, and subtlety.

While Minto probably knew more about Canada and its problems than most novice Governors-General, he had no precise knowledge of

[1] F. H. Underhill, "Lord Minto on His Governor-Generalship," *Canadian Historical Review* (June, 1959), 122.

[2] D. M. Farr, "Lord Dufferin: A Viceroy in Ottawa," *Culture*, 19 (1958), 161.

the powers and limitations or the ordinary mechanics of his office. Nor had his years with Lansdowne given him any real insight into the nature of the viceregal position. His friends and well-wishers proved even less helpful. Although Lord Strathcona, the Canadian High Commissioner, plied him with travel brochures, provincial and federal yearbooks, and a copy of George R. Parkin's The Great Dominion, apart from the last item this literature scarcely proved inspiring or particularly helpful. Other friends with an intimate knowledge of Canada, such as Lord Lorne, Lord Lansdowne, Sir Garnet Wolseley, and Lord Mount Stephen, offered advice and counsel, but none seemed to rise above the well-worn platitudes. Moreover, men and circumstances, on which so much depended, had changed considerably since they had been in Canada. Even the constitutional experts, Alpheus Todd and Walter Bagehot, and the instruments of his office, Letters-Patent, Instructions, and the British North America Act, tended to concentrate on the routine duties and crisis powers of his office.[3] A man bent on a more creative role possessed little guidance apart from experience and common sense, qualities which Minto seemed to possess in rather short supply.

Many scholars have tended to see the post-Confederation Governor-General as a mere figurehead. He has been described as a glorified postman or "the decorous cover for the practices of the colonial politician."[4] Yet the legal instruments constituting and describing the office provided for wide power and authority. For example, the British North America Act, though vesting the executive government of Canada in the Queen personally, contemplated the administration of the government by the Governor-General "on behalf and in the Name of the Queen." Read with the common law, the B.N.A. Act permitted the Sovereign to delegate to the Governor-General nearly all her powers of executive government. And by its own terms the Act conferred a great many of these powers directly on the Governor-General, simply by virtue of his commission. The royal Letters-Patent, by which the Sovereign constituted the office of Governor-General, went further. These empowered him to keep and use the Great Seal and to constitute and appoint, to suspend or to remove, judges, commissioners, justices of the peace, and other Canadian officers and ministers, including the Prime Minister himself. The Letters-Patent also empowered him to summon, prorogue, or dissolve Parliament. The Royal Instructions added the power of pardon. In law all these powers, taken together, made the Governor-General the local repository of strong constitutional executive authority. But in practice, he usually exercised these powers only on the explicit advice of his ministers, either collectively or in some in-

[3] See Maurice Ollivier, British North America Acts and Selected Statutes (Ottawa, 1962), particularly Part VI, "Documents Relating to the Office of Governor-General of Canada...."

[4] Goldwin Smith, Canada and the Canadian Question (Toronto, 1891), 149.

stances individually. Consequently what was legal might not necessarily be constitutional, that is to say, customary.

In short, a Governor-General's duties ranged from the routine to the exceptional. He administered the oath of allegiance to all persons holding public positions of profit or trust in the Dominion. He granted pardon, on the advice of his Cabinet, and played postman to the British and Canadian governments. And as the Queen's Canadian representative, he also assumed the position of Commander-in-Chief of the land and naval militia in Canada. In fact, he performed all the regular duties of a head of state.

In general terms, the British North America Act and Letters-Patent, read together, conferred on him both common law and statutory powers, but these powers were often of uncertain scope. Moreover, the practice and custom governing their proper exercise were frequently more nebulous still. The British North America Act referred to these when it conferred on the Governor-General all the unspecified powers and authority which, under imperial and local acts, had been vested in his predecessors at the time of Confederation. Some of these had become immutable and binding, while others had changed or evolved beyond the settled judgment of the precedent-conscious constitutional expert. During Minto's administration a dispute over customary rules governing honours recommendations constituted one example which caused a great deal of difficulty. The Governor-General's classic right to encourage, advise, and warn was another more general but nebulous power. Effective use of these powers required intimate knowledge of men and circumstances, combined with suasion, sympathy, and moderation, Lord Elgin's trinity of essential viceregal virtues. As early as 1839, Joseph Howe, in his famous open letters to Lord John Russell, demonstrated the impotence of an uninformed Governor. And all colonial Governors were essentially itinerant rulers, learning and then leaving. Given the nature of the office, a good Governor-General needed to possess, practise, and appreciate the art of politics without becoming partisan. He had not only to be correct, but also to appear to be so. That is to say that he had to understand the spirit of the law as well as its letter. Minto's early failure to appreciate this subtle dimension of his office would soon limit his effectiveness and create many unnecessary difficulties.

Before 1926 and the appointment of a British High Commissioner to Ottawa, the Governor-General possessed an additional cumbersome responsibility. He doubled as a prototype British Ambassador charged with defending the rights and interests of the imperial government. Saddled with this function he had to reconcile in himself the conflicting interests and demands of two governments. But as so many Governors-General discovered, the line between Canadian and imperial interests remained hazy and undefined. A skilful, experienced Viceroy could avoid much intergovernmental friction by foresight and diplomacy. On the other hand, a clumsy, inexperienced ruler could create much mischief, strife, and tension.

The pre-1926 Governor-General, acting as British agent in Canada, worked under instructions from the British government which were conveyed through the Colonial Office. The Letters-Patent constituting his office made this perfectly clear. It enjoined him to exercise his several powers and responsibilities by virtue of, among other things, such instructions as the Queen in her Privy Council from time to time might choose to give. Normally these instructions came through the Colonial Office, although during Minto's administration both the War Office and Admiralty often communicated directly. Then, too, there was the usual semi-private network of letters to friends in places of trust or authority. The efficiency of this network depended upon influence and personal friendship and could often be as effective as the official channels.

Contrary to popular belief, the Colonial Office gave Minto no specific instructions. Chamberlain simply requested a formal interview with Minto soon after he accepted the post, presumably to give Minto whatever initial direction the Colonial Secretary desired. Much to Minto's disappointment, Chamberlain, while pleasant and very civil, had nothing important to say, except to request from him a quarterly written report. Above all, Chamberlain issued no marching orders and unveiled no grand imperial blueprint or strategy. Indeed, Chamberlain's apparent indifference to the larger imperial vision remained a recurring viceregal complaint.

The Governor-General had other duties, too. These duties, though more intangible, were nonetheless essential. As the Queen's Canadian representative he became the personal embodiment and central symbol of the monarch and the monarchical system in Canada. His hospitality, presence, and patronage created a sense of community and participation in society and government which cut across the diverse lines of party, region, religion, and culture. The pageantry, pomp, and circumstance which usually accompanied him, combining the familiar and spectacular, provided the means for popular celebration and reaffirmation of loyalty and allegiance. Entertainment, tours, and civic ceremonies with their interminable patriotic addresses were an important, though often tedious, part of a Governor-General's duties.

A Governor-General's success and popularity in this sphere depended very much upon the incumbent's temperament, generosity, staff, and sheer physical stamina. Although Minto loved parades and pageantry and enjoyed uniforms to a fault, he disliked civic ceremonies, receptions, and dinners with their endless toasts and pompous speeches. Consequently he avoided or suppressed them when he could. He preferred small, intimate parties, games and sports. In fact, during his time, some people complained that Rideau Hall became nothing more than an exclusive resort of the Ottawa sporting set. Unlike many of his predecessors and successors he did little or nothing for the arts and letters, although he dutifully patronized what he must. Moreover, given the legacy of his immediate predecessor, Lord Aberdeen, Minto's distaste for mass entertainment created disappointment and dissatisfaction.

Of course, the cost of entertainment and tours bore heavily upon a Governor-General's private purse, particularly those who, like Minto, possessed only relatively moderate means. The Governor-General's annual salary and fixed expense account which amounted to $76,000 had remained unaltered for thirty years. This sum covered only about three-quarters of his average yearly expenditure, that is, an estimated sum of $103,500. The rest, something like $27,500, came from his own pocket, which proved a heavier financial burden than Minto initially anticipated.[5] Later, he tried to alter the viceregal financial settlement, at least for his successor, Lord Grey, who seemed even more impecunious than he. Faced by this burden, Minto tried to reduce expenditures, and with some success. But the saving may well have been at the expense of much good will. For example, he discontinued the habit of holding periodic regional courts in Halifax and Victoria, which had enjoyed such success under his immediate predecessor. Instead, he confined himself to an annual season in Montreal and Toronto, as well as the traditional residence at the Quebec Citadel, which Minto enjoyed immensely. This cut saved him something like $6,000 annually, but doubtlessly lost him many potential friends and defenders, particularly in the Maritimes, which he neglected more than most of his predecessors.

In other ways, too, the Aberdeen legacy proved an onerous initial burden. Extravagant tales of the Aberdeens' doings and misdoings regaled British society, and as they passed by word of mouth, they lost nothing in the retelling. The unfortunate pair were ridiculed openly in journals like *Vanity Fair*, which irreverently dubbed them *Ego et Rex meus.*[6] Friends twitted Minto before he left Britain about the social chaos he would encounter at Rideau Hall. They warned him that he might "find it a little awkward just at first to sit down to dinner with the housemaids," but assured him that "tea and prayers bring them together—don't forget."[7] When Minto arrived in Ottawa, he reported with some merriment the alleged state of Rideau Hall under his predecessors:

[5] Minto Papers, "Memorandum for His Excellency the Governor-General," January 26, 1899. Aberdeen estimated that the office had cost him £5,000 a year more than his salary and fixed cost allowances. Minto Papers, Chamberlain to Minto, July 19, 1898. Although Minto complained of the viceregal costs, the office still may have been preferable financially to remaining in Britain. This was certainly the case with Lansdowne and Grey. One unidentified newspaper clipping made the point quite brutally but accurately when it wrote: "It is an open secret that Lord Minto was sent to Canada to allow him to patch up his fortunes, which were sadly dilapidated. He was poor for his station according to English standards, and a few more years at home would have left him financially stranded. When he came to Canada he rented his estates at Home." Minto Papers, scrapbook.

[6] *Vanity Fair*, December 31, 1896.

[7] Minto Papers, Wenlock to Minto, July 31, 1898.

The establishment was too awful—punctuality for anything unknown—dinners sometimes not till 10 p.m. His A.D.C.'s starving and always picking up what they could. . . . The Haddo Club (or terms of equality with servants every Thursday night) when subjects were brought forward for discussion in which I hear on one occasion the butler considerably bested H.E.—the servants consequently odious to everyone.[8]

Nor did the Aberdeen influence cease once they had left Canada. The chief offender, Lady Aberdeen, had decided to retain a close association with her National Council of Women and had planned a return visit and tour of Canada within the first year of Minto's administration. The Mintos, who magnified the possible terrors of Lady Aberdeen's return, appealed in vain to Chamberlain and eventually to Lord Aberdeen to stop "this infernal woman prowling about."[9] Her visit passed off smoothly enough and without incident, although Minto thought her antics disgraceful, because, according to him, she visited every public institution in Ottawa, distributed prizes, and spoke from a public platform. Obviously in Minto's eyes these activities were outside the pale of Victorian female respectability. In fact, Lady Aberdeen displayed far more discretion than they had imagined possible. The Mintos always tended to exaggerate the social ills of the Aberdeens. Consequently their prescribed remedy seemed out of all proportion to the disease.

The Mintos, particularly Lady Minto, came to Canada with a self-imposed mandate to restore order and decorum to the social life of Rideau Hall. This was a task scarcely designed to win friends.[10] John Anderson, the Chief Clerk at the Colonial Office, when he visited Canada in 1901 with the Duke and Duchess of Cornwall, blamed Lady Minto for much of the petty criticism which plagued the Mintos' term.[11] She enforced punctuality rigidly, curtailed entertainment, and purged guest lists. Only those "entitled" to official recognition were entertained and a strict observance of precedent and court etiquette, which had often been abridged or ignored under the Aberdeens, was re-imposed. Although the Mintos might chuckle to themselves about the nervous Nanaimo mayor who consistently addressed them as Your Majesty, or the terrified Chatham, New Brunswick, official who bowed deeply before an aide-de-camp while offering the Governor-General, attired in plainer civic dress, a hearty handshake, their rigid and elaborate adherence to rules did nothing to endear them to their terrorized guests. While greater order might have been desirable following the Aberdeen years, the Mintos probably went too far. Generally Canadians tended to see Minto as "a stately grey-haired gentleman," a sedate, correct, dignified official who moved as the

[8] Minto Papers, Minto to Arthur Elliot, December 25, 1898.

[9] Minto Papers, Diary, November 1, 1899; Minto to Chamberlain, August 20, 1899.

[10] Minto Papers, Minto to Arthur Elliot, February 26, 1899.

[11] Joseph Chamberlain Papers, John Anderson to Chamberlain, January 6, 1902.

shadow of royalty, a man who "never unbends."[12] Few would have recognized the joyous, boyish, middle-aged man who, during Lady Minto's absence in Quebec, joined a servants' dance at Rideau Hall and danced and sang in the drawing room until the party's end. "I had visions of Lady Aberdeen emerging from a sofa," he reported to his horrified wife.[13]

Unfortunately Minto's staff did nothing to ease the transition. Their inexperience and naïvety simply compounded his own. Minto's military secretary, Laurence Drummond, a close friend and sporting companion, might have proven invaluable had he remained in Ottawa and put his mind to the task. But he, too, lacked previous administrative and political experience. According to a Rideau Hall companion, Drummond was a hard-working, "elderly young man of thirty five, married and settled down to a life he takes most seriously."[14] More to the point, Drummond was a professional soldier, billed by the Scottish press as "one of the heroes of Omdurman."[15] Just back from military service abroad, he had agreed to accompany Minto to Canada more out of friendship than conviction, and he remained restless and anxious to depart and did so as soon as the South African war began. His departure left Minto without a proper military secretary for over a year and a half. Drummond's replacement, Major F. N. Maude, a retired military engineer and a former editor of the United Service Magazine, was only thirty-six, a meticulous administrator and something of a perfectionist. He took command immediately and became a pillar of strength, although his encounters with the Canadian public, who complained of his predilection for polishing "our manners," were far from cordial.[16] In the interim, Minto acquired a private secretary, S. F. Sladen, a devoted, competent assistant, who performed the duties of military secretary. He remained in Canada after Minto's departure and became for many years something of a permanent fixture in the Governor-General's office.

Minto's aides-de-camp, W. F. L. Lascelles, later Lord Harewood (Scots Guards), and J. H. C. Graham (Coldstream Guards), were both young, unmarried Lieutenants, entitled to $12,000 per annum for their services.[17] As Minto soon learned, they were of little practical value and often a decided liability. These men give the impression of being two jovial, frolicking school boys, bent on a lark, who were brought out for their decorative and entertainment value rather than any practical talent. Graham described himself as "a Scotchman by birth, an Englishman by occupation, a dilettante with a turn for writing inferior doggerel, a taste for literature, an ear for music, a

[12] The Montreal Gazette, November 18, 1899.

[13] Minto Papers, Minto to Lady Minto, October 28, 1899.

[14] Minto Papers, Harry Graham, "Across Canada to the Klondike," MS, 4.

[15] Weekly Scotsman, October 29, 1898.

[16] Montreal Sunday Sun, November 20, 1904.

[17] Minto Papers, Minto to John Anderson, November 26, 1898.

retentive memory and a prodigious thirst."[18] Graham's penchant for doggerel once caused Minto considerable embarrassment. Just before the American presidential election in 1904 he foolishly published, in an American magazine under his own name, a poem poking fun at Roosevelt. Fortunately nothing came of his indiscretion, though it caused Minto many anxious moments.[19] Lascelles, a man more of Minto's tastes and temperament, a sporting, manly, outdoor type— although, Minto complained, credulous in the presence of strong-minded women—left as Drummond did before his first year was up. His replacement, Lieutenant Arthur C. Bell (Scots Guards), a man not unlike Graham, became a great favourite in Ottawa society. An amusing, flamboyant companion, but with no particular love of camp life, he shared Graham's prodigious thirst, literary pretensions, and irresistible compulsion to publish. His letter to the *New York Times*, decrying Chamberlain's tariff campaign, for example, caused Minto as much if not more pain than Graham's poem.[20]

The fourth important member of Minto's household, Arthur Guise, came highly recommended by his former employer, Lord Crew, and became Comptroller of Rideau Hall. According to Graham, who never sacrificed poetry for accuracy, Guise was "a wild warm-hearted Irishman . . . a bonvivier of Bohemian tastes, an Imperialist with Radical tendencies."[21] It is difficult to say whether it was his Bohemian tastes, radical tendencies, or sheer boredom—since he hated Ottawa—which betrayed him into what Chamberlain and King Edward VII considered a grave indiscretion. In December 1901, he and Bell attended what in Minto's mind appeared to be an inoffensive public lecture in Ottawa by John Redmond, an Irish journalist and a leader of the Home Rule movement. Perhaps what was more offensive was that Redmond had some time previously prayed publicly for the defeat of British arms in South Africa. There was no question of Guise's sympathies. During Minto's Klondike tour of 1900, Guise had created a great stir by trying to throw a large American with pro-Boer sentiments out of a Yukon saloon into a river. Guise's attendance at the Redmond lecture, however, brought down upon Minto and his household the undiluted wrath of Chamberlain and Edward VII. Neither was amused, and Chamberlain lost no time informing Minto of their displeasure. This led to a heated exchange between Minto and Chamberlain, the only one of his Canadian career, which terminated with Chamberlain's terse warning that Minto was never again to permit such "Improprieties."[22] Although Minto considered the whole affair a lot of d----d nonsense" and wondered "how a big man like J. C.

[18] Minto Papers, Graham, "Across Canada to the Klondike," 5.

[19] Minto Papers, Minto to Lady Minto, July 7, 1904.

[20] Minto Papers, Minto to Lady Minto, July 9, 1903.

[21] Minto Papers, Graham, "Across Canada to the Klondike," 3.

[22] Joseph Chamberlain Papers, Francis Knollys to Chamberlain, December 10, 1901.

can fuss over it," nevertheless, at times like these, his staff seemed to be more trouble than assistance.[23]

Yet, whatever their public shortcomings, together they appear to have been a very jolly household. Above all, they were a stark contrast to the pious band of concerned people which had haunted the Aberdeen establishment. One could scarcely have imagined Lord Aberdeen, for example, watching with any degree of humour the departure of an A. D. C. (Bell) for St. Louis in a private rail car costing $50 a day loaded with cocktails.[24] Nor could one conceive of Lady Aberdeen's formidable reaction upon learning, as Lord and Lady Minto did, of their staff's propensity for nude, early morning dips in the Banff Hot Springs Hotel's swimming tank, a sport they refused to renounce despite the caretaker's threats and pleas that he and they were liable to a fine of $25.[25]

There was a kindly, affectionate, joyous private side to Minto, which inspired devoted loyalty from his staff and friends, and presented a stark contrast to his stiff, wooden, exacting public image. Those who remained outside the charmed circle of his confidence tended to magnify every blemish of his character or career; those admitted to the inner sanctum tended to excuse, defend, or deny any imperfections. Throughout Minto's administration his private and public images never matched.

[23] Minto Papers, Diary, December 23, 1901.
[24] Minto Papers, Minto to Lady Minto, June 23, 1904.
[25] Minto Papers, Graham, "Across Canada to the Klondike," 34.

Chapter Five

The Wooden Governor

Minto's apologists have often seen him as "a shrewd constitutional governor," a type of Tory-democrat, whose honest, straightforward "broad humanity enabled him sometimes to read more correctly the heart of the plain man than the plain man's official exponents."[1] A glance at his early actions, however, scarcely supports this unqualified conclusion. On the contrary, Minto's first year in Canada is a curious and often tedious tale of discord and dissension. From this period he emerged, in the eyes of many, as the "Wooden Governor," the stiff pro-Consul intent on ruling Canada.

Adversity plagued Minto's first months in Canada. Trouble began on the St. Lawrence River. Until then the ten-day crossing from Liverpool aboard the comfortable 6,000-ton vessel, the *Scotsman*, had been smooth and pleasant, despite the lateness of the season. But on Friday, November 11, 1898, the day before his party was due to reach Quebec City, his eldest son, Larry, became seriously ill with a bronchial ailment, and for a time the doctors feared for his life. Acting upon two doctors' advice, Minto cut the Quebec City reception to an abso-

[1] Buchan, *Lord Minto*, 121; Gundy, "Sir Wilfrid Laurier and Lord Minto," 28.

lute minimum and decided to move on almost immediately to Montreal by ship. He remained in the provincial capital only long enough to take the oath of office, a brief but impressive ceremony in the Quebec Legislative Council, and reply to the Mayor's traditional address of welcome. Then he returned to the ship and sailed slowly toward Montreal, leaving the Aberdeens to bask in the undivided attention of newsmen and politicians who had come to honour both the new and departing Governors-General.

In Montreal Larry's continued illness prevented even a modest reception, and on Sunday, amidst slush and snow, Lord and Lady Minto toured the city with the anonymity of private citizens. By Tuesday Larry had recovered sufficiently to travel on to Ottawa, but there, too, they enjoyed no public reception. It had been cancelled. Throughout the ordeal Minto stoutly refused to talk to newsmen and not until Saturday, over a week later, did he consent to an official civic reception. By this time public curiosity had abated or had been diverted by other public issues.[2]

Judged by press comment, Canadians' reception of Minto seemed as cool and uncertain as the inclement weather which greeted him. While most noted his previous Canadian experience and the fact that his eldest daughter, Eileen, was a Canadian by birth, an air of reserve and apprehension characterized their initial reaction.[3] One paper wrote later that many Canadians felt Minto's appointment a sacrifice of the traditions of the office and the dignity of Canada.[4] Others dismissed the position's importance and described it as one befitting a nonentity. Some Liberal journals were clearly apprehensive. They evidently feared that the advent of a soldier might compromise Sir Wilfrid Laurier's 1897 colonial conference victory where he had cleverly evaded imperial military commitments. Their fears were fed by Minto's widely reported parting comment to a Scottish military group in which he had promised to continue his work with the Canadian militia.[5] This casual remark had been compounded by the indiscreet prophecy of British journals that Minto, in cooperation with Major-General E. T. H. Hutton, the newly appointed General Officer Commanding the Canadian militia, would give Canada "five years of vigorous rule."[6]

The man that Canadians saw step smartly ashore at Quebec that cold November day and exchange welcoming greetings with the small group who waited to escort him to the Legislative Council seemed quite capable of providing vigorous rule. According to one

[2] The spell of personal misfortune continued into the spring of 1899 when Minto learned of the *Labrador's* wreck off Newfoundland. This vessel contained many valuable personal effects.

[3] *Canadian Gazette*, July 28, 1898, contains a valuable résumé of Canadian press reaction.

[4] Toronto *News*, November 14, 1904.

[5] *Scotsman*, October 15, 1898.

[6] Toronto *Telegram*, December 26, 1899; *Canadian Gazette*, October 20, 1898.

observer, this small but erect, athletic, gray-haired, middle-aged gentleman with an iron-gray moustache gave the impression of a "man of determination."[7] And as he drove to the Legislative Council to take the oath of office and thereby become Canada's seventh post-Confederation Governor-General, the critical state of his son's health probably gave his drawn, bronzed features an air of unusual severity.

The Canada Minto first encountered in 1898 appeared little changed since the 1880s. Fortunately, the old capital of Quebec remained intact. In Minto's opinion it was still the finest city on this side of the Atlantic. And, although Montreal had grown a good deal since the 1880s, the old town and commercial section appeared comfortably familiar. As he moved west the changes became more obvious. Even Ottawa, that city of sawdust and civil servants, now had a more settled look. It boasted a new tramway, electricity, and more and better streets. In the far prairie west things were in a state of constant change and would remain so throughout his administration.

Men and politics had changed too. The familiar Tory party had been driven from office and with it many of the old Ottawa hands. Their old Chieftain, Macdonald, was dead. Others too had departed or were languishing in the shades of opposition. Yet Sir Charles Tupper, leader of Her Majesty's opposition, was a familiar landmark. In government, the bookish deskmate of Edward Blake, the Liberal opposition leader in the 1880s, was now Prime Minister and known as Sir Wilfrid Laurier. But apart from a few old stalwarts like Cartwright and Scott, Laurier's Cabinet colleagues had been known to Minto largely by name and reputation. It would take time to appreciate the nature and extent of the changes which had occurred. However, Minto was anxious to begin at once and determined to set the right tone. Things would not be run as they had been run under his predecessor. With all the impatience of a novice, he plunged immediately into the affairs of his office. The results were often unfortunate.

For example, Minto's needless embroilment in a musical dispute in the spring of 1899 was not only petty but downright silly. It was reminiscent of his old, trivial quarrels with the Reverend Galloway. The quarrel began only a few months after Minto arrived. In February 1899, Samuel Aitken, a representative of the Associated Board of Musical Examiners of the Royal College of Music and the Royal Academy of Music in London, came to Canada with a mission to establish a standard musical examination for the Empire. According to Aitken the system would be "unimpeachable, impartial and imperial," and bring Canadian musical standards into conformity with those in Britain and the colonies, notably Australia, New Zealand, and South Africa.[8] Aitken's crusade had all the characteristics of a late Victorian period piece. Unfortunately, he began his campaign without consulting established Canadian colleges and conservatories and

[7] Montreal *Gazette*, November 18, 1898.

[8] Samuel Aitken, *The Case of the Associated Board* (Toronto, March 29, 1899), 1.

throughout his crusade he stoutly refused to consider any conciliatory proposals of cooperation or coordination with these institutions.
A disagreeable and tedious feud followed. Almost immediately
Canadian musicians, whose incomes depended largely on examination fees, formed a large and representative protective association to
protest Aitken's intrusion and to defend their professional interests.
First they took their case to the press, which gave them sympathetic
support. Undaunted by the storm he had aroused, Aitken fought back,
and his crude and illogical means of persuasion soon obscured the
original merits of his case. Of course, he was not a man one would
normally choose for an ally. In the press he ruthlessly attacked the
reputation of musicians and musical institutions. The Dominion College of Montreal, the Toronto College of Music, and the Toronto
Conservatory of Music were, he claimed, mere "trading institutions"[9]
and A. S. Vogt, a distinguished Canadian musician, a foreigner who
possessed no musical talent.[10] His intemperate accusations aroused
strong opposition outside the musical world, in French and English
Canada and among men who might otherwise have supported Aitken's campaign if only by their silence. The Canadian Club of Toronto, for example, entered the fray and gave its full support to the
Canadian cause.

To stop Aitken a Canadian protest committee led by James L.
Hughes, the respected Toronto school supervisor, appealed directly
to Minto, who earlier had been persuaded by Aitken to become honorary president of the Associated Board in Canada. The Governor-
General had unwisely consented because of the Colonial Office's
unofficial endorsement in 1897 of the Board's efforts to improve
musical standards in the "British colonies." Although this blanket
recommendation was cleverly used by Aitken to justify his Canadian
crusade, the Colonial Office knew nothing of Aitken or his methods.
On the other hand, Minto was the man on the spot and in a position to
make a more perceptive assessment and, if necessary, to persuade the
Colonial Office to withdraw or qualify its support. Alternatively,
Minto might have played peacemaker; instead, he simply aggravated
matters more by assuming the role of a partisan, seemingly convinced
of the validity of Aitken's course.[11]

Consequently, when the Canadian committee presented its
closely reasoned forty-seven page petition, Minto replied, not by
calling for mutual understanding and settlement or by issuing a
formal, noncommittal perfunctory statement, but with an ill-advised
defence of Aitken and the Associated Board. More seriously, his
defence seemed to impugn by implication the reputations of Canadian musicians and their institutions. Elated by Minto's support,
Aitken seized upon his words and quoted him freely in his press
defence against the Canadian committee's attacks. Understandably

[9] Toronto Globe, February 28, 1899.

[10] Toronto World, March 10, 1899.

[11] Colonial Office 42 (868), Minto to Chamberlain, March 15, 1899.

offended by Minto's remarks which Drummond, his military secretary, had communicated to the press, Canadian musicians replied in kind. They questioned Minto's judgment and impartiality and contested and repudiated many of his assertions.[12]

Aitken's mismanaged Canadian campaign soon ended in ignominious failure, leaving Minto discredited and in possession of a lost and unpopular case. In London the news of Canadian resistance to Aitken's tactics received sympathetic support and the Associated Board wisely decided to recall him.[13] This left Minto in an even more awkward and embarrassing but typical position. A more cautious, perceptive, and experienced man, or a less impatient one, might have avoided entanglement in this silly affair. A shrewder man might have attempted to seek or impose peace where he found misunderstanding and strife. But as subsequent events would demonstrate, Minto was at first none of these things.

Laurier's prolonged absences from Ottawa and his preoccupation with Canadian-American relations during the first months of Minto's administration did nothing to make it easier for the Governor-General. Although Laurier and many of his chief ministers had gone to Quebec to greet Minto, Larry's illness had reduced their contact to polite formalities. Laurier then left for Washington to participate in the second sitting of the International Joint High Commission convened to settle outstanding Canadian-American differences, and he remained there until February 1899, except for brief, hurried visits to Ottawa. When he returned to Ottawa and recovered from six months of tough, unsuccessful negotiations he plunged immediately into a parliamentary session which he planned to be the last before a general election. Consequently Minto failed to establish close ties of friendship with Laurier until much later. In Laurier's absence, Sir Richard Scott, the irascible old Secretary of State, acted as Prime Minister. Meanwhile the other Cabinet ministers, except for Sir Richard Cartwright, the Minister of Trade and Commerce, and Louis Davies, the Minister of Marine and Fisheries, who assisted Laurier in Washington, performed their perfunctory official duties or attended to private and political matters in their constituencies.

As a result, Minto associated with a small, closely knit circle of imperial officers: Colonel Gerald Kitson, Commandant of the Royal Military College; Colonel Hubert Foster, Chief Staff Officer of the Canadian militia; Minto's old friend, Major-General E. T. H. Hutton; and George Parkin, Principal of Upper Canada College and author of The Great Dominion. Insulated from Canadian public life, they simply reinforced all his old misconceptions and prolonged Minto's initial period of adjustment. Indeed, the friendship of one member of this group, that of E. T. H. Hutton, proved the greatest cross of Minto's early administration. Very soon this querulous officer embroiled himself in a series of interminable disputes, dragging the Governor-

[12] Montreal Gazette, March 11, 1899; Toronto Globe, March 9, 1899.
[13] London Truth, February 2, 1899; London Musical News, April 1, 1899.

General with him. Nothing poisoned Minto's relations with his government more than his unfortunate support of Hutton's many causes. Conscious of Hutton's lack of tact and common sense, the Colonial Office had tried to block his appointment to Canada.[14] However, the War Office insisted, confident that he had learned a lesson since his command of the New South Wales militia in 1893-96, which had ended in a ministerial crisis. Both Wolseley and Sir Redvers Buller had tried to warn Hutton before he left London to ride a bit more gently in Canada, and to urge and flatter rather than drive and abuse. In their words, "you can lead them [the colonials] anywhere with a silken noose."[15] But before long Hutton had quarrelled with F. W. Borden, the Canadian Minister of Militia, Sam Hughes, the opposition military critic, and Lord William Seymour, the General Officer Commanding British troops in Halifax. He had also annoyed or irritated many other military and civilian personages of greater and lesser import.[16]

Having arrived in Canada two months before Minto, Hutton met the new Governor-General in Quebec, anxious to secure viceregal support for his self-imposed mission to reform the Canadian militia. As an old friend of Minto's, Hutton had easy access to Rideau Hall, where he soon found he possessed a firm, loyal, and influential supporter, and it was not long before he decided to test his friendship. Minto had not been in Canada two weeks before Hutton sought his assistance in settling a minor matter between himself and his Minister. It seemed that Borden had recommended to Cabinet the appointment of a Dr. Napoléon Chevalier to the Medical Officer's post at the military school at St. Jean, Quebec. Although Borden sought Hutton's perfunctory approval, when the new General Officer Commanding requested more information, Borden ignored the request and sent the recommendation directly to Cabinet where it received general approval. Understandably annoyed by Borden's apparent discourtesy, Hutton asked Minto to intervene. Without hesitation, Minto agreed with Hutton and refused to sign the Order-in-Council until Hutton's approval had been obtained. However, when Borden firmly and somewhat superciliously reminded Minto that he must either accept a

[14] Colonial Office 42 (865), Minute, John Anderson, June 2, 1898.

[15] Hutton Papers, British Museum, "Memorandum of the Hutton-Wolseley Interview," July 29, 1898.

[16] Hutton, despite his good reputation with some Canadian historians, was a notoriously difficult man. Although he himself was convinced that he was "the very humble instrument of an All-wise Providence," other men saw him in a somewhat different light. His Canadian predecessor described him as a "dangerous martinet," and he seemed to quarrel with anyone who crossed his path. Hutton's Australian posting after the South African war, for example, ended with similar difficulties. The Australian Governor-General wrote Arnold-Forster in 1904 that there seemed more than a fair chance the colonial government would dismiss the General. Arnold-Forster, while conscious of Hutton's shortcomings, was reluctant, however, to bring him home since, as he confessed to his diary, Hutton "cannot keep his mouth shut, and would talk us into a difficulty every week." H. O. Arnold-Forster Papers, British Museum, Diary, February 27, 1904.

minister's advice or request his resignation, the Governor-General, confused and uncertain of his position, capitulated and signed the order. It was a bad beginning.

There is no question that Minto possessed the right to request additional information before signing the Order. To make his signature contingent upon Borden's compliance with the demands of a subordinate official was quite another matter. Its results were twofold. It encouraged Hutton to seek at Government House what he failed to obtain from his minister. This fed rather than tamed that officer's considerable pretensions. Second, it gave Minto an unfavourable reputation among Liberal journalists, who quickly spread an unflattering version of the incident. Almost immediately they created the popular notion that "both Hutton and Minto misunderstood their duties and responsibilities."[17]

According to Buchan, Minto at first resolved to avoid close association with Hutton's military reform crusade. If this is so, he renounced his resolve a month after his arrival. For in a speech to the Toronto Club in December 1898, he left his audience in no doubt of his sympathies. On that occasion he informed his audience that E. T. H. Hutton was an old friend of his and if tact, knowledge, and competence could assure success, he would predict that "he is bound to succeed"; but to assure success the Canadian public must support the General and prevent his work being hampered by "political influences."[18] This was an obvious reference to the Chevalier case as well as a public notice that Minto would tolerate no corruption in the public service. Minto's remarks were as deliberate as they were pointed and indiscreet, and they immediately raised the hackles of the sensitive party press. Yet Minto was not entirely blind to Hutton's faults, as an examination of his intervention in the Domville fracas will indicate.

Although the roots of the Domville case lie lost in the morass of New Brunswick politics, superficially the facts seemed simple and straightforward. Lieutenant-Colonel James W. Domville, Commanding Officer of the 8th Princess Louise (New Brunswick) Hussars, was obliged to resign under General Order 90. This Order had been issued by Hutton's predecessor, N. Y. Gascoigne, and by it the tenure of a commanding officer was limited to a five-year period. Only in exceptional circumstances could it be extended to eight years. Both Borden and Gascoigne agreed that Domville's time had come and that he must go, despite his protests.

However, things were not that simple. Domville's military claims for an extension of his term were not without merit. Educated at the Royal Artillery Academy at Woolwich, Domville, then a Conservative, had once been considered a candidate for the post of General Officer Commanding the Canadian militia. Even in 1897, at the age of

[17] Willison Papers, Public Archives of Canada, George Simpson to J. S. Willison, November 24, 1898.

[18] Minto Papers, draft of Toronto Club Speech. Toronto Globe, December 15, 1898.

fifty-five, Domville was far from incompetent. In the opinion of his military superiors, he was well above the calibre of most commanding officers. In fact, his District Officer Commanding, Lieutenant-Colonel George J. Maunsell, had recommended him for the three-year extension. Domville's reasons for seeking the extension, however, were not military but political.

Put another way, Domville might have resigned without incident, except that he disliked the political persuasion of his successor, Lieutenant-Colonel Alfred Markham, whose newspaper, the Saint John Sun, had opposed Domville's election to the House of Commons in 1896. According to Domville, regimental patronage affected close to five hundred votes which it would be foolish to transfer to his political opponent, particularly before an impending provincial election. Moreover, after 1896, Domville occupied a somewhat unusual political position. A former Conservative Member of Parliament, Domville had contested successfully the King's County constituency in 1896 for the Liberals, where he had bearded the Conservative Minister of Finance, George Eulas Foster, in his own political lair. While Domville's victory had enhanced his reputation among Liberals, New Brunswick Conservatives remained bitter and resentful and ready for revenge.

Now safely installed in a Toronto seat, Foster was particularly anxious to destroy Domville's political influence in King's. He began his attack by charging Domville in the House of Commons with misappropriation of militia funds. According to Foster, Domville had obtained and cashed a cheque in the amount of $300 from the militia department for the rental of his regimental armouries. The Auditor-General had brought this error to Domville's attention and the latter had rectified it at once. Undeterred by his failure to impugn Domville's reputation, Foster, under parliamentary immunity, went farther, and accused Domville of other irregularities. But Gascoigne had investigated them and found insufficient evidence to substantiate them, and had recommended that they be dropped and Domville retire in honour. At this point there was no disagreement between the Minister and the General since Borden had backed Gascoigne's demands and had insisted on Markham's right to succeed.[19] However, Domville had no respect for Borden's opinions or judgment and appealed over his head to Laurier. There the case rested until E. T. H. Hutton arrived, gathered the tangled threads of the dispute, and acted. Without consulting Borden, Hutton immediately ordered Domville to surrender the regimental stores to his successor.[20]

Unable to await his victory, Markham foolishly ordered his agent to enter Domville's armouries, often the property of the commanding officer, to seize the military supplies. Markham's illegal actions gave his opponents the cause they sought and they began to question his

[19] Laurier Papers, Public Archives of Canada, Borden to Laurier, February 18, 1898.

[20] Minto Papers, Minto to Hutton, June 3, 1899.

right to succeed. In an effort to end this absurd controversy plaguing his command, Lieutenant-Colonel Maunsell suggested that both men resign in favour of a third, more neutral candidate. Borden endorsed Maunsell's suggestion at once, since it seemed just and reasonable, but Hutton would not consent and Domville would not retire.

Meanwhile Borden, as anxious as anyone to be rid of Domville, persuaded him to retire voluntarily following the New Brunswick provincial election. But when the election was over Domville refused to budge until the Commons public accounts committee, investigating Foster's charges, cleared his reputation. This seemed a reasonable request and Borden, with Hutton's consent, agreed to it. But to forestall the committee's report, Domville delayed appearing before the committee. Annoyed by Domville's devious tactics, Hutton decided to force him out, and in May 1899, without Borden's approval, Hutton persuaded Foster to withdraw his charges and then put Domville on leave of absence pending his retirement. Placed in the disagreeable position of defending Domville, Borden demanded the cancellation of Hutton's order. At this point Minto entered the controversy, not that he had been ignorant of its details until then.

Since Borden's request had placed Hutton in a delicate position he went at once to the Governor-General. Although at first Minto assured Hutton of his "most thorough support," upon second thought he was less confident that he could back him so unequivocally.[21] Despite Hutton's good will and intentions, Minto readily recognized the General's incorrigible vanity, tactlessness, and indiscretion; a brief conversation with Borden convinced him of Hutton's stupidity on this occasion and he lost no time telling the General so. Whatever the rights and wrongs of the case, Borden's request that Domville remain in command until the public accounts committee reported on Foster's charges seemed to Minto to be just and reasonable. In his view, any gentleman had the right to clear his reputation. Yet to see that things were done properly Minto agreed to devise a formula for the settlement of this feud. According to Minto's plan, Hutton must cancel the order as Borden demanded, on the condition that Domville state in writing the date he intended to appear before the public accounts committee. Then, following the committee's report, Domville was to retire. Markham would take command for a week, after which he would be replaced by a third man. Essentially these were the terms Borden had originally suggested.[22]

In August 1899, then, the contentious Colonel retired as planned, following the public accounts committee report. The committee's report had found financial irregularities in Domville's regimental administration but it had cleared Domville of personal guilt or responsibility. This done, the dispute might have ended there, but Hutton, in contravention of the Minto agreement, attempted to retain

[21] Minto Papers, Minto to Hutton, June 9, 1899.
[22] Laurier Papers, Minto to Borden, June 11, 1899.

Markham in command during summer camp. Understandably annoyed by Hutton's duplicity, Borden insisted on Markham's retirement and Hutton capitulated.[23]

To friends Hutton boasted that he had won a great moral victory for a purer militia, supported by a Governor-General who had backed him "like a hero."[24] This claim deserves little serious attention, since under viceregal pressure Hutton had conceded Borden's position. Moreover, if his own later charges contain a shred of truth, the militia remained unpurified. Neither Hutton nor Minto gained much from this petty feud. However, it does provide an insight into their perception of men and circumstances. Throughout, they tended to see things in simplistic terms. To them, Borden was the protagonist, the protector of Domville and the Liberal party. They failed to realize that neither Borden nor any of his Cabinet colleagues held any brief for Domville. In fact, Borden had insisted on Domville's resignation from the start. He regarded Domville as a troublesome nuisance who, as Richard Scott said, exaggerated the political importance of his command.[25] Domville reciprocated Borden's dislike. A personal and professional tension had existed between the two men ever since Borden accepted the portfolio Domville had solicited in 1896.[26] On an earlier occasion, over another matter, Domville had even threatened to assault Borden. Oblivious to the subtleties of Canadian politics, both Hutton and Minto tended to exaggerate the partisan nature of the dispute. More serious, Minto's and Hutton's actions endangered, rather than assisted, militia reform. In Desmond Morton's words, they failed to see that Borden was the "most powerful force for [militia] reform in Laurier's government."[27]

Many Liberals suffered from similar illusions. They believed that Hutton and Minto were political partisans who favoured Conservatives over Liberals in the race for places in the militia. They compared Domville's struggle for an extension with the easy acquiescence to a similar request made by William White, Commanding Officer of the 30th Battalion, who had made no secret of his Conservative leanings. They noted how closely Hutton worked with Sir John Carling, the Conservative Senator, while reorganizing the 7th Fusiliers of London. In Toronto, Liberals complained that Hutton had placed the entire organization of the new medical unit in Conservative hands; but they were wrong. Hutton's battle with the redoubtable Conservative Member of Parliament for North Victoria, Sam Hughes, proved that the General respected no man's politics, particularly when they clashed with his personal ambitions.

[23] Hutton Papers, Hutton to F. W. Borden, August 11, 1899.

[24] Hutton Papers, Hutton to Sir Redvers Buller, June 18, 1899.

[25] F. W. Borden Papers, Public Archives of Nova Scotia, Richard Scott to Borden, April 14, 1899.

[26] See Laurier Papers, vol. 12, 4753-5059.

[27] Desmond Morton, "Authority and Policy in the Canadian Militia, 1874-1904" (unpublished Ph.D. thesis, University of London, 1968), 431.

Hughes and Hutton seem to have clashed almost from the first time they met. They were too much alike to get on well with each other. Although competent officers, both were impulsive, vain, and intemperate; both craved rank and distinction and saw war as a means to advance their claims. Understandably, their most bitter altercation occurred over the leadership of the proposed South African war contingent. In May and again in July 1899, Hughes, an early exponent of imperial federation, had anticipated war in South Africa and had offered to recruit and command a Canadian volunteer contingent. Hutton, on the other hand, who had little respect for the martial virtues of Canada's non-permanent militia, had larger ambitions. He dreamed of commanding the combined colonial contingents, and he felt that he could obtain this goal only if he played a conspicuous part in organizing and despatching Canada's contribution. In this way he would reap whatever credit it earned. Given his position, this meant an official government-endorsed contingent as opposed to Hughes's private plans.

Since the details of Canada's entanglement in the South African war are fairly well known, only those facts relevant to the focus of this study will be recalled. It was in July, 1899, that Chamberlain first wrote to Minto asking whether Canada might provide military assistance in the event of war in the Transvaal and what form this aid might take.[28] Minto immediately informed Hutton of Chamberlain's letter and Hutton, without waiting for the Canadian government's response, began preparing a contingency plan for the despatch of 1,200 Canadian men. When he completed his preparations he wrote directly to Wolseley, enclosing a detailed set of plans for his information. He also took the opportunity of offering his personal services to lead the combined colonial forces of Australia and Canada.[29] Although Hutton later boasted that he spent the summer working up "a spirit of patriotism and military enthusiasm . . . to a white heat throughout Canada," his greatest task consisted not of persuading English Canada to send volunteers, but of persuading the federal government to accept his and not Hughes's plan.[30]

Initially Hutton planned to give Hughes a conspicuous place in the proposed official contingent. But unaware of the General's plans and fearing the worst, Hughes made his own arrangements. Then on July 24 he again offered to raise and command a Canadian volunteer contingent, but he was more insistent this time. In his triple capacity of militia officer, Canadian citizen, and British subject, Hughes submitted his offer through three channels, the General Officer Commanding, the Minister of Militia, and the Colonial Secretary. The first never got beyond Hutton's desk, and Hughes received not so much as an acknowledgement of his offer. The second, Borden endorsed and

[28] Minto Papers, Chamberlain to Minto, July 3, 1899.
[29] Hutton Papers, Hutton to Wolseley, September 4, 1899.
[30] Hutton Papers, Hutton's MS, "Memoir," 149.

sent to Cabinet, despite Hutton's objections. In turn, the Cabinet sent
the offer to Minto and asked him to transmit it to the Colonial Office.
But Minto, after consulting Hutton, returned the Privy Council minute covering Hughes's offer and explained to the Cabinet that he
considered Hughes incapable of serving with British officers.[31]
Hughes's third offer was acknowledged graciously by Chamberlain,
who asked Minto to thank Hughes for his patriotism and loyalty.

Irritated by Hughes's success, Minto showed Chamberlain's letter
to Hutton. Without considering the consequences of his request, he
asked the General to reprimand Hughes, a subordinate officer, for his
unusual military behaviour in communicating directly with Chamberlain. Hutton needed no prompting. He immediately informed
Hughes of the Governor-General's "command," adding that all subsequent communications must pass through the General Officer
Commanding.[32]

Minto's actions were somewhat irregular at best. Hughes, like
many Canadian citizens before and since, had addressed the British
government directly. In the past, Minto had offered no objection to
this procedure. Not only had he forwarded these communications to
the appropriate department, but he had conveyed their response
promptly and courteously. But Hughes was another matter. Blinded
by his personal feelings, Minto chose to regard Hughes as a troublesome militia officer trying to short-circuit and undermine Hutton's
authority through a direct appeal to the imperial government. Even
so, the means Minto chose to demonstrate his displeasure was most
unusual. Minto knew that as Commander-in-Chief of the Canadian
militia he had no executive authority. His official access to Hutton ran
through the Minister of Militia; and although Hutton and Minto never
tired of fussing over the stupidities and inconvenience of red tape, no
two men insisted more on the strict adherence to proper procedures.
In fact, had not this been Hughes's initial offence?

Minto's intrusion did nothing to diffuse the Hutton-Hughes feud
since Hughes never suffered rebuff silently. Stung by Hutton's communication and the Governor-General's complicity, Hughes struck
back with all the recklessness of a doomed man, and Hughes understood only one type of battle—total warfare, in which no quarter was
given. In a fit of passion, he wrote to Hutton and demanded to know by
what authority the Governor-General had ordered his reprimand. He
also took the occasion to denounce Hutton's vindictiveness and remind him of the stupidities of British regulars through the ages. He
ended his tirade by predicting certain defeat for British troops in
South Africa "if ordinary British tactics be employed."[33] Hughes's
retort lacked any suggestion of subtlety and his insulting language
together with his dubious historical references convinced both Hut-

[31] Minto Papers, Minto to Hutton, August 10, 1899.
[32] Laurier Papers, Hubert Foster to Hughes, August 24, 1899.
[33] Hutton Papers, Hughes to Hutton, August 28, 1899.

ton and Minto that the man was slightly mad and certainly unfit to command troops.

Hutton, who resembled no one more than Hughes himself, replied in kind. He decided to answer Hughes by ridicule. Canadians were, he asserted, utterly unprepared to serve alongside British regulars. "You might as well try to fly to the moon," he told Hughes, "as to take the field alongside of British regulars."[34] Hutton's unkind comments opened an old contention between the two men on the relative virtues of the militia as opposed to the regulars.

However, Hughes remained undaunted by Hutton's rebuff and decided to prove to Hutton, the Canadian government, and Chamberlain himself, that he could collect a contingent of Canadians willing to serve under his command. He immediately wrote to several newspapers requesting volunteers to contact him, an action which only gave Hutton additional cause for offence. Hutton retaliated by charging Hughes with violation of the Army Act, which forbade unauthorized recruiting for the regular army, and threatened to remove him from command of his regiment if he persisted.

At this point the Canadian government intervened. It rejected the contention that Hughes's press poll constituted a violation of the Army Act. It realized, too, that Hughes, although a Conservative, was an efficient and popular militia officer, and it had no desire to defend Hutton's persecution of him; but it had another motive as well. As war approached, some Cabinet members saw Hughes's volunteer scheme as a means of avoiding the tortuous dilemma of Canadian official participation.

Laurier made this perfectly clear soon after receipt of Chamberlain's famous telegram of October 3, thanking "the people," as opposed to the government of Canada, for loyal offers of military assistance and suggesting the organizational form these offers ought to take. While some Canadians regarded Chamberlain's message as a heavy-handed means of coercing their reluctant government, others saw it as an open invitation to begin recruiting the type of private force which Hughes had suggested. Anticipating Cabinet dissension over Canadian participation, Laurier attempted to dodge the issue by encouraging the latter interpretation. On October 4, Laurier not only denied the existence of a government contingency plan, which the *Canadian Military Gazette* confidently assured Canadians existed, but explained that the wording of the Militia Act prevented militia service abroad. On the other hand, he went to great pains to remind Canadians anxious to aid Britain of Chamberlain's words and promised that the Militia Department would readily transmit "individual offers to the Imperial Government."[35] While agreeing with the validity of Laurier's interpretation of Chamberlain's cable, Minto felt, like the *Canadian Military Gazette*, that it would be "a criminal act of folly

[34] Laurier Papers, Hughes to Laurier, October 27, 1898.
[35] Toronto *Globe*, October 4, 1899.

to appoint an amateur militia officer without army experience to command a battalion."[36] He decided, therefore, that Hughes must be stopped and at once.

In the end the Minto-Hutton thesis triumphed and Hughes had to make a bitter peace with them in order to go to South Africa. Still Hughes had not been left friendless. The Canadian government refused to support Hutton's demands for peace based on Hughes's unconditional surrender. Richard Scott, for one, was furious at Hutton's outrageous behaviour, particularly the General's boast that he might have to overturn the Canadian government as he had turned out the government in New South Wales. As Acting Prime Minister he summoned the General to appear before the Cabinet to explain his feud with Hughes. There Scott accused Hutton of driving Hughes into insubordination.[37] Despite his sympathy and friendship with Hughes, Borden defended Hutton against Scott's wrath, and outside the Cabinet tried to play peacemaker. First, he spoke to Hughes and invited him to go to Quebec ready to sail with the first contingent. Meanwhile, on the train down to Quebec, Borden, trading on Hutton's temporary good will, arranged a compromise. According to Borden's plan, Hughes was to be permitted to accompany the contingent in civilian clothes in return for a full apology to Hutton for his literary excesses, which had so offended the General.[38] Anxious to be off, Hughes agreed, but before he reached Father Point he began to regret his unquestioning compliance and to demand a place of command in the Canadian contingent. Only then did he realize how very shallow his apparent victory had been.

In South Africa Hughes found his career blocked at every turn. Everywhere Hutton's and Minto's missives preceded him. Using their personal influence with the commanding officers in the field, they bent every effort to discredit Hughes. Dissatisfied with Hughes's initial qualified apology, Hutton insisted that Hughes receive no responsible military post until he had made a more complete and public confession of fault. Minto supported Hutton's demand and wrote to Lord Roberts, the new Commander-in-Chief, describing Hughes's extraordinary behaviour. When Hughes complied with Hutton's demands, Minto withdrew his objections on the condition that Hughes never command Canadian troops.[39] Hughes then obtained a post with the British Intelligence Corps for five months before Roberts, at Minto's behest, finally ordered him home.

In South Africa Minto was able to keep a close eye on Hughes through correspondence with Canadian officers and his military secretary, Laurence Drummond, who had accompanied the first con-

[36] *Canadian Military Gazette*, October 3, 1899; Minto Papers, Minto to Laurier, October 6, 1899.

[37] Hutton Papers, Hutton's MS, "Memoir," 159.

[38] Hutton Papers, Hutton's MS, "Memoir," 161.

[39] Colonial Office 42 (892), Minto to Chamberlain, July 23, 1903.

tingent.[40] Hughes, of course, was his own worst enemy. He was "a species of lunatic," Hutton once accurately predicted, whom "I should never be surprised to see Minister of Militia."[41] In February, 1900, the case was re-opened during a Commons debate on Hutton's recall. Unfortunately, the government decided to publish the Hughes-Hutton correspondence, perhaps to embarrass the Conservative opposition. As a public man, sensitive of his reputation, Hughes attempted to defend himself by remote control; but his intemperate methods caused him more harm than good. In countless letters to friends at home Hughes described at some length the incompetence of British regulars in South Africa, together with highly coloured accounts of his own heroic exploits. These were designed to provide proof of his early predictions and to reply to Hutton's sneering public remark that he was "utterly unfit for military service" and "practically insane."[42] Erstwhile friends published Hughes's intemperate, egotistical effusions in the Canadian press. The whole affair created much mirth at Hughes's expense. But Minto and Hutton, utterly humourless on this subject and overly sensitive to British blunders, were mortally offended. Minto wrote Roberts, first through the Colonial Office and later directly, to inform him of Hughes's latest indiscretions.[43] Roberts investigated Minto's complaints and called upon Hughes to explain and then sent him back to Canada.

Still the feud did not end. When Hughes returned and began to boast of his exploits which had gone unrecognized by envious, incompetent British regulars, Minto decided upon more drastic action. In his secret files he possessed the full story of Hughes's dismissal. Although Minto piously informed the Colonial Office that he "always treated Lord Roberts' command for Hughes to leave South Africa as secret," in September 1900 he authorized Colonel Kitson to release the true story of Hughes's dismissal to the press.[44]

Minto carried this vindictive campaign against Hughes to extravagant limits. In 1902 he refused to sign a recommendation for Hughes's promotion.[45] The following year when he learned Hughes had appealed directly to the War Office to recognize his South African war services and had demanded at least one Victoria Cross, Minto wrote the Colonial Office a detailed four-page account of Hughes in which he dismissed him as an eccentric whose opinions were no longer "taken seriously by his political friends or opponents."[46]

However, Minto seems to have overplayed his hand. Not that the Colonial Office failed to recognize Hughes's eccentricity. On the con-

[40] Minto Papers, Laurence Drummond to Minto, January 12, 1900.
[41] Laurier Papers, Borden to Laurier, March 23, 1900.
[42] Minto Papers, Hutton to Minto, August 20, 1900.
[43] Minto Papers, Minto to Frederick Roberts, July 13, 1900.
[44] Colonial Office 42 (892), Minto to Chamberlain, July 23, 1903.
[45] Minto Papers, Minto to St. Jean Brodrick, May 27, 1902.
[46] Colonial Office 42 (892), Minto to Chamberlain, July 23, 1903.

trary, they regarded Hughes's flamboyant appeals to Chamberlain as "extraordinary productions it would be hard to beat outside Billingsgate."[47] Still, they were not deceived by Minto's explanations either. At first the Colonial Office refused to believe that Minto had ordered Hutton to reprimand Hughes for his "unauthorized" offers of troops. They chose instead to believe that Minto had acted "under order from the Govt."[48] Yet they considered it "spiteful of Hutton" and by implication Minto, to prevent Hughes from commanding troops in South Africa.[49] While recognizing that Hughes's letters to the press were indiscreet, still they felt Hughes "had some justification, in view of the publication of the Dom. Govt. of his correspondence with General Hutton."[50] In the end, the Colonial Office became very suspicious of Minto's impartiality. "The statement in para. 2 of Lord Minto's desp. is not quite correct," one perceptive Colonial Office clerk noted.[51] In other words, this feud did little to enhance Minto's reputation with the Colonial Office.

In Canada Minto's actions were even less popular. Neither the government nor the opposition approved or condoned his vindictive behaviour. For as eccentric and difficult as Hughes undoubtedly was, he was extremely popular among many militia officers and they resented his punishment, particularly by imperial officials. On this issue Minto had lost all sense of proportion.

Long before the Hughes dispute ended, Minto, unfortunately, had become involved in yet another of Hutton's feuds. Although Hutton's quarrel with Lord William Seymour, the General Officer Commanding British troops in Halifax, began as a minor power struggle, in which the Canadian government played the part of an interested third party, it quickly degenerated into a petty personality conflict which obscured the main point at stake.

The existence of two distinct military commands in Canada had continued to be a source of conflict ever since British regulars withdrew from central Canada in 1871. Their departure meant that the burden of land defence was shifted to the recently created Canadian militia, a force called into existence by Canadian statute and under a Canadian Minister of Militia. The small garrison of British regulars which remained to guard naval installations in Halifax, however, remained a separate command, responsible to the War Office and commanded by a man senior and superior to the Canadian General. In the event of war the two commands were to be consolidated under the authority of the Halifax General, who also doubled as Administrator in the Governor-General's absence. To complicate matters more, the Canadian militia's Commanding Officer was, by law, a British regular

[47] Colonial Office 42 (879), Minute, John Anderson, July 5, 1900.

[48] Colonial Office 42 (874), Minute, John Anderson, November 7, 1899.

[49] Colonial Office 42 (874), Minute, John Anderson, January 2, 1900.

[50] Colonial Office 42 (879), Minute, John Anderson, July 5, 1900.

[51] Colonial Office 42 (879), Minute, John Anderson, July 5, 1900.

army officer loaned to the Canadian government. In order to increase the efficiency of his weak land force he often employed the services of other British officers. In the past the War Office had often asked the Halifax General, being the superior officer in Canada, to report on all regulars serving in Canada, including those loaned to the Canadian government. Lord William Seymour assumed, therefore, that he possessed command and authority over these officers not in their capacity as Canadian officers, but as British officers, a rather tenuous claim which Hutton haughtily rejected.

However, Hutton's hauteur must be seen in a larger context. In his mind, Seymour's routine request was not simply a convenient, established short-circuiting of the proper lines of command but the first installment of a larger plan to subordinate his militia command to the Halifax General. Soon after Hutton arrived in Canada in August 1898 a "Canadian" Commission of Defence under the presidency of Major-General E. P. Leach began hearings on the state of Canadian defences. Hutton declined to be part of the Commission on the assumption that its report would possess greater force if he remained unassociated with its anticipated indictment of Canadian defences. The Leach Commission naturally discussed at length the relationship between the two commands in Canada. Although Hutton later boasted that the report, which did indict Canadian defence, was made with his "direct collusion," he remained somewhat unhappy with its call for closer cooperation between the two commands. Their suggestions were, he felt, both unworkable and a threat to his authority, particularly given the personality of the incumbent Halifax General, Lord William Seymour.

According to Minto the personal quarrel between Seymour and Hutton began at Ottawa in the autumn of 1898 over a petty matter of protocol. Seymour had come to Ottawa to confer with the new Governor-General and Hutton had decided to honour Seymour with a dinner party. Colonel Hubert Foster, Hutton's pliant Chief Staff Officer, himself a British officer on loan to the Canadian government, arrived at the dinner party in civilian clothes. Seymour interpreted Foster's actions as a calculated slight. In his opinion, Foster's dress was a refusal to recognize Seymour's position as Foster's superior officer, and Foster was nothing more than Hutton's shadow. Foster, an unsophisticated and ingenuous man, apologized profusely, but his apology was scarcely credible given his prior knowledge of Seymour's presence.[52] Then Seymour asked Foster for a copy of a secret report entitled "Reconnaissance of the Eastern U. S. Frontier." This was not an unreasonable demand, given Seymour's respon-

[52] Foster later fell from viceregal favour and accommodated himself as easily to Borden's views as he had to Hutton's. In fact, Minto later blocked Foster's ambitions to succeed Kitson at the Royal Military College and persuaded him that he had a better chance of military employment in Britain. "The vulture," as Kitson and Minto called him, returned to Britain to find no position waiting or available. Minto Papers, G. Kitson to Minto, February 20, 1901.

sibilities in the event of war. Foster agreed to oblige, but insisted on sending it through the Governor-General's office. The procedure was unusual but would have been correct if it had gone to the Governor-General's office through the Minister of Militia, but it had not. At the time Seymour said nothing about the incident, but he clearly grasped its significance and waited his time and turn.

It came in April 1899. This time it was Seymour's turn to stand on his dignity. He complained to Minto that Hutton had spoken publicly on the problems of Great Lakes' defence, thereby infringing upon his naval jurisdiction. Minto replied by admitting Hutton's fault but pleading for understanding and sympathy, given Hutton's difficult role.[53] Seymour accepted Minto's apology and the matter ended there, although the resentment remained.

Then a month later the War Office ordered Seymour to make the routine report on all British officers in Canada, including those serving with the Canadian militia. Following established custom and practice, Seymour wrote directly to Hutton to ask for the information requested by the War Office. Hutton rejected Seymour's request and refused to supply the information. Instead, he appealed directly to Minto, not to Borden, to stop Seymour's intrusions. Although Minto agreed to write Seymour and to explain Hutton's position, Minto himself felt that Hutton was being unduly sensitive and told him so. He reminded Hutton that confidential reports regarding "officers serving the Colonial govnt. go home through the G.O.C. Halifax" and pressed him to do everything possible to cooperate.[54]

Minto, however, shared Hutton's fears of Seymour's ulterior motives. Moreover, his own refusal to understand or accept Seymour's contentions simply complicated matters more. In a letter to Seymour Minto explained somewhat needlessly that Canada was a self-governing colony with a militia command controlled directly by and through its government. Yet Seymour never claimed control or authority over the Canadian militia and made that clear on several occasions. For example, on one occasion Borden, in a moment of exasperation, had appealed to Seymour to curb Hutton's insubordination but Seymour had refused because any action on his part "as Lt. General was resented by Lord Minto as an unwarrantable interference with the militia of Canada."[55] On other occasions, Seymour tried, although his attempts may not have been without some malice, to make clear his claim on British regulars in the Canadian militia by addressing them by their inferior British regular rank. This was a procedure which immensely annoyed Foster and Hutton, who enjoyed exalted colonial ranks. Finally Seymour agreed to abandon the informal mode of direct communication with Hutton and address him directly through the Governor-General and Minister of Militia. But

[53] Minto Papers, Minto to Seymour, April 18, 1899.
[54] Minto Papers, Minto to Hutton, July 15, 1899.
[55] Colonial Office 42 (876), Seymour to Selborne, September 18, 1900.

this procedure, although perfectly correct, entailed even greater terrors for Hutton and Minto.

Neither Hutton nor Minto seemed to see or accept the logic of
their position, for if, as they both asserted, they wished to affirm the
autonomy of the Canadian militia, they would have accepted
Seymour's final proposal, since the proper chain of communication
between two autonomous commands would, in that case, pass
through the responsible minister; but they did not accept it. As one
authority has pointed out, this dispute "would have ended very
quickly if Hutton had taken it to the Minister"—that is, if it involved
only a question of autonomy.[56] However, autonomy had only been a
debating point, not a serious argument. Above all, they had no desire
to admit Borden to the cosy confidence of imperial defence communications.

Terrified by the implications of Seymour's suggestion, Minto
wrote directly to Lord Lansdowne. With scant regard for logic he
called upon Lansdowne to define Seymour's powers and curb his
pretensions since the Canadian government would never permit its
militia to "Become an appanage to the Halifax command." Moreover,
he continued, trying to conjure the ghost of the Leach report, "from
what I have seen of Lord William it would be fatal to give him further
control."[57] The autonomy argument, however, again proved a
double-edged sword.

The War Office responded promptly to Minto's request. In October 1899 it outlined its proposed redefinition of Seymour's powers.
Although the War Office supported Minto's call for a clearer separation of commands, a point not really in contest, it read a good deal
between the lines. For example, one War Office official noted that
Hutton was an officer "constitutionally deficient in every atom of
tact—and constitutionally incapable of even acquiring and exercising
the elements of it."[58] While reaffirming the separation of commands,
the War Office also insisted that the General Officer Commanding the
Canadian militia must keep the Halifax General informed at all times
on the state of his force and report regularly on the imperial officers
serving under his command. Finally, the War Office, accepting
Seymour's suggestion, proposed that all future communications between the two commands pass through the Canadian Minister.

Minto and Hutton objected immediately to the War Office's
proposal regarding the proper line of communication, and insisted on
the need to eliminate the Canadian minister. Already, relations between Seymour and Borden were too intimate for their liking. Instead,
they suggested that all future communications should pass directly
through the Governor-General's Military Secretary.[59] The Colonial

---

[56] Morton, "Authority and Policy in the Canadian Militia," 400.

[57] Minto Papers, Minto to Lansdowne, August 30, 1899.

[58] Quoted in R. A. Preston, Canada and "Imperial Defense" (Durham, N.C., 1967),
256.

[59] Colonial Office 42 (875), Hutton to Borden, November 29, 1899.

Office at once detected the absurdity of the suggestion: "it wd. be anomalous to have one servant of the Dominion Govnt. reporting on the services of another of its servants without the Dominion Govnt. knowing anything about the matter. It is in one sense a mere matter of form but it involves a not unimportant principle."[60] Neither Minto nor Hutton seemed to appreciate the irony, not to mention the hypocrisy, of their position as self-appointed defenders of the Canadian militia's autonomy.

Once the imperial arbitrator had spoken, the dispute ought to have ended, but from the start this quarrel had been infected by personal animosity and bitterness, which grew with time. This fact became painfully clear a few months later when the Canadian government dismissed Hutton from command of the Canadian militia. Seymour, who made no secret of his feelings toward Hutton and to a lesser extent also toward Minto, decided to write an official memo to the Canadian government condemning Hutton's conduct while in command of the militia. Minto naturally feared the potentially damaging effect of this document coming from an imperial officer, and he refused to transmit it to Laurier.[61] Annoyed at Minto's refusal, together with his failure to inform him officially of Hutton's dismissal, Seymour foolishly sent the document directly to Borden. He had clearly gone too far, and had laid himself open to the rebuke which followed.

Minto readily seized the opportunity and reported Seymour to the War Office. The War Office promptly informed Seymour that he had acted improperly. Seymour resigned immediately, convinced that Minto had misrepresented his actions and had made his position at Halifax untenable. Minto's victory now seemed complete. Later, however, Seymour's friends persuaded the aggrieved General to request a board of inquiry to clear his reputation. The board decided that Seymour had at no time contravened military law or practice. Their judgment compromised Minto's victory.

Since this quarrel had been shrouded in the secrecy of official despatches and private correspondence, Canadians generally had remained ignorant of its existence. Consequently, this dispute, unlike the Hughes and Domville affairs, did little to damage Minto's public reputation. Yet together they form a curious pattern less suggestive of the shrewd, level-headed, constitutional ruler of men than of a man, as Laurier saw him, who was absolutely untrained in constitutional practice and knew little but horses and soldiering.[62] Time, of course, would teach Minto subtler means of exercising power and of persuading men and solving problems. But the old image formed during these years of the stiff, arbitrary pro-consul intent on ruling Canada with a firm hand, persisted, to be traded on by his detractors long after it ceased to hold any real vestige of truth.

[60] Colonial Office 42 (875), Minute, John Anderson, March 6, 1900.

[61] Minto Papers, Minto to Seymour, March 20, 1900.

[62] Skelton, The Life and Letters of Sir Wilfrid Laurier, 207.

Chapter Six

The Heavy Dragoon

Soon after Sir Wilfrid Laurier died in 1919, a Liberal-Nationalist interpretation of Canadian history gained wide popularity, an interpretation not unflattering to the late and distinguished leader. It depicted Canadian political development as a relentless struggle for increased Canadian autonomy against a jealous and reluctant imperial government. As an interpretation it reflected more the mood of post-war Canada than historical fact. Its chief authors, O. D. Skelton, Laurier's official biographer, J. W. Dafoe, an erstwhile disciple, and L.-O. David, a long and faithful friend, raised this theory to the level of a national myth.[1] But all heroic stories must have villains, and no man seemed better suited to fill this bill than Minto. To them Minto had been Chamberlain's hand-picked agent sent to entangle Canada in an expensive network of imperial obligations against which Laurier struggled for six long years.

The crux of their case, which is based largely on circumstantial evidence, rests upon the unwarranted conclusion that Minto con-

[1] Skelton, *The Life and Letters of Sir Wilfrid Laurier*; Dafoe, *Laurier: A Study in Canadian Politics*; L.-O. David, *Laurier: Sa vie, ses oeuvres* (Beauceville, 1919).

spired to force Canadian participation in the South African war. They contend that the campaign for participation began many months before the outbreak of war in the Transvaal. According to them, it started at least as early as March 1899, when the War Office, through Minto, requested an interpretation of Section 79 of the Militia Act which defined the Canadian militia's territorial liability in the event of war. Laurier's "patriot" response supposedly gave Chamberlain his first victory on the road to Canadian commitment. Although H. Pearson Gundy has argued a convincing case against this conspiracy theory he inexplicably ignored the March request. However, a closer examination of this episode merely confirms Gundy's conclusions.[2]

The conspiracy theory's first difficulty is one of chronology; it should be noted that the circumstances leading up to the March request predated Minto's arrival in Canada. In September 1898, when Britain seemed on the brink of war with France over Fashoda, the War Office and the Admiralty, anticipating a more global struggle, turned their attention to British North American defence. Sir John Fisher, Admiral of the North Atlantic Fleet, in cooperation with Lord William Seymour, was ordered to prepare a defence plan for British North America's Atlantic coast. They immediately decided that upon the outbreak of war Britain ought to sever all French cable communications with British North America and to occupy the French colonial islands in the American hemisphere. The most expeditious means of occupying Martinique, St. Pierre, and Miquelon, they argued, would be to send Canadian militia units directly to the islands or to Halifax to relieve British garrison troops for the task. But Seymour, more familiar with Canadian affairs, anticipated Canadian political and constitutional difficulties and suggested a consultation with the Governor-General. Since Seymour's despatch reached Ottawa just before Minto arrived, Aberdeen had time to make only a superficial response. Therefore, if there was a conspiracy, it had obviously begun well before Minto arrived.

The second difficulty with this explanation is that it ignores Minto's true role in the ensuing controversy, since Minto, not the Canadian government, played the real role of antagonist to the War Office plan to employ the Canadian militia on the French Islands. Essentially Seymour's despatch raised two questions: one, did His Excellency foresee any internal disturbance within the Dominion which might affect any disposition of troops? Two, could the War Office count on "either reinforcements or a relief from the Dominion to the Imperial Troops" in the event of an occupation of St. Pierre and Miquelon?[3] In Aberdeen's opinion, there would be no adverse political reaction to the occupation of the islands apart from a few disaffected persons in Montreal and Quebec. The second question he left to his successor to answer.

[2] Gundy, "Sir Wilfrid Laurier and Lord Minto."
[3] War Office 32/275B/83/266/Canada, Seymour to Under Secretary of State for War, December 14, 1898.

To Minto the subject must have seemed fortuitous. The first substantive issue of his administration was a military matter of primary importance and one, though technical, not totally unfamiliar. The matter of Canadian enlistment for foreign service had arisen during his term as Lansdowne's Military Secretary over fourteen years ago, and at that time he had sounded out John A. Macdonald himself on the subject. This, then, was an opportunity to take a firm lead and to demonstrate his knowledge and sound judgment to both his Canadian and imperial colleagues.

Minto immediately consulted his Minister of Militia, F. W. Borden, whom he found fully acquainted with Seymour's despatch. Borden assured Minto that Canadians could and would probably join an expeditionary force to the French islands. However, Minto disagreed since Section 79 of the Militia Act, he explained to Borden, appeared to restrict the militia's use to "active service either within or without Canada at any time when it appears advisable so to do by reason of war, invasion, or insurrection, or danger of any of them." In other words, Minto believed that the Militia Act forbade the force from being "transported beyond the seas for offensive purposes" and he had a letter from John A. Macdonald to prove it. He had corresponded with the former Prime Minister on the subject in 1885. However, Borden remained unconvinced.

Although Minto reported Borden's opinion to Seymour, he made it perfectly clear that he did not share his Minister's interpretation. He still believed that the Militia Act prohibited the use of the Canadian militia in the occupation of St. Pierre, Miquelon, and Martinique, despite the generality of the concluding phrase of Section 79. Given this unfortunate limitation of the Act, Minto continued, the British government might use Canadian troops to garrison Halifax or, better yet, recruit a contingent in Canada. There would be no practical or legal difficulty, Minto confidently assured Seymour, in recruiting a large body of men; 2,000 or more could be raised without dificulty.[4] John A. Macdonald himself had told him in 1885 that there were no legal barriers to British regular recruitment in Canada.[5] But this was not the point, since neither Seymour, Fisher, nor the War Office was interested in recruiting in Canada.

In London Minto's peculiar interpretation seemed utterly absurd. To forbid the Militia to cross the Canadian border would make a mockery of the force, particularly in the event of a war with the United States. Therefore, Seymour was instructed to speak to Minto at his earliest convenience and inform the Governor-General of the War Office's considered opinion, confident that Minto would acquiesce to its sounder judgment.

However, Minto remained uncowed by the full weight of War Office wisdom. Even when Seymour went to Ottawa to discuss the

[4] Minto Papers, Minto to Seymour, November 22, 1898.

[5] War Office 32/275B/100/266, J. A. Macdonald to Lord Melgund, February 10, 1885.

matter with the Governor-General he found Minto as adamant as ever, although very much more on the defensive. The Governor-General, conscious of Section 79's ambiguity, now based his interpretation almost entirely on the Macdonald letter which he quoted as though it were divinely inspired. On Seymour's return to Halifax he reported to the War Office his failure to persuade Minto to abandon his interpretation.

The Admiralty and War Office were astonished at Minto's intransigence. They had originally thought that Minto's peculiar interpretation was simply the result of ignorance and inexperience, not a firmly held and considered opinion. To overcome Minto's objections the Admiralty suggested a new tactic, an appeal to the Canadian government, which it may have learned from Seymour would be more sympathetic to their views. This second appeal, however, contained a subtle change of reference from a European colonial conflict to one with the United States. This deliberate change was probably an effort to conceal their secret preparations or an obvious effort to strengthen their argument. It was clearly not, as one writer has suggested, evidence of military plans for a possible war with the United States following the failure of the International Joint High Commission's meetings in Washington.[6] Although by March 1899 the Fashoda crisis had all but passed, the British maintained their invasion plans for the French islands for several years. More important, the Canadian Governor-General had inadvertently raised an important theoretical question which demanded a solution.

Minto was not deceived by their tactics, and when he wrote to Laurier on March 25 to seek the Canadian government's official opinion he carefully described the origins of this request, explained his own views, and drew attention to the subtle change of reference. He admitted the absurdity of his own position in the event of war with the United States, but insisted that in no circumstances could militia troops be used "outside the American continent." He felt sure, however, that if the Empire were ever threatened Canada would make a "sentimental offer which could not be considered with purely business calculation."[7]

Laurier shrewdly refused to be drawn into the political question of a "sentimental offer." Consequently, he confined his reply to the legal side of the case. Before he committed his government, however, he sought and received the advice of Borden and his Minister of Justice, David Mills. Their conclusion was unequivocal. In their opinion, the imperial government possessed the undisputed power "to move troops anywhere within or without the Dominion." When Laurier reported the Cabinet committee's response to Minto, the Prime Minister added that it might be unwise, nevertheless, to utilize French-Canadian troops on the islands, but "in saying this he in no

[6] Norman Penlington, *Canada and Imperialism, 1896-1899* (Toronto, 1965), 190-91.

[7] Minto Papers, Minto to Laurier, March 25, 1899.

way qualified the right of the Imperial Government to do so."[8] This was a position which he maintained firmly, despite Minto's attempts to dissuade him with the ubiquitous Macdonald letter.

Unmoved by Laurier's response, Minto made one last futile effort to convince the Admiralty. While he appreciated Laurier's "Imperial and friendly inclination," he wrote Seymour, he could not agree with his conclusions. Then he repeated all the old familiar arguments he had used before and pondered anew the possible mysteries of the Macdonald letter. In short, his words were scarcely those of a conspiring imperial agent.

Finally, the conspiracy theory's assumption of Colonial Office complicity fails to correspond with the facts. To see this March request as part of "Mr. Chamberlain's" imperial strategy or as the beginning of "negotiations concerning Canada's share in a possible South African war" is to ignore the fact that Chamberlain learned of the March request only after March 25.[9] Previously, all correspondence had been confined to Minto, Seymour, the Admiralty, and the War Office. And when the Colonial Office and Chamberlain learned of the Minto-Seymour correspondence, the War Office appeared acutely embarrassed and explained the circumstances of the request more in terms of an apology than a plot. It disclaimed any intention of using Canadian troops on the French islands and assured the Colonial Office it would not think of "employing such troops in another hemisphere"; it was, or so it said, simply interested in a technicality raised by Lord Minto.[10] Moreover, as subsequent events proved, Chamberlain had no interest in the *right* of the imperial government to compel Canadian troops. When war came what Chamberlain wanted was a "sentimental offer" or, in other words, a demonstration of imperial unity and solidarity. This may account for the fact that it took Chamberlain two months to thank Laurier for his "patriotic" response.[11]

Minto's part in the Canadian contingent crisis which preceded Canada's decision to send troops to South Africa, though somewhat more ambiguous, is equally unimpeachable. Friends and critics, unable to appreciate Minto's enigmatic position, have devised unwarranted explanations for his behaviour which bear little relationship to his personal notes and correspondence. Several years later, for example, L.-O. David claimed that at the time of the Boer War, Minto had forced Laurier to send troops. According to David, Minto had offered Laurier the alternatives of providing troops or resigning. This story gained a considerable contemporary popularity and was reiterated time and again in the French-Canadian press. David explained that

[8] War Office 32/275B/92/266/Canada, "Memorandum of Meeting with Laurier," March 27, 1899.

[9] Wade, *The French Canadians*, 477.

[10] War Office 32/275B/100/266/Canada, G. F. Wilson to Colonial Office, May 29, 1899.

[11] Minto Papers, Minto to Laurier, June 17, 1899.

the Prime Minister chose the former course simply to prevent the Conservatives from taking power, since he knew that they would despatch 5,000 men to Laurier's 2,000.[12] While one might dismiss this extravagantly partisan tale as the confused mental meanderings of an octogenarian, Minto's friend, E. T. H. Hutton, appeared no better informed. Some years later, while preparing "an appreciation" of Minto's Canadian career for a prospective biographer, Hutton boasted that he and Minto had forced "the weak-kneed and vacillating Laurier Government with their ill-disguised French and Pro-Boer proclivities to take a part—nay a leading part—in the great movement which has drawn the strings of our Anglo-Saxon British Empire so close."[13] Yet he confessed that he could never understand how Minto, despite his coercive actions, managed to retain "the confidence and goodwill of his Government." Hutton would never have believed the answer: Minto had given neither Laurier nor his government any cause for complaint.

Personally, Minto was not a convinced war partisan. Almost until the outbreak of war, Minto maintained an ambivalent attitude toward the coming conflict, its justice, and Canada's obligations. His equivocations regarding the war grew out of a larger perspective of British life and politics than that possessed by so many ardent Canadian imperialists. It was a view stripped of the romance engendered by distance. His suspicion of the leading politicians, his intense dislike of Rhodes and the Chartered Company, and the lingering fear that Chamberlain had never satisfactorily severed himself from this sordid lot caused him many grave doubts, and these doubts were fed by a close correspondence with his brother Arthur, a prominent Liberal-Unionist Member of Parliament who opposed the war in South Africa from the start. Consequently, Minto could never quite regard the war as a righteous crusade and he lacked the sense of Anglo-Saxon racial mission which blinded many of his contemporaries. For example, when the South African League Congress, following its April meeting in Kimberley, appealed to the Canadian British Empire League to support the Transvaal Ouitlanders' struggle for political rights, an Ottawa rumour suggested that Minto would press the Canadian government for a similar expression of sympathy. Minto did nothing of the sort; nor did he have any intention of doing so. In fact, he wrote to Laurier in quite a different vein to warn him against precipitate action or mingling "in any way with South African complications." Minto, who regarded the South African League as the hirelings of the Chartered Company, added that there would be plenty of opportunity later "to show our good-will," when the imperial government had declared itself.[14]

In his official correspondence Minto was particularly circumspect; he was more the impartial imperial postman, than the dedicated,

[12] Le Devoir, 1, 5, and 19 décembre, 1924.

[13] Hutton Papers, Hutton to Minto, January 10, 1902; Hutton's MS, "Memoir," 153.

[14] Laurier Papers, Minto to Laurier, May 2, 1899.

clever, imperial conspirator. For one thing he lacked the subtlety and finesse of an effective conspirator, a fact Chamberlain discovered when he first canvassed colonial support for a possible war in South Africa. Despite the reserve of some of his more cautious colleagues, Chamberlain, following the failure of the Bloemfontein Conference in June 1899, began to plan for war in the Transvaal. As a means of convincing his wavering colleagues, Chamberlain decided to seek the support of the self-governing colonies in order to demonstrate to doubters in the Cabinet, the country, and abroad, the solidarity of the Empire.

Early in July, Chamberlain wrote Minto two letters clearly stating his intentions. In these letters he explained to Minto that the South African situation had deteriorated and there existed a real possibility that force would be necessary to settle the trouble brewing there. But if colonial governments could be persuaded to make "a really spontaneous" offer of military assistance, it would "have a great moral effect and might go far to secure a pacific settlement" by demonstrating "the solidarity of the Empire." He also made it perfectly clear that if trouble began the imperial government would accept and utilize offers of colonial troops. In closing, he warned Minto against any word or action which might be construed as "external pressure or suggestion."[15] The letter gave Minto wide scope, leaving things very much in his hands. It even failed to stipulate that Minto must consult the government. It simply requested him to ascertain "the views of those concerned."

Minto, however, wrote directly to Laurier, and made no effort to disguise the gravity of the crisis or the implications of the despatch of Canadian troops. While noting that things had improved slightly since Chamberlain had written the letters, he felt it might possibly be "only the lull before the storm." He frankly, but perhaps unwisely, drew Laurier's attention to the serious future implications of a Canadian offer. In Minto's opinion it would "signify the acceptance of a principle which . . . would I believe do much for the future history of the Mother Country and her colonies." Then he bluntly asked Laurier if Canada would supply troops to support British claims in the Transvaal. On his part he confessed that he quite understood "that questions of Imperial emergency may arise in which a colony deeply interested in its own development might justly not see its way to assist."[16]

Minto's letter, and his talk of imperial federation, did nothing to still Laurier's fears. It also suggested an easy escape, and Laurier was not one to miss an opportunity. After several interviews with Minto, Laurier made a clever and diplomatic reply much along the lines Minto had inadvertently suggested. While Laurier piously protested his own personal desire to see troops go and expressed his

[15] Minto Papers, Chamberlain to Minto, July 3, 1899.
[16] Minto Papers, Minto to Laurier, July 19, 1899.

confidence in the righteousness of the Ouitlanders' cause, he regretted that his government would be unable to field a contingent. He gave three major reasons for this decision: the need to retain troops in Canada, owing to the uncertainty along the Alaskan border; the great tax a contingent would make on the Canadian treasury; and French-Canadian hostility to imperial expeditions of this nature.[17]

Laurier's well-reasoned and polished reply did not deceive Minto entirely. Despite the Prime Minister's protests, he detected Laurier's "luke-warm" attitude toward imperial questions. "The Frenchman in him," he informed Chamberlain, "precluded the possibility of any British enthusiasm." But Minto also recognized the difficulties a Canadian contingent might create in French Canada, although in his own mind there was no question that "in any real emergency the British determination to assist the Mother Country would be irresistible by any government."[18] Then, after consultation with Hutton, but without any authority from the Canadian government, Minto provided Chamberlain with an outline of "the probable composition of the force," should one ultimately be sent.

The South African crisis, however, did not rest there, but continued to cause Laurier and Minto difficulty. No sooner had they disposed of the Chamberlain despatch when the secretary of the Capetown and London South African Association, J. Davis-Allen, arrived in Ottawa armed with letters of introduction to prominent Canadians. His mission was to solicit a parliamentary resolution of support for the Transvaal Ouitlanders. Nor was he to be put off easily. When the Commons' Speaker, J. D. Edgar, a close friend of Laurier, refused Davis-Allen the use of the Railway committee room, the intrepid secretary persuaded the Senate to find him a room in the Senate's quarters, where he promptly founded a Canadian parliamentary branch of the South African Association.[19] Then he met with Minto, Laurier, and Tupper, the opposition leader. After his interview with the Prime Minister, Davis-Allen, either by mistake or design, cabled Chamberlain, informing him that Laurier wished to introduce a resolution in the Commons affirming Canada's support for the Ouitlanders, but stating that Laurier would do so only if it were the Colonial Secretary's desire. Chamberlain needed no further prompting. He immediately informed both Minto and Lord Strathcona, the Canadian High Commissioner in London, that a resolution from a non-British imperial leader would be of immeasurable assistance.[20]

Annoyed, but compromised by Davis-Allen's misrepresentation, yet afraid Tupper might seize the initiative and embarrass the government, Laurier reluctantly agreed to move a resolution.[21] On July

[17] Minto Papers, Minto to Chamberlain, July 25, 1899.

[18] Colonial Office 42 (869), Minto to Chamberlain, July 20, 1899.

[19] Laurier Papers, J. D. Edgar to Laurier, July 14, 1899.

[20] Joseph Chamberlain Papers, Lord Strathcona to Chamberlain, July 30, 1899.

[21] Minto Papers, Lord Lorne to Minto, August 8, 1899.

31, he introduced a cautiously worded resolution endorsing the Ouit-landers' call for political liberty but cleverly avoiding any promise of military aid. In his speech he appealed to the conscience of mankind rather than to the threat of physical force.

Minto approved of the resolution and wrote to congratulate Laurier after it had received the unanimous support of the House. Nevertheless, he refused to associate himself too closely with Davis-Allen's activities. Minto himself would have preferred "to see an offer of material assistance" since he had less faith in the conscience of humanity than Laurier had. In his letter of congratulations, however, he again reminded Laurier that there was no question of Britain asking for or needing help; rather, it was for the Canadian government to decide "whether Canada should think it advisable for Imperial reasons to offer troops."[22]

Soon after the Ouitlander resolution passed both Houses, Parliament was prorogued. The politicians returned to their constituencies and Ottawa settled into its familiar but deceptive August quiet. According to Hutton's faulty reminiscences, it was during this period of August and early September that he and Minto conspired to commit Canada to participation in the impending South African conflict. However, Hutton's contention is unsupported by any existing written evidence.

As soon as the session ended, Minto himself fled to the Quebec Citadel where he remained until the end of September, except for a brief visit to Halifax and two short trips to Ottawa on public business. The spring and summer session had been long and tedious and Minto was anxious to get away on a long deserved vacation, his first since his arrival in Canada. While he was in residence at Quebec he spend a good portion of his time hunting and fishing with his aide-de-camp, W. F. L. Lascelles, far from the reach of official correspondence. Then on September 28, he left with Lady Minto for a ten-day trip to New York, where, among other things, he planned to see the children off for school in England. Consequently, he returned to Ottawa only three days before the outbreak of hostilities in South Africa. His itinerary, then, scarcely suggests that of a busy imperial conspirator, nor does his correspondence. In fact, if one can judge from the extant correspondence during these months, Minto seemed much more concerned about Lady Aberdeen's impending trip to Canada than Kruger's activities in South Africa. News seemed scarce and the little he received encouraged his confidence that war would be avoided.

However, the vacation gave Minto time for reflection, and the more he thought, the more uncomfortable he felt about a war in which money and the yellow press played so prominent a part.[23] Late in September he confided to his brother that he saw no reason why Canadian statesmen should "commit their country to the expenditure

[22] Minto Papers, Minto to Laurier, July 31, 1899.
[23] Laurier Papers, Minto to Laurier, February 9, 1900.

of lives and money for a quarrel not threatening imperial safety and directly contrary to the opinion of a colonial government at the Cape."[24] While in this mood of growing uncertainty, he wrote Chamberlain that although there existed a strong, enthusiastic element in Canada pressing for a force, on the other hand there was "a great deal of irresponsible and unreliable talking connected with it."[25] He also warned Chamberlain that it would be a serious mistake to push Laurier too far on the subject of troops for the Transvaal. He argued a similar line with his impetuous friend Hutton, and made every effort to dampen his friend's growing enthusiasm. For example, when Hutton wrote Minto early in September, announcing the completion of his plans for an official Canadian contingent and his own personal desire to lead the combined colonial contingents in the coming campaign, much to Hutton's chagrin, Minto replied that there seemed little chance now that Canada would send troops, and even if it did he might not support Hutton's request to leave Canada.[26] During this period Minto felt caught between two fires and could not make up his mind on the justice or necessity of the coming conflict. He explained his predicament confidentially to his brother Arthur: "My Chief at home [is] thirsting for blood, all my friends here ditto, and myself, while recognizing imperial possibilities, also see the iniquity of the war, and that the time for colonial support has hardly yet arrived."[27] Minto wrote these lines only three weeks before fighting actually began in the Transvaal.

Minto, of course, was scarcely ignorant of the growing tide of English-Canadian sentiment demanding Canadian participation. But, at this point, he dismissed it as small, unimportant, and unrepresentative. Yet all during the late summer this loosely knit group of war protagonists, largely urban-based and led by a few sensational city dailies, supported by military institutes, patriotic societies, and churches, began mobilizing support for Canadian participation. Davis-Allen, who remained in Canada several weeks after his Ouitlander resolution passed Parliament, worked Montreal, Ottawa, and Toronto as thoroughly as possible.

Apart from French Canada, there existed small, scattered pockets of English-Canadian resistance, consisting of farmers, radical labour, "advanced" Protestant clergy, and Anglophobic Canadians, usually of Irish descent, but their opposition lacked any semblance of organization and active popular support.[28] During a mid-September fence-mending tour of Ontario, Laurier tried to cultivate this group which drew sympathy from many "old hard headed, close fisted rural Liber-

---

[24] Buchan, *Lord Minto*, 130 n.

[25] Minto Papers, Minto to Chamberlain, September 23, 1899.

[26] Minto Papers, Minto to Hutton, September 5, 1899. He repeated his belief in the improbability of war to Laurier. Minto Papers, Minto to Laurier, September 24, 1899.

[27] Quoted in Buchan, *Lord Minto*, 130 n.

[28] Carman Miller, "English Canadian Opposition to the South African War as Seen through the Press," *Canadian Historical Review* (December, 1974), 422-38.

als."[29] But he made little headway against the persistent appeals of the urban press, and in the end, it was the almost hysterical rhetoric of this latter group, not the threats and schemes of a blundering General aided by a doubting viceroy, which forced Laurier into participation.

It was Chamberlain's October 3rd telegram announcing the acceptance of colonial offers of troops and describing the military organization they should follow (small units of men easily attached to British regiments) that first startled Minto out of his confidence that war could be avoided. Then things began to happen quickly. Minto, still in New York when Chamberlain's telegram arrived, offered to return to Ottawa at once. But since Laurier did not insist, he stayed another three days. Nevertheless, he remained apprehensive, for the terms of Chamberlain's telegram disturbed him. Did Chamberlain want individual, private offers, the type of scheme Sam Hughes had fathered? Or did he want a government-sponsored contingent, that gesture of moral support of which he had often spoken? While in New York, Minto felt very much isolated, and, to make matters worse, he had no confidence in his deputy, Lord William Seymour.

Fortunately, Laurier made every effort to keep Minto well informed. He apologized for the unauthorized release of Chamberlain's telegram by Colonel L.-J. Pinault, the Deputy Minister of Militia, and requested Minto's, not simply Seymour's, permission to publish it in the official Canada Gazette, since he wished to advertise as widely as possible Chamberlain's desire for private offers.[30] Troubled by the Prime Minister's attempts to promote private recruiting, and taking advantage of Laurier's friendly gesture, Minto decided to give Laurier the benefit of his advice and opinion. While he admitted that Chamberlain's telegram seemed to encourage individual offers, personally he thought it would be a grave mistake. In his opinion, if troops went they ought to be sent by the Canadian government and reflect Canada's size and imperial importance, since their value would be as much symbolic as practical. In keeping with this notion, he argued that Canada ought to reject flatly the War Office suggestion that Canadian troops be divided into small units of 125 men, to be attached to British regiments. If Canadian troops went, they ought to go as a full-fledged Canadian contingent under Canadian officers. In closing, Minto expressed the desire that no action be taken until he returned to Ottawa. He also asked to see Laurier briefly on October 7, the day he planned to return from New York. Regrettably that was the day before Laurier left for Chicago to help open a new Post Office building in that city, and it was impossible to arrange an interview. It is unfortunate that this meeting failed to take place because up until this point Laurier's relations with Minto were open and friendly and seemingly devoid of suspicion. If war were declared Laurier had even promised to invite

[29] Quoted in Paul Stevens, "Laurier and the Liberal Party in Ontario" (unpublished Ph.D. thesis, University of Toronto, 1966), 205.

[30] Minto Papers, Laurier to Minto, October 3, 1899.

Minto to attend the Cabinet meeting which decided for or against participation. While Minto had no desire to attend this meeting, the Prime Minister's invitation suggested his friendly intent. Thereafter the situation changed quickly.

Meanwhile, Minto cabled Chamberlain for a more precise interpretation of his October 3rd telegram. Minto feared that in his absence the government might act hastily and accept the recruitment of individual offers. This would kill any chance of a government-sponsored contingent. He also feared that Seymour, ignorant of "what has hitherto been decided," that is to say the existence of plans for an official contingent, would make no effort to dissuade the government.[31] In his cable to Chamberlain, Minto explained his personal objections to non-official offers. Some days later Chamberlain replied, and made it perfectly clear that he had no intention of accepting "any offers from Volunteers."[32] This relieved Minto's mind immensely, but it also left Laurier with the option of an official contingent or no troops at all, and the English-Canadian imperialists would never accept the latter choice.

When Minto reached Ottawa late in the evening of October 7, Canada faced a serious crisis. Laurier had already departed for Chicago, leaving behind a Cabinet rocked by strife and dissension and a country, at least the English-speaking section of it, calling for immediate action. The afternoon before Laurier had left Ottawa he had held a Cabinet meeting.[33] At this meeting Scott and Israël Tarte, the Minister of Public Works, convinced of a conspiracy to force Canada into participation, had identified Hutton and Minto as the two principal conspirators. Someone, they argued, had inspired the Chamberlain October 3rd telegram and had released the Militia Department's plan for a contingent to the *Military Gazette*. Its release had embarrassed the government considerably, since Laurier had previously denied its existence. Then Laurier, apparently confident that the storm in the Cabinet and country would blow itself out, had departed for Chicago. In his absence Scott, an irritable Irish Catholic and the most anti-British member of the Cabinet, became Acting Prime Minister. Thus it was he, not Laurier, who met Minto upon his return from New York to report the unpleasant results of the Cabinet meeting.

Minto's encounters with Scott were always less harmonious than those with Laurier. During the interview, Scott, in a direct and accusing manner, asked Minto if, to his knowledge, Hutton had released or authorized the release of the Department of Militia's contingency

[31] Laurier Papers, Minto to Laurier, October 9, 1899.

[32] Although Garvin (*Life of Joseph Chamberlain*, vol. 3, 531-32) states that Chamberlain informed Minto on October 6 (this letter, dated October 7, 1899, is found in the Hutton Papers) that he did not "intend to accept any volunteers," this communication, probably sent to Ottawa, could not have reached Minto until two days later since, in the interim, Minto cabled Chamberlain from New York privately, discouraging non-official, private offers; Hutton Papers, Minto to Hutton, October 9, 1899.

[33] The Montreal *Gazette*, October 7, 1899.

plan. Minto assured Scott of Hutton's innocence, but Scott remained suspicious until Minto agreed to wire the Major-General, who was then in British Columbia. The General's bland denial, however, failed to convince Scott and he reworded his question: Did Hutton at any time offer or suggest to British authorities that they might depend upon Canadian troops? Of course, both Minto and Hutton had given the War and Colonial offices precise, although unauthorized, information on the possible composition of a Canadian contingent, together with the assurance that in any real crisis they could count on Canadian aid. Perhaps because the question struck so dangerously close to home, Minto flatly refused to pursue the subject any farther since he insisted that it impugned the integrity of the General Officer Commanding. Minto's refusal simply rekindled Scott's suspicions and he was in no mood to brook opposition.[34] He therefore asked Borden as the Minister of Militia to make the inquiry. Although in the Cabinet Borden had denied categorically the Scott-Tarte charge, he agreed to wire Hutton, more to appease Scott's wrath and confirm his own affirmation than to accuse the General.[35] Hutton's second denial still failed to convince Scott—only a confession could have done that; nor, in his eyes, was Minto above suspicion.

When Laurier returned to Ottawa he found a Cabinet and country even more divided than when he had left. War had been declared and a decision could no longer be avoided. The English-Canadian press made that perfectly clear. The language of some papers was shrill and menacing, often bordering on hysteria. Hugh Graham's Montreal Star led the way. It spoke ominously of the "cowards" in Ottawa and their "Boer-like delays," while train loads of English women and children were meeting a cruel death at the hands of savage Boers.[36] It sent prepaid and often preworded wires to all the reeves and mayors across the country seeking their public stance on the war. Then after careful editing, it printed all the replies supporting the war, together with a carefully selected number of those opposed. Not surprisingly, most of these were from French Canadians.[37] The Toronto World talked loosely of the Boers in Canada with whom Canada itself might soon have to deal.[38] Still very sensitive about his own "race and religion," Laurier clearly understood the meaning of their message.

Yet to the last he tried to side-step the issue, confident that war would be avoided. All the way back from Chicago, even after he learned of the declaration of war, he argued with his Liberal entourage against Canadian participation. On the other hand, John Willison, editor of the Toronto Globe and a close confidant of the Prime Minis-

[34] Minto Papers, Minto to Queen Victoria, November 12, 1899.

[35] Hutton Papers, MS, "Memoir," 156.

[36] Montreal Star, October 12 and 13, 1899.

[37] Laurier L. LaPierre, in "Politics, Race, and Religion in French Canada: Joseph Israël Tarte" (unpublished Ph.D. thesis, University of Toronto, 1962), 373, states that the Star destroyed over 3,000 negative replies.

[38] Toronto World, October 10, 1899.

ter, pleaded with him for immediate action, and it was he who warned Laurier that "he would either send troops or go out of office." According to Willison, when they parted in Toronto, Laurier, "still reluctant, unconvinced and rebellious," knew that he could no longer depend upon the loyalty of the Liberal English-language press. Indeed, it was this "manifestion of public feeling" in the English provinces, Laurier later confessed to Willison, which persuaded him "he could not safely resist."[39]

Laurier called his Cabinet into session as soon as he reached Ottawa. For two days it debated the question of participation. The meetings were long and stormy, lasting from noon until 5 p.m. There were three factions. Tarte and Scott opposed any official military contribution. Their opponents, led by Borden and William Mulock, the Postmaster-General, demanded a full Canadian contingent, re-cruited, equipped, transported, and paid by the Canadian government, along the lines envisaged by Minto and Hutton. Between these two extremes, the moderates, composed of men like W. S. Fielding, the Finance Minister, while acknowledging the political wisdom of a Canadian contingent, wished to keep the financial burden to an absolute minimum. To them, Chamberlain's October 3rd cable offered the best blueprint for Canadian aid, that is, small units confined to 125 men each which were to be paid, armed, supplied, and transported at the imperial government's expense. Although this was the plan which eventually triumphed, when the Cabinet rose on the first day, Tarte and Scott seemed to have gained the upper hand. They had come well prepared and had concentrated their attack on the audacity of the "imperial conspirators," Chamberlain, Minto, and Hutton, whom they had denounced for their crude attempts to force the government's hand. However, during this stormy session no decision had been taken except to meet again on the following day.

During the two-day Cabinet crisis Minto communicated with Laurier three times, twice in writing and once personally. Minto's first letter, dated October 12, simply reiterated the old arguments favouring a full contingent. In this letter he reminded Laurier of the need to send a force "worthy of Canada," one which "would find favour with the Canadian public," a point which in no way contra-dicted Laurier's own opinion. If "we were to send a force to Africa," Laurier reassured Minto, "it should not be on the puny scale pro-posed, but on some plan more in consonance with the importance of Canada."[40]

Minto's interview with Laurier, though less congenial than usual, was still frank and friendly. Their discussion, which probably took place after 5 p.m. on October 12, centred on three subjects—the

[39] John Willison, *Reminiscences Political and Personal* (Toronto, 1919), 303-304. David accompanied Laurier to Chicago and participated in the Willison-Laurier discussion.

[40] Laurier Papers, Minto to Laurier, October 12, 1899; Hutton Papers, Laurier to Minto, October 12, 1899.

probability of Canadian participation, Chamberlain's telegram of October 3, and the dissension in the Cabinet. While Minto scarcely expected Cabinet unanimity, Laurier's account of the Cabinet animosity and strife somewhat startled him at first. Still he could not see why the majority in the Cabinet were so unreasonably "frightened by their French colleagues." He also realized that the Chamberlain cable still rankled with many Cabinet members and lay at the root of much resentment and bitterness. Laurier made that unmistakably plain in a terse note he wrote Minto before the interview. The "clandestine attempt which is made to force our hands," he had written, "must unavoidably result in impeding rather than in facilitating whatever action we may have to take."[41] Minto wondered if perhaps Laurier was beginning to believe the Scott-Tarte charges. Laurier certainly returned to the point during the interview. In an almost accusing tone he demanded to know to what actual offers of troops did Chamberlain's cable refer? "What were those communications and from whom and through what channels they were sent?"[42] Therefore, to dispel the awful suspicions and to clarify the issue Minto agreed to cable Chamberlain immediately. In his cable he explained the situation as best he could and requested a denial from Chamberlain. When Laurier had finished his tale Minto was convinced, as he later told Chamberlain, that the Cabinet would refuse to send a contingent. On his part, he tried to persuade Laurier of the wisdom, particularly the practical political wisdom, of sending troops—if for no other reason, he argued, than that the majority of Canadians seemed to desire some form of participation. In fact, Minto even went so far as to suggest that Laurier ought to summon Parliament immediately to secure approval for the Cabinet's decision, a proposal which Laurier firmly rejected. Finally Minto gave up, conscious that he had failed to move Laurier.

The next day, however, Minto made one more effort. Chamberlain's reply to Minto's inquiry provided a good pretext to reopen the subject. The telegram itself removed any suggestion of threat or conspiracy. In fact it went farther by making it perfectly clear that while the imperial government would appreciate troops as a "practical demonstration of unanimity throughout" the Empire, it had no intention of asking for troops.[43] Once Chamberlain had spoken, Minto, even if he had wished, could scarcely have used stronger language, much less threaten to dismiss his government if it refused to despatch troops. But Minto had no intention of doing anything of the sort; in fact, in his final communication he went out of his way to emphasize the voluntary nature of the decision. He reminded Laurier, "as you are aware there has never been any request from the Impl. govnt. that troops should be sent from here."[44] There remained but one more point which Minto had failed to raise the day before and which, he

[41] Hutton Papers, Laurier to Minto, October 12, 1899.

[42] Colonial Office 42 (869), Minto to Chamberlain, October 13, 1899.

[43] Colonial Office 42 (869), Chamberlain to Minto, October 13, 1899.

[44] Minto Papers, Minto to Laurier, October 13, 1899.

felt, Laurier ought to consider. This point was that Canada's failure to respond to the imperial crisis might possibly be misinterpreted in Britain at a time when Canada depended a good deal upon imperial support to maintain its position in Alaska. The point did deserve consideration, but it contained no threat or hint of a threat. It was also Minto's last word before the Cabinet made its final decision.

When the Cabinet reconvened for its second day of deliberations, the majority of the Cabinet seemed to have shifted toward support of a Canadian contingent, although their opponents were far from vanquished. The climax to the discussions came when Muloch stormed angrily from the meeting, seemingly never to return. Laurier, who, to the last, had hoped to avoid a commitment, realized he could temporize no longer. During his first term of office he had pursued a political strategy of appeasing English Canada and particularly Ontario. His acceptance of a knighthood, his imperial preference policy, and his Manitoba school settlement had all won him wide popularity among English Canadians. The defection of an important Ontario colleague at the height of this crisis, when the English-language press seemed to speak as with one voice, would, he felt, seriously jeopardize his carefully cultivated electoral strategy. A compromise would have to be arranged. At the close of the Cabinet meeting, W. S. Fielding announced the decision, while Laurier left for Rideau Hall to inform Minto. The government would recruit and equip 1,000 men, divided into 8 companies of 125 men each. It would also accept the War Office's offer to transport, pay, and return the troops at the imperial government's expense. The slight expenditure of Canadian funds required to recruit the troops was, Fielding informed the press, "under no circumstances to be regarded as a departure from the well-known principles of constitutional practice, nor construed as a precedent for future action."[45] To Ontario, the government declared that its actions were tailored to adhere strictly and faithfully to Chamberlain's October 3rd cable. To Quebec, it described the decision as a harmless formula to permit English Canadians to join the British army, if they so desired. The government's compromise deceived no one. Essentially it represented a capitulation to the demands of English Canada.

Clearly the Cabinet had agreed to send troops not because it feared Minto's wrath, but because it feared electoral defeat. Moreover, Minto's ambiguous attitude toward the growing South African crisis, his moral equivocations, and his feeling that the crisis would be resolved short of war precluded the conspiratorial role assigned him by both friends and detractors. When war came, the pack instinct prevailed and he rallied loyally to the cause, but all during the two-day crisis his conduct remained correct and constitutional. Whatever his past or future faults, on this count of dragooning Canada into the South African war, his slate was clean.

[45] Laurier Papers, "Memorandum of the Privy Council Decision," October 13, 1899.

Chapter Seven

The Imperial Pro-Consul

Although Minto had not dragooned Canada into participating in the South African war, his innocence did nothing to improve his relations with the Canadian government. Suspicions remained among Liberal politicians that Minto had conspired to force the government's hand. Minto, too, felt bitter toward his accusers. Consequently, as the war continued Minto's relations with his government grew progressively more strained. Official encounters turned into confrontations, petty incidents became serious issues, as Minto assumed the role of the stiff, imperial pro-consul depicted by the Liberal-Nationalist historians, though this role was neither inspired nor condoned by the Colonial Office. In these circumstances a collision seemed almost unavoidable.

Several factors help explain the deterioration of Minto's relationship with his government. First, the euphoric enthusiasm which seemed to characterize English Canada's reaction to the outbreak of war altered a number of Minto's own attitudes and perceptions. His initial doubts and hesitations as to the war's justice and necessity were temporarily silenced by more pragmatic considerations. Whatever the rights and wrongs of the war, and Minto still did not see it as a righteous crusade for the Ouitlanders' rights, he did not think that this was the time to weaken the war effort with moral quibbles. The war had come and it must be fought to a finish and the sooner the better. He himself had offered to go to the front if he were needed, but his offer had been declined and he consoled himself that there was much to be done here, particularly given the unrepresentative nature of the Canadian government.

Second, in the months which followed Minto became increasingly sensitive to what he considered to be the wishes of the imperial government and determined to uphold imperial interests against his own weak, incompetent, and disloyal administration. For a time, even his old opposition to formal schemes for imperial reorganization seemed to falter. Surprised by the receptive colonial response to the war, a response which he had not anticipated, Minto now wondered if perhaps the imperial moment had dawned and Chamberlain would unveil some larger scheme for imperial union. The pre-war campaign for Canadian participation now seemed to him to have been moved by more than the shrill rhetoric of a few influential hotheads anxious for medals and glory, the image he had painted to Chamberlain only a few weeks before. It now seemed to him that there was a wide popular support for imperialism unrepresented by Canada's own government and, as the man on the spot, he felt that he must find a means of giving voice to these larger public sentiments.

Finally, what initial sympathy Minto had possessed for the Canadian government's difficulty had been eroded by the contingent crisis. The Cabinet's shameless bickering, their weak and vacillating search for compromise rather than principle confirmed his worst impressions of politicians. On a personal level, their attempt to find an imperial scapegoat and their ready sacrifice of imperial interests to political expediency remained a source of gnawing private irritation. In the future he felt he must insist on stricter control and accountability. The government must learn that he was no mere figurehead or rubber stamp but a forceful guardian of imperial interests, a man who could and would insist upon his rights.

Minto's "downright contempt" for his government's behaviour became painfully clear soon after the government announced its decision to make a military contribution which Minto considered "unworthy and unrepresentative of Canada." From the start he had been opposed to the division of the Canadian troops into the small units requested by the War Office. These units which were to be attached to and submerged in British regiments would destroy the character and significance of a "Canadian" contingent.[1] With Borden's support, Minto sought and received Laurier's permission to alter the contingent's organization, although Laurier later claimed to

[1] Some people later claimed that Minto, the servile imperial conspirator, had supported, indeed insisted on, the 125-unit scheme suggested by the War Office. They did not think him capable of a more Canadian view. See Ottawa Citizen, August 19, 1900.

have misunderstood the exact nature of Minto's request. What Minto wanted was a full-dressed contingent under Canadian officers along the lines initially suggested by Hutton. The Colonial Office recognized at once the political advantage of Minto's request, and Chamberlain himself wrote Lansdowne privately, insisting that he would "not accept" the War Office's refusal.[2] The War Office offered no objection and the change was made. But it remained officially secret, much to Minto's disgust, almost until the day the contingent sailed. This desire for secrecy was based on the anticipated hostility from Cabinet ministers, notably Tarte. The majority of the Cabinet, Minto explained to Wolseley, were simply terrified "by their French colleagues. . . . I must say it is perfectly sickening."[3]

Minto never really understood the wiles of politicians, and he failed to appreciate the problems of political power in Canada, particularly those associated with the Province of Quebec. He mistakenly dismissed Laurier as a pleasant but weak man who, like all the rest, remained "terrified of Tarte." In Minto's mind Tarte, the wicked wizard of Canadian politics, had to be brought to heel. Minto was not afraid of Tarte, and he always believed that most problems could be solved through frank, forthright, and manly discussion. He decided, therefore, to confront the recalcitrant minister himself.

Scarcely a week after the Cabinet had decided to despatch troops, Minto invited Tarte to his parliamentary office, determined to have it out with him. He began by sternly rejecting Tarte's claim that the imperial government had forced Canada to send troops. Minto explained that this charge not only did violence to the facts but reflected adversely on the Governor-General. He then pointed out that the strong popular support for the government's decision disproved the validity of Tarte's assertion. Tarte politely conceded Minto's point. Then Tarte went on to explain his own constitutional stance. In his reply he cleverly couched his argument in terms of his public support for imperial federation, and insisted that "a colony should not accept pecuniary or military responsibility on behalf of the mother country, unless that colony had some representation."[4] He spoke to the Governor-General so clearly and simply that even Minto conceded the "theoretical" soundness of his case.

During this interview Minto found Tarte, not the malignant maverick he had expected, but a charming, disarmingly honest "strong man" who knew his own mind. In fact, Minto seemed to develop a particular respect and affection for the man, although he still did not entirely trust him. His distrust grew, too, the more he thought back over their meeting, since it seemed to him that Tarte had masked his true feelings behind a constitutional quibble. In Minto's opinion Tarte's real objections were probably a lack of sympathy "for

[2] Colonial Office 42 (869), Minute, Chamberlain, October 15, 1899; Joseph Chamberlain Papers, Chamberlain to Lansdowne, October 14, 1899.

[3] Minto Papers, Minto to Wolseley, October 22, 1899.

[4] Colonial Office 42 (869), Minto to Chamberlain, October 20, 1899.

British enterprise," the "ultramontane pressure" and his "anxiety for the security of the Quebec vote."[5]

But the more Minto continued to reflect on their meeting, the more he decided that perhaps Tarte was not the sole source of difficulty in Laurier's Cabinet. Clearly the Cabinet, with a few exceptions, was not all that it ought to be. Some members appeared weak, others incompetent, and still others, disloyal. He concluded that even Laurier himself, though a polished, charming gentleman, could be trusted only so far and his lack of strong leadership had a debilitating effect on the Cabinet. Taken all together, the Cabinet seemed to Minto to have lost touch with or to have deliberately frustrated the will of the people. Their attacks on Hutton, Chamberlain, and himself were simply attempts to assuage their wounded feelings, or cheap efforts to divert public attention from their shameful handling of the war crisis. In these circumstances Minto's duty seemed clear: he must hold the line firmly; he must insist that they keep the record straight; and if necessary he must protect the people from the capricious conduct of their elected leaders, and give voice to the true feelings of the people.

The festivities marking the despatch of Canada's first South African contingent brought the growing friction between the Governor-General and his government to a head. The carnival mood of the estimated 10,000 people who came to Quebec to see the troops depart belied the bitterness and recrimination existing behind the scenes. Trouble started on the evening of October 28 during the Quebec Garrison Club's banquet for the officers of the Canadian contingent, and it began predictably with Major-General Hutton, who could never resist an oratorical occasion. When asked to address the banquet, Hutton, intoxicated by his "flattering reception" in Quebec, soon extended his "few brief remarks" well beyond the discreet realm of duty. He began his address by directing saccharine but condescending compliments toward the Minister of Militia. He praised him for the generous and impartial manner in which he administered his department—particularly during the last few weeks. Then he passed on to a loftier subject, Canada's imperial obligations, and predicted that the time would come when Canada would send not 1,000 men but 50,000 to 100,000 to maintain the Empire's integrity. Hutton's declaration, emanating from an important public official, in the heart of Quebec and before members of the press, seemed to Laurier like a deliberate repudiation of the Prime Minister's own promise, that no precedent had been set by the current decision.

The next evening during Minto's reception at the Citadel for the senior officers and captains of the contingent, Minto's excessive praise of Hutton, whom he described as the best General since Confederation, both drew attention and lent authority to Hutton's words the previous night. It also suggested design and coordination. Although Minto went out of his way to disassociate the despatch of

[5] Hutton Papers, MS, "Memoir," 159 and 162.

troops from the broader question of imperial federation by declaring his opposition to written constitutions which might prove irksome and create ill feelings, the Canadian press gave more space to his praise of Hutton.[6] Originally, Minto had intended simply to bolster the General's tenuous position, but given the tense relations between the government and the General, his words were probably inopportune and ill chosen. In fact, most of the hard work, recruiting and despatching the contingent, had been done by Borden and his department. Many of the senior men, following the Minister's example, had worked literally day and night. Their work, completed in less than three weeks, was a tribute to the spirit and stamina rather than the organization and efficiency of the department. Meanwhile, Hutton remained in the North West until October 25, and when he returned to Ottawa he immediately began to quarrel with senior staff. On one occasion even Minto had to intervene and beg Hutton to be more reasonable.[7] Borden and his senior staff, therefore, had some reason to expect greater recognition than they received from the Governor-General, whose lavish praise of Hutton understandably irritated them.

Borden himself did nothing to ease the growing tension between the General and the government. Although in the past he had defended Hutton against the harsher criticism of his Cabinet colleagues, and had tried to play peacemaker, he was no longer in any mood to tolerate Hutton's impertinence. When he arrived in Quebec, strained and tired, Borden began to drink, and when he drank he became belligerent. The afternoon of Minto's reception Borden and Hutton had quarrelled on the parade square and Hutton had stomped off in a huff, and before the evening was out Borden, now in no condition to reason, had also fought with a retired officer of the 8th Royal Rifles who had attempted to defend Hutton's honour.[8]

The next day, during the official farewell ceremonies for the contingent, Minto's remarks not only fuelled these flames but started a new conflagration. At the stroke of noon Minto, always punctual, arrived on the Esplanade. Accompanied by his staff in full military regalia he took his place beside Laurier. A brief inspection followed. Then Minto began a round of platitudinous speeches. After the usual pleasantries, an allusion to the historic setting, and the need for national unity, Minto went straight to the point of his oration. The contingent, he declared, would remain a tribute to the people of Canada. They had insisted that troops go and they had "rejoiced when they had been graciously accepted." Moreover, they had "no desire to consider the quibbles of colonial responsibility." Minto's reference to "the quibbles of colonial responsibility" was a direct and deliberate attack on Laurier's "no precedent" clause. Nor was it an oratorical slip caused by the heat of the moment. A poor and deliberate public

---

[6] Montreal Gazette, October 31, 1899.

[7] Minto Papers, Minto to Hutton, October 26, 1899.

[8] Minto Papers, Hutton's confidential memo to Minto, January 31, 1900.

speaker, Minto had carefully chosen and rehearsed his lines. When Laurier rose to speak he did his best to correct or qualify Minto's assertion. He explained that Canada would, in future, send troops only "when and where she sees fit."[9] But it was too late, the press already had its issue. Minto's words, the Montreal *Star* thundered, "imply a grave censure upon some of His Excellency's Ministers."[10] Minto himself enjoyed the publicity. He had obviously decided to become a tribune of the people. "The fact is," he wrote his wife, "that since Monday & Tuesday your poor humble boy has been the hero of the hour—the papers are full of my speeches, and extracts from them, and I think I may say to my girl I have put a lot of life into things and have spoken out."[11]

Delighted by the public reception of his Quebec speech, the next night, as the guest of honour at the Montreal Caledonian Society's annual concert, Minto repeated his assertion. His words were slightly changed but the meaning was clear. He began by stating that the Canadian contingent was a capable force and a credit to the Dominion, and it had gone out, he declared to this excited assembly, "because you insisted upon its going, and I am very glad you did so."[12] He went no farther, but he had already gone too far. The audience, worked up to a fever pitch by the events of the past few days and "the stirring" songs, poems, and oratory of the evening, had clearly expected much more. Other speakers followed Minto. One, A. A. Stevenson, the Conservative President of the Caledonian Society, berated those who had tried to stifle the voice of the Canadian people, while another Conservative, Senator Donald MacMaster, perhaps hoping to provoke an indiscretion, asserted that Minto possessed the constitutional power, as Commander-in-Chief, to call out the Canadian militia and hence circumvent the unpopular policy of an obstinate government.

To Liberals, the Society's meeting bore all the rhetorical characteristics of a Conservative party rally presided over by the Governor-General. In the confusion which followed, the press attributed to Minto some of the remarks uttered by the other speakers, particularly Stevenson's promise that other contingents would depart shortly. The press reacted immediately. Tory papers praised the bravery, loyalty, and gallantry of the Governor-General,[13] while Liberal ones attempted to refute the validity of MacMaster's constitutional interpretation as though it were Minto's.[14] Minto himself realized that he had been captured by the Tory press but he regretted not a word. He informed his wife that the government "deserve anything in all this business."[15] Yet, he thought it best to explain to Laurier that the press, particularly

[9] Montreal *Star*, October 30, 1899.

[10] Montreal *Star*, October 31, 1899.

[11] Minto Papers, Minto to Lady Minto, November 3, 1899.

[12] Montreal *Star*, November 1, 1899.

[13] Montreal *Star*, November 1, 1899.

[14] Montreal *Herald*, November 2, 1899.

[15] Minto Papers, Minto to Lady Minto, November 3, 1899.

the Montreal *Star*, had misquoted his speech and that Stevenson's "words seem to have been put in my mouth."[16]

Laurier had watched the events of the last few days with growing anxiety. Minto's explanatory note gave Laurier the opportunity he sought. The *Star* may or may not have misquoted Minto but Laurier himself had heard his Quebec Esplanade address which, together with his previous and subsequent orations, came perilously close to public censure. Aware of Minto's inexperience but uncertain of the degree to which he had allowed himself to be used by the Tory press and party, Laurier sought an appropriate form and occasion to warn Minto. The Prime Minister was well aware that Minto's remarks might inadvertently lead to a serious controversy, but he himself could scarcely rebuke the Governor-General, privately or publicly. He needed a more subtle method. He decided, therefore, to reproach Minto by protesting Hutton's less offensive remarks.

A few days later Laurier wrote Minto a stern note deploring Hutton's Garrison Club speech. In it he reminded Minto that it was not in the tradition of the British army to permit soldiers "of high or low rank" to venture on political ground. That "ill advised speech," Laurier continued, came close to, if in fact it did not constitute, a breach of "the duties entrusted to the General." Determined to remain faultless, Laurier made it clear that he blamed Hutton not for holding "his views, but the promulgation of these views." Then Laurier passed quickly to generalities. A recent letter from Chamberlain thanking Canada for its generous gift provided the pretext. The Colonial Secretary, Laurier wrote, seemed to understand the grave difficulties faced by the Canadian Cabinet. "I am sorry," Laurier added rather pointedly, "that what is obvious to him is not apparent to others, who by their position ought to know better."[17]

Minto rose immediately to Hutton's defence. He tried to explain that imperial questions were inevitably closely related to military matters. He also pleaded with Laurier to understand the difficult position of the General, since Hutton was doing such a fine job and required tolerance and sympathy from the Canadian government. This was a standard argument Minto had already worked to exhaustion in Hutton's defence. He stood on much firmer ground when he reminded Laurier that if he objected to Hutton's comments the proper disciplinary redress was not through the Governor-General but the Minister of Militia "as his immediate chief."[18] Minto had obviously missed the point, probably purposely.

Laurier certainly understood the correct constitutional relationship between Hutton and Borden. He also knew of the delicate relations between the two men and had no desire to fuel the flames. Although Laurier conceded Minto's constitutional point and agreed to speak to Hutton himself, he was not prepared to let the matter rest; Minto must learn his lesson.

[16] Minto Papers, Minto to Laurier, November 3, 1899.

[17] Hutton Papers, Laurier to Minto, November 7, 1899.

[18] Laurier Papers, Minto to Laurier, November 8, 1899.

There were many reports respecting Hutton's attitude toward the Liberal government, Laurier replied, but he had dismissed them since he was confident Hutton was a loyal soldier. Yet the party press had made a good deal out of some of Hutton's public addresses. To prevent all future suspicion, Laurier suggested, Hutton ought to avoid "not only political ground but everything approaching it."[19] The analogy was clear and, this time, Minto seemed to grasp it.

In reply, Minto admitted that Hutton had a real weakness for oratory which laid "him open to misconstruction as well as criticism." But he assured Laurier that Hutton had no intention "whatever of utilizing party politics to further his own views."[20] With that, Laurier let the matter drop, confident that Minto understood. However, on closer reflection, Minto soon realized how very pointed Laurier's admonition had been and he wrote the next day to the Prime Minister, adding that he, too, understood "how important it is for me to avoid the merest suspicion of associating myself with party politics."[21] Imperial matters were another question, he protested, and Laurier must understand that he would not tolerate for a moment anything detrimental to imperial interests.

This feud, however, was soon overshadowed by another double-headed quarrel, which one author has, rather extravagantly, called "a precursor to the King-Byng dispute."[22] The first of the two issues arose over Minto's precipitate release of an imperial telegram. The second began as a press dispute between Tarte and J. Castell Hopkins, the American-born secretary of the Imperial Federation League, who was an editor and publicist of untiring imperial conviction. In each case, Minto's actions acutely embarrassed the Colonial Office. As the self-appointed guardian of the imperial cause, on both occasions, he went well beyond the call of public duty.

Late in the evening of November 1, Laurier arrived at Rideau Hall to inform Minto that the Cabinet had decided to offer Britain a second contingent. Somewhat surprised by the Cabinet decision, Minto agreed to cable the offer immediately to the imperial government. To Minto, Laurier seemed unhappy with the Cabinet decision. He had mentioned it only toward the end of their conversation, and then wondered if the offer "would make too much of the danger in South Africa." Convinced that Laurier was seeking a pretext to annul the offer, Minto tried to reassure Laurier. This offer, he informed Laurier rather gratuitously, would be well received in Britain and Canada and would help dispel the general feeling that the government had not "kept pace" with imperial sympathies.[23] Thus reassured, Laurier announced the offer to the press. But much to Minto's surprise, the public took little notice of it.

[19] Hutton Papers, Laurier to Minto, November 8, 1899.

[20] Laurier Papers, Minto to Laurier, November 8, 1899.

[21] Laurier Papers, Minto to Laurier, November 9, 1899.

[22] James A. Colvin, "Sir Wilfrid Laurier and the Imperial Problem: 1896-1906" (unpublished Ph.D. thesis, University of London, 1954), 215.

[23] Colonial Office 42 (869), Minto to Chamberlain, November 21, 1899.

Determined to provoke a more enthusiastic response, Minto decided to give greater publicity to the imperial government's reply. Several days later the Colonial Office declined the Canadian offer but thanked the Canadian government and assured it that should occasion arise they "will have no hesitation in availing themselves of it." Minto sent the cable to Laurier and advised him to release it to the press before the Colonial Office did so. Laurier agreed to give it to the press, but he was on his way to Quebec for a week's political tour, and wishing to discount the importance of the offer in that province, he released only the substance of the message—the imperial government's refusal.[24] Minto protested immediately and Laurier agreed to release the full text of the message. However, before Laurier could do so Minto gave the telegram to the press. His purpose was to destroy the impression that Britain would never need more troops.

Laurier complained at once of Minto's discourteous action, since it seemed to him that the Governor-General lacked confidence in his written word. From this charge Minto defended himself in lofty constitutional tones. He declared that his instruments of office gave him the undisputed right to publish any or all imperial despatches, and that such a procedure was backed by endless precedents in the Governor-General's Office. Laurier, however, had never questioned that right. Moreover, Minto informed Laurier, the people of Canada had a right to know and as an imperial agent he would see that they did know. Minto's haughty stand was neither inspired nor condoned by the British government. The Colonial Office easily grasped the point which seemed to elude Minto. Laurier, they could see, had been shabbily treated. "It is a pity," John Anderson, the perceptive Chief Clerk at the Colonial Office, noted, "that Lord Minto took it into his head to give our telegram to the press without giving his ministers notice."[25]

Minto's actions during the next dispute, his further attempt to tame Tarte, threatened to create an even more serious crisis. The immediate cause of Minto's wrath was an exchange of letters between Tarte and Hopkins in the Toronto *Globe* dealing with Canada's imperial obligations. In his letter Tarte outlined all the old familiar arguments he had often used before, the failure of Parliament to authorize the despatch of troops, Canada's lack of representation in imperial councils, and the coercive character of Chamberlain's October 3rd cable inviting troops.[26] Many of these arguments, Minto felt, were heresies which Tarte had renounced soon after their earlier interview. He also seemed to hold Tarte personally responsible for much of the bitterness and misunderstanding toward Quebec in English Canada and strongly suspected him of influencing Laurier "to suppress" the Colonial Office telegram in order to save political embarrassment in Quebec. Once again Minto decided to take Tarte in hand and try to curb his antics, but this time he intended to use sterner methods.

[24] Colonial Office 42 (869), Laurier to Minto, November 9, 1899.

[25] Colonial Office 42 (869), Minute, John Anderson, December 6, 1899.

[26] Toronto *Globe*, November 8, 1899.

When Minto read Tarte's open letter in the Toronto *Globe*, he wrote at once to Laurier in Montreal, informing him that he objected strenuously to many of Tarte's assertions, particularly his charge that Canada had been forced by the imperial government to send troops. These charges, Minto wrote, "coming from one of my ministers," places an entirely "erroneous view of the position of Her Majesty's Government before the public of Canada."[27] Then Minto, invoking his constitutional powers and prerogatives as guardian of "Imperial interests in Canada," threatened to repudiate publicly Tarte's statement unless the Minister explained himself satisfactorily and at once. Minto's repudiation would, of course, have forced the resignation of the Minister or the entire government. Fortunately, he first decided to seek the advice of the Colonial Office.

Meanwhile, Laurier rose to Tarte's defence. He pointed out that Tarte had made no assertion of facts but simply drew an inference from undoubted facts. His conclusion, Laurier added somewhat sardonically, "is that Canada should be represented at Westminster. From this conclusion perhaps Your Excellency will not dissent."[28] Laurier himself did not think the matter warranted much serious attention. Nevertheless, he suggested that Minto ought to speak privately to Tarte.

But Minto had no intention of speaking to Tarte. He had done that on a previous occasion and it had had little effect. In Minto's opinion this was a very serious matter and Laurier must face the consequences. Thus, he informed Laurier that if Tarte failed to retract his assertions, then he as Governor-General would publicly repudiate them.

Fortunately, this time Minto's threats were mostly idle bluster. Two days before he replied to Laurier Chamberlain had answered Minto's earlier request for advice, and had instructed Minto to take no notice of Tarte's letters. Above all, he had cautioned Minto to avoid any communication with the press. It will "do no harm," John Anderson noted, "to let him [Tarte] go on advocating Canadian representation, and if he has got any ideas on the subject it would be a pity to repress him."[29] When the Colonial Office later learned the full details of the Tarte feud, it had even less sympathy for Minto's case. "I hope this matter is now at an end," Anderson wrote, "and that Lord Minto will let it drop."[30] Once he had received Chamberlain's advice, Minto had no choice but to let it drop.

Unaware of the Colonial Office's reaction, Laurier called upon Minto as soon as he returned from Montreal. He wanted to settle both the Tarte dispute and the quarrel over Minto's premature release of Chamberlain's telegram. This conversation, really their first serious

[27] Colonial Office 42 (869), Minto to Laurier, November 9, 1899.

[28] Colonial Office 42 (869), Laurier to Minto, November 10, 1899.

[29] Colonial Office 42 (869), Minute, John Anderson, November 10, 1899. See also Chamberlain to Minto, November 11, 1899.

[30] Colonial Office 42 (869), John Anderson to C. T. D. Cox, December 6, 1899.

general discussion on Canadian affairs since Minto arrived, turned into a long, intimate, and friendly exchange of opinions. It gave Minto some appreciation of Laurier's political position, particularly in Quebec, and laid the basis for a closer friendship. Minto began the conversation by stiffly standing on his imperial dignity. But Laurier, perhaps sensing that Minto's position had weakened and that now the Governor-General simply sought a graceful exit, reminded Minto of the difficulty in distinguishing clearly between imperial and purely Canadian matters. Laurier then shifted the conversation to more general topics. He explained to Minto his political difficulties with friends in Quebec and dismissed Tarte's actions as a result of poor health and bad friends, particularly Henri Bourassa, the nationalist young French-Canadian politician. Soon the discussion ranged freely over a wide variety of subjects—the prospects of imperial federation, national unity, and the influence of history teaching on the formation of French- and English-Canadian opinion. Minto used the occasion to express many of his curious perceptions of French Canadians. He wanted to know the degree of affection for France among French Canadians and the extent to which their press was manipulated by "editors and managers from Old France." While reminding Minto "that it is only fair to remember the difference of races," Laurier assured him that no French Canadian would exchange English rule for that of France. He also told Minto that he felt certain that as the years went on "the two races will unite in Imperial sympathy" but that it would take time and that he was doing all in his power to persuade French Canadians to "throw in their lot entirely with the rest of Canada."[31] Minto was delighted by this frank and informative discussion and wrote at once to the Colonial Office to report in detail the essence of their conversation. He seemed to feel that the Colonial Office would find Laurier's remarks as useful and revealing as he had. But the Colonial Office seemed far less impressed by Laurier's revelations. "There will always be two nations in Canada," Anderson blandly commented in reply.[32]

While Minto's interview with Laurier cleared the air considerably, it did not eliminate all friction. In retrospect, it seemed more like the calm before the storm, the prelude to the cause célèbre of Minto's Canadian career, the firing of Major-General E. T. H. Hutton.

Although cast in the role of Hutton's guardian and protector, Minto had become increasingly conscious of the General's erratic behaviour. As the war continued and Hutton became anxious to go to the front, he became even more difficult and erratic. He seemed to want to do everything by himself and at once, but found it impossible to settle down and do anything well. Even his friends found him impossible. On two occasions before the Canadian government initiated action to rid itself of his services, Minto's own relations with Hutton had become somewhat strained.

[31] Colonial Office 42 (869), "Minto's Memo on the 2nd Contingent controversy," November 16, 1899.

[32] Colonial Office 42 (869), John Anderson to C. T. D. Cox, December 6, 1899.

First they fought over the composition of Canada's second contingent. In mid-December the War Office, reeling from the defeats and humiliations of Black week, reversed its earlier stand and informed the Canadian government it could use more Canadian men. After three months of tough Boer warfare the War Office now knew the type of men they wanted. What they wanted were not infantry but mounted men who were good rifle shots, the type of unorthodox soldier who could meet and beat the Boer on his own terms. Consequently, the War Office decided that the second Canadian contingent should consist of three batteries of field artillery, three squadrons of mounted rifles, and one squadron of scouts.

Hutton set about immediately to raise the men. The mounted rifles, he felt, ought to come from the militia cavalry. Any glory they might attain would obviously reflect directly and favourably upon him. On the other hand, Minto argued that the Militia Department ought to cast a much larger net and recruit extensively in the North West. In Minto's opinion, raw North Western recruits who could ride and shoot and had experience with rough terrain would be preferable to the notoriously inefficient, ill-trained city cavalry. He also felt that Hutton ought to stick more rigidly to the War Office's request for small units rather than insist on a full-dressed contingent, since small units would give the War Office greater mobility. But Hutton would hear nothing of this and Minto soon despaired of ever persuading him. In Minto's opinion, Hutton had not grasped the lesson of the war and he clearly did not understand the first thing about mounted rifles. "He can not get out of his head the popular effect of the organization," Minto confided to his diary, "and thinks a great deal about the hats they are to wear."[33]

In despair, Minto wrote privately to Lansdowne to explain how unreasonable Hutton had become[34] The War Office agreed to do what it could and wrote at once to Hutton suggesting a reduction in the number of guns and a corresponding increase in the number of mounted men, thereby destroying the perfect harmony of Hutton's contingent plan and stressing the need for irregular troops. Lansdowne also suggested that they be of the North West Mounted Police class, but Hutton refused to consider the idea.

Finally Minto appealed to Laurier, hoping that the Canadian government would see the point and overrule Hutton.[35] But Laurier coyly refused to tamper with a subject within the competence of a military expert and Minto resigned himself to defeat. Still he regretted that the General could "not see things in a more practical light." Hutton might be "an excellent organizer," Minto recorded in his diary, "and a capable fellow but there is something verging on the theatrical in him."[36] Soon after the second contingent arrived in South

[33] Minto Papers, Diary, December 24, 1899.
[34] Minto Papers, Minto to Lansdowne, December 17, 1899.
[35] Laurier Papers, Minto to Laurier, December 25, 1899.
[36] Minto Papers, Diary, December 24, 1899.

Africa it was broken into the more manageable units Minto had suggested.

The second altercation between Minto and Hutton arose over a somewhat trivial matter. Since the beginning of war Minto had considered several plans to care for the dependents of sick, wounded, or dead soldiers. What he wanted was a comprehensive plan which would command national support. Already several organizations—the Red Cross, the Soldiers' Relief Fund, and the Soldiers' Wives' League—had introduced limited and competing relief funds. To eliminate administrative duplication and competition and to provide a sound scheme for relief for soldiers' dependents, Minto decided to create the National Patriotic Fund. But before he launched the National Patriotic Fund he had given his support and patronage to the Red Cross, since it seemed to be the most comprehensive and representative existing organization.

Then early in January the British journal the *Daily Mail* offered to sponsor a music recital in Ottawa, the proceeds of which would go to the sufferers in the war who belonged to the Canadian contingent. Minto agreed to attend the concert and to give a dinner at a later date for the people who organized the Ottawa recital. It was understood that the funds would go to the Red Cross Relief Fund. However, Hutton had other ideas, and without consulting Minto, he had arranged that the money, approximately $5,000, should go to the Soldiers' Wives' League, of which his wife was President. Minto disliked this organization since it was not solely Canadian, but simply a branch of a larger Imperial League. Consequently, there was no guarantee that the money would be used for Canadian soldiers.[37] When Minto learned of Hutton's arrangement—and he learned of it only during the recital—he was furious. He cancelled the dinner and during the concert's intermission gave Hutton a severe dressing down.

Yet when Laurier arrived at Rideau Hall on January 19, 1900, demanding Hutton's resignation, Minto rose immediately to the General's defence. He reacted partly out of loyalty but also out of a sense of self-preservation. Laurier's request had scarcely taken Minto by surprise. He had been expecting a "blow up" for some time. In fact, just the night before, Hutton had explained to Minto in great detail the cause of his latest feud with Borden, some sordid row over horse dealing.

To avoid charges of partisan patronage in the purchase of horses for the second contingent, Borden and Hutton had created a purchase board under the direction of Colonel Gerald Kitson. Borden's political friends, however, soon complained of the board's discrimination against Liberal horse dealers. They pointed particularly to Kitson's purchase of large numbers of horses from a Hamilton dealer, Captain Hendrie, who happened to be a prominent political opponent. Borden ought to have ignored these inevitable complaints. Instead, he summoned Kitson to answer the charges. Understandably wounded by

[37] Minto Papers, Diary, January 4, 1900.

Borden's insinuations, Kitson complained to his friend Hutton who offered to speak to Borden on Kitson's behalf. But before this meeting took place, Borden sent a Liberal horse dealer, Robert Beith, to London, Ontario, to oversee all future horse purchases. When Beith arrived in camp at London, Hutton, whom Borden had failed to inform of Beith's arrival, refused to permit him to inspect Kitson's horses. Beith telegraphed Hutton's refusal to Borden and Borden then ordered Hutton to purchase no more horses without Beith's prior approval.

Hutton complied with Borden's order and, according to the General, Beith found only five horses unfit and prices too high in only a few cases. Although Hutton found no fault with Beith's opinion, he deeply resented Borden's behaviour, and he told the Minister so in unmistakable terms on January 12. The next day Borden, evidently unreformed and unrepentant, wrote Hutton himself seeking additional information on horse purchasing. Hutton refused to supply answers on several points. He saw the request as an insult and decided to return Borden's letter unanswered. When Borden received Hutton's reply he wrote, "most unsatisfactory if not intentionally rude" across the letter and sent it back to the General.[38] There the matter rested for two days while Laurier tried to mediate the dispute. But when he failed, Borden requested Cabinet approval for Hutton's dismissal, and threatened to resign himself if he failed to receive it.

Minto shared Hutton's sense of outrage. He deplored this gratuitous slur on the honour of his friends, Hutton and Kitson. He felt that no government would dare dismiss an important public officer, a man of Hutton's rank and reputation, over so trivial and indecently petty an issue and one which reflected so unfavourably on the government's behaviour. Minto also seemed to see Laurier's request for Hutton's removal in larger terms, as an assault on the imperial tie, and an attempt to weaken the militia and prevent the despatch of additional troops to South Africa. He believed that several Ministers— Tarte, Scott, Borden, and perhaps Laurier himself—had decided months before to make of Hutton the scapegoat and to pin on him all the faults falsely attributed to the General, Chamberlain, and himself. In his opinion, this despicable horse-dealing incident was simply a trumped-up pretext to obscure the government's own lack of imperial sympathy. He had seen that a confrontation was coming for some time, and had decided to stand between Hutton and his accusers, to defend the imperial tie and expose them for what they were.

Consequently, Minto informed Laurier that the government had no grounds on which to ask for Hutton's recall or dismissal. When Laurier protested that the present difficulties were only the last on a very long list of grievances, Minto dismissed these as gossip and hearsay. Seizing the initiative, Minto insisted that he had watched things closely in the Militia Department and had remained impartial and uncommitted—an absurd claim—and had made up his mind

[38] Hutton Papers, "Hutton's Demand for a Royal Commission of Inquiry into State of the Militia," February 3, 1900, item 13.

what ought to be done if serious friction arose between the two men. Laurier, Minto declared, ought to get rid of Borden, who was an intemperate, incompetent man who regarded the militia as a patronage machine. Once this was done he should be replaced by a more suitable man like James Sutherland, then a Minister without Portfolio. Laurier replied that whatever Borden's faults, no other Cabinet minister would accept the portfolio with Hutton as the General Officer Commanding, least of all Sutherland who thoroughly disliked the General and told Laurier "he would have split with him long ago."[39]

How, then, did Laurier propose to get rid of Hutton? Minto asked. There were two methods, Laurier replied: the General might be recalled for active service in South Africa and might even lead the third "Canadian" contingent, the Strathcona Horse, or else the Canadian government might dismiss him. Laurier pointed out that the former solution might well be preferable since it would save Hutton as well as the British and Canadian governments much embarrassment. But Minto rejected Laurier's suggestion as a makeshift arrangement. General after General had come and failed in Canada, he lectured Laurier, and the time had come to settle this issue "once for all." If Laurier wanted Hutton's recall his government must state in writing the precise reasons for their request. Then he would transmit the request to the imperial government with a strong covering despatch stating his own opinions on the subject, which, he warned Laurier, were "strong." Such a despatch would, in effect, have amounted to a recommendation to reject the Canadian request. Minto did not propose to stop there. He also threatened to write Laurier an official memorandum stating his personal views on military administration, a document which might be laid before Parliament upon request. Laurier's curiosity was doubtlessly aroused by Minto's threats. And he asked the Governor-General if he would mind first making an unofficial statement of his views which Laurier might show, at his discretion, to members of Cabinet. It would be understood that this statement would not preclude the writing of a more official document later. Meanwhile, Laurier promised to try once more to "adjust matters" but he warned Minto that should he fail and Minto continue to block Hutton's dismissal, the government would resign. The interview terminated at this point. The Hutton affair had now become a first-class crisis.

Closer thought and reflection confirmed Minto's determination to resist, come what may. Apart from losing Sir Wilfrid, he explained to Chamberlain later that day, "it would be a great thing for Canada generally if the govnt. resigned on the question."[40] In his opinion, it would expose the graft and corruption in the Militia Department and in the government generally. More important, it would lead to "an expression of public opinion on political corruption and provide an opportunity to reconstitute the office of General Officer Commanding along proper lines." If Chamberlain disapproved, he added cau-

[39] Minto Papers, Memo of Laurier-Minto interview, January 30, 1900.
[40] Minto Papers, Minto to Chamberlain, January 17, 1900.

tiously, the Colonial Secretary ought to cable at once and he would do his best to postpone matters.

Meanwhile Minto, convinced of the firm support of both the imperial government and Canadian public opinion, began preparing the unofficial memorandum he had promised Laurier, in which he set out to expose the error and corruption of the Canadian government. The resulting document was an absurd treatise which badly discredited Minto's case. It was divided into two parts, the first part attempting to explain the proper constitutional relationship between a General and the Minister of Militia. However, Minto constantly confused what existed in law with what he felt ought to exist. Although he admitted that "the supreme authority in a constitutionally governed country will rest with the Government of the day," he seemed to believe that the law had constituted the Minister of Militia and his General as co-equals. Minto also seemed to think that the Orders and Regulations issued by the Department of Militia which defined the specific duties of a General Officer Commanding—discipline, mobilization of troops, offensive and defensive operations, and recommendations for commissions, staff, and other appointments—had limited or reduced the general powers of administration and responsibility vested in the Minister by the Militia Act. "The machinery of government as approved by Act of Parliament," he argued in summary, "is certainly not intended to be upset by the powers vested theoretically in the Government." The second part consisted of a rather pointed arraignment of the corruption of his government, particularly in the Militia Department. In it he warned the government that Hutton's "recall would not be passed over, in England or in Canada, without much public comment . . . [since] a very large portion of the Canadian public would sympathize with General Hutton."[41]

Minto confessed very shortly afterwards that this document had been hastily devised and badly written.[42] More to the point, it played directly into his opponents' hands. They now possessed the measure of the man and the essence of his case. Altogether, Minto's attack on his government's integrity and the sweeping range of his charges rallied and solidified the Cabinet to the cause of Hutton's dismissal. Armed with this document which, contrary to Minto's intentions, Laurier circulated to the entire Cabinet, the Prime Minister reconvened his ministers to reconsider their request for Hutton's recall. In Cabinet, David Mills, the Minister of Justice, demolished Minto's constitutional treatise and tore its arguments to shreds. In Mills's opinion, it was a very dangerous document which subverted the notion of responsible government. It took the Cabinet little time to reach a decision. It decided almost immediately that it would dismiss the troublesome General from service with the Canadian militia if the War Office refused to recall him.

[41] Minto Papers, Minto's memo to Council, February 3, 1900.
[42] Colonial Office 42 (875), Minto to Colonial Office, February 8, 1900.

Yet Laurier had no desire to precipitate a crisis which might force him from office and into a premature general election, particularly given the uncertain state of English Canadian opinion following his government's equivocal stand on the war. Therefore he decided to make one last effort to reconcile his government's differences with Hutton and Minto. During Laurier's second interview with Minto the two men retraced the chief arguments of their initial discussion, the horse-dealing row, and the proper relationship between ministers and generals. In a more conciliatory mood, Laurier declared that he refused to believe that Hutton was anything more than "a straightforward honourable officer." He admitted that Borden had made a mistake initially but felt that Hutton's subsequent actions had placed him in the wrong. Still he warned Minto that he could not agree with the Governor-General's constitutional position outlined in his unofficial memorandum and he restated the case in favour of Hutton's recall rather than dismissal.[43]

Minto seemed to mistake Laurier's conciliatory manner for weakness. Convinced that the government would back down eventually and victory would be his, Minto decided to hold firmly to his original position. The government's attempts to settle the dispute confidentially, he informed Laurier, were totally unacceptable. The government must accept public responsibility for its actions. If the government insisted on Hutton's recall he would do as he had promised previously. He would protest their request to the imperial government and write a formal memorandum which could come before Parliament. Such a document, he stressed, would expose publicly the government's sordid record. Although Laurier warned Minto that his government might refuse to accept responsibility for the Governor-General's actions the interview ended amicably. Both men agreed to speak again to their "clients" and Minto confessed that he knew Hutton had often been indiscreet.

Much to Minto's surprise, two days later Laurier returned to Rideau Hall, with a short draft despatch asking for Hutton's recall. Minto protested immediately that the despatch was too short and lacked a precise explanation for this unusual request. He insisted that a demand of this nature must be made by Order-in-Council, complete with explanation. However, Laurier seems to have been much firmer this time. He reminded Minto of the Letellier affair, when the Quebec Lieutenant-Governor's decision to force the resignation of his ministry had been repudiated by the federal government. The constitutional reference seemed lost on Minto, who persisted in calling it the "Boutellier incident," and he confidently denied its relevance.[44] His own position, he declared, was quite different. Yet despite Minto's bold exterior, Laurier's remarks had unsettled him. He became even more distressed when he learned that Laurier had circulated his unofficial memorandum to the entire Cabinet. Minto knew that this document was a blunt, unpolished statement which he had no opportunity "to

[43] Minto Papers, Memo of Laurier-Minto interview, January 27, 1900.
[44] Minto Papers, Memo of Laurier-Minto interview, January 30, 1900.

tone down" and which had never been intended for general circulation. Later Minto was so embarrassed by this document that he apologized to Borden for the pointed references to him and his department. Unsure of his constitutional position and the propriety of his memo, Minto decided to play for time. He therefore appealed to Laurier to make one final effort "to patch up the affair." He, in turn, promised to speak to Hutton at once, but the time for conciliation was long past.

The next morning Laurier returned with an official request recommending Hutton's recall in the form Minto had earlier demanded. During the ensuing interview Minto, surprised by Laurier's prompt return, betrayed his own doubts and insecurity. Throughout the interview he vacillated between supplication and intransigence, desperately seeking a defensible position. He first hesitated to sign the order, despite his earlier assurances. His refusal, he mused aloud, might well be unconstitutional, but given "the present anxious condition of the Empire," might be justified. Then he tried to impress upon Laurier the gravity of the government's decision to dismiss Hutton in the midst of a serious imperial crisis and the threat of a Fenian invasion. It would be impossible, he declared, to fill Hutton's place with a competent imperial officer at this time and no Canadian seemed fit to occupy the post.

Laurier remained unmoved by all these arguments. The imperial government, Minto then protested, might refuse to recall Hutton. Then, Laurier replied, the Canadian government would simply dismiss him. Minto again suggested a Cabinet shuffle but Laurier would not hear of it. Finally, Minto suggested that Laurier withdraw the Order for further consideration. But Laurier refused; he had made up his mind. The Order must remain and he would represent Minto's views to the Cabinet at his earliest convenience. Laurier had displayed a toughness unexpected by Minto.[45]

Yet Minto was far from defeated. He had failed to stay the Canadian government, but he was still confident that he had the imperial government's support. Yet, there too, he sought reassurance. After a day's reflection he cabled Chamberlain explaining the more serious turn of events. In this despatch he recited all the well-worn arguments for Hutton's retention: the imperial crises, the problem of his replacement, the reputed Fenian threat, and the need to "make a firm stand once for all." He made no effort to disguise the seriousness of the crisis. If the British government failed to recall Hutton, he told Chamberlain, the Canadian government would dismiss him. However, he pointed out that there was still one final alternative. He could simply refuse to sign any Order-in-Council dismissing the General, thereby forcing his government to resign or submit.[46]

Alarmed at the turn events had taken in Canada, Chamberlain lost no time replying to Minto's cable. He agreed immediately, without

[45] Minto Papers, Memo of Laurier-Minto interview, January 30, 1900.
[46] Colonial Office 42 (875), Minto to Chamberlain, February 1, 1900.

consulting the War Office, to comply with the Canadian government's request for Hutton's recall. He intended to insist that Hutton's offer of services for South Africa be accepted. Although Chamberlain regretted the Canadian government's decision, he warned Minto that it would be foolish "to force an officer on your Govt—who is distasteful to them."[47] Other members of the Colonial Office concurred and in the privacy of intra-departmental correspondence they did not mince words. They were appalled at Minto's rash attempt to "coerce" his ministers, particularly over as indefensible an issue as Hutton, a man "unfit by temperament and manners" for the position he occupied. According to their testimony, his weaknesses were "known both to the W.O. and this dept. before the appointment was made—and which we pointed out (unofficially) to the W.O. at the time, and they persisted in the selection against our objections."[48] Without the aid or sanction of the imperial government Minto was left defending a hopeless case.

He also possessed a hopeless client. For Hutton seemed incapable of keeping out of trouble even for the duration of the crisis. The government's resolve to risk a serious political crisis had been strengthened by its discovery of another example of Hutton's gross insubordination which in itself would have destroyed any chance of retaining his services. In December, Borden, while checking a proposed list of officers for a staff course at the Royal Military College, asked Hutton to omit the names of Lieutenant-Colonels White and Vince owing to their age and infirmity. White, whose command had been extended several times previously, was due to retire in a few months. Borden argued that their places should be given to younger men of greater use to their regiments. Hutton agreed and stated his approval in writing, adding that "it would be inadvisable to extend this officer's tenure of command."[49] Nevertheless he instructed his chief staff officer, Lieutenant-Colonel Foster, to inform White that he had been removed "by the Honourable the Minister" on the grounds that he had taken "an active part in politics on behalf of the opposition."[50] Hutton's actions would have been unacceptable to any government.

Even so, despite his poor case and worse client, Minto had not lost hope. He still believed he possessed one final card, an appeal, direct or indirect, to the Canadian people. At this point he had completely lost perspective. For his proposed plans violated both the letter and spirit of Chamberlain's instructions. Convinced of the righteousness and popularity of his cause, Minto felt that the success of his efforts would vindicate his methods. In an attempt to forestall dismissal procedures the Colonial Office had complied immediately with Laurier's request for Hutton's recall. Yet Minto gave Laurier no

---

[47] Colonial Office 42 (875), Chamberlain to Minto, February 1, 1900.

[48] Colonial Office 42 (875), Minute, John Anderson, February 7, 1900.

[49] F. W. Borden Papers, Hutton to F. W. Borden, December 11, 1899.

[50] Minto Papers, Hubert Foster to W. White, January 29, 1900; Foster to White, February 1, 1900.

indication of Chamberlain's favourable reply. Indeed, Minto carefully cultivated the impression that the imperial government might refuse
the request, obviously trying to force the Canadian government to the
more extreme measure of dismissal. In his opinion, this would bring
the sordid affair out in the open. Meanwhile, Minto submitted to his
government his long-awaited official memorandum, which was simply a polished, less pointed version of his earlier "unofficial" document.

The Cabinet replied immediately in a long twenty-page statement, challenging Minto's constitutional interpretation and denying
his charges of public corruption. In their indictment Minto later
recalled that they attributed to the Governor-General all the failings of
a Stuart king. Mills, the author of the government's counter constitutional treatise, used the strongest possible language. "There is no
executive officer," he reminded Minto, "who is not under the jurisdiction of some Minister" who is responsible before Parliament for
"every administrative act." It "is true," he continued, that Hutton may
be regarded as a specialist, but, "so too, are many scientific men."
According to Mills, Minto's constitutional interpretation would reduce Canada to the condition of a "Crown Colony." Then he turned to
the viceregal charge of public corruption, which he rejected categorically. "There are," he asserted, "but few instances in the history of
English Parliamentary Government in which the Sovereign, or Her
representative, have censured a Minister."[51]

The government had taken a firm stand, and it had almost completely turned the tables on Minto. It flatly refused to accept responsibility for Minto's official communication, thereby offering him the
simple choice of withdrawing his own document or accepting the
resignation of his government. For Minto the battle had taken a
strange turn. Only a short time before Minto had seen himself leading
the attack from what he considered impregnable defences; now he
held a rather tenuous position.

At last Minto seemed to face the logic of his position. He wrote at
once to Laurier informing him that he adhered unequivocally to
Mills's statement. His own position, he felt, had been "so well known
and so incontrovertible" that he could not imagine "how he could
have been supposed to have expressed an opinion counter to them."[52]
However, he did admit some days later to the Colonial Office that his
constitutional position was "somewhat crude" yet written on the
assumption "that in frequent conversation I had fully recognized the
responsible position of the General toward his Minister." Although
he repeated this explanation in a more private letter to Chamberlain, it
was a poor defence for a man who had earlier proposed to pen a public
exposé of his government.[53]

Fresh from its victory over the Governor-General, the government
decided to press its advantage and dismiss Hutton. In this way, they

[51] Colonial Office 42 (875), Memorandum signed by David Mills and Laurier, n.d.
[52] Colonial Office 42 (875), Minto to Privy Council, February 6, 1900.
[53] Minto Papers, Minto to Chamberlain, February 7, 1900.

would establish beyond a doubt their constitutional authority. Although Laurier knew through his correspondence with the Canadian High Commissioner to Great Britain, Lord Strathcona, of the Colonial Office's efforts to recall Hutton, it took the War Office over a week to find the contentious General suitable employment in South Africa. This delay soon became intolerable owing to Hutton's insubordination. Meanwhile, much to Minto's delight, Laurier drew up a Privy Council Order dismissing the General from service with the Canadian militia. Minto signed the Order immediately despite his earlier threats. And while Minto informed Chamberlain the next day that he had done all in his power to prevent Laurier's actions, this is not so,[54] since he had promised Laurier the previous day that he would sign the Order because it appeared so important "in the public interest that my govnt. should accept responsibility" for the General's withdrawal.[55]

The Privy Council Order suited Minto's latest plans precisely. He had lost a battle but not the war. Once he signed the Order he cabled to the Colonial Office urging it to delay action "as to his [Hutton's] employment in South Africa . . . till things further develop."[56] Several days before, Minto had persuaded Hutton to avoid resignation and allow the government to dismiss him, then demand a Royal Commission of Inquiry into the militia's affairs.[57] Hutton had already begun work on his brief for the proposed Commission. The brief was a detailed twenty-point list of his grievances dating back to his arrival in Canada. He had also decided upon a more general public appeal, consisting of a promise to eliminate party politics from the Militia, make it an efficient force for Canadian defence, maintain the Empire and restore the constitution and liberties of the Canadian people![58] Indeed, he had planned a campaign of no mean measure which, he told Minto, he would fight à outrance. The Colonial Office, however, had other ideas.

News of the Canadian government's precipitate actions came as a sharp surprise to the Colonial Office. The reason was not difficult to surmise. "Lord Minto," Anderson guessed, "did not tell his Ministers that we were trying to get Hutton to S.A."[59] Chagrined by Minto's failure, the Colonial Office lost no time securing Hutton's recall which it hoped would erase the effects of Minto's blundering. It wrote the War Office demanding immediate action. The War Office, they argued, had got them into the difficulty by insisting on Hutton's appointment; it could now get them out. Under this sort of pressure the War Office responded. The next day Chamberlain instructed Hutton to return at once for service in South Africa. Then it asked the Canadian government to rescind the Privy Council Order, to avoid

[54] Colonial Office 42 (875), Minto to Chamberlain, February 7, 1900.

[55] Laurier Papers, Minto to Laurier, February 6, 1900.

[56] Colonial Office 42 (875), Minto to Chamberlain, February 7, 1900.

[57] Minto Papers, Hutton to Minto, February 7, 1900.

[58] Hutton Papers, "Memo on Canadian Career," 27-37; Minto Papers, Hutton to Minto, February 3, 1900.

[59] Colonial Office 42 (875), Minute, John Anderson, February 9, 1900.

public debate.[60] Although anxious to comply, Laurier could not, since Hutton had already unleashed a public attack on the government which had appeared in the press. The next day, an opposition member asked for an explanation in the House and Laurier had to admit that Hutton had been dismissed from service with the Canadian militia.

The tempest aroused by Hutton's dismissal subsided quickly once the General left Canada. Laurier ignored Hutton's request for a Royal Commission since it had been made typically but improperly through Minto rather than the Minister of Militia. Hutton's dismissal provoked a brief Commons debate, but the opposition had little desire to defend a man who had persecuted Sam Hughes, a prominent member of their party. Much to Minto's disappointment, no mass popular protest arose outside Parliament to defend the outraged honour of the departed General. Minto and Hutton had (Fred White, the respected Commissioner of the North West Mounted Police, told Minto frankly during the crisis) "entirely overrated" the support they were likely to receive from the Canadian people.[61]

Even Minto soon recognized the folly of his course and the fatal flaws of the General. "I quite agree," he wrote Chamberlain over two months later, "that strong action [against] my govnt. would have been a mistake."[62] He also confessed to Lansdowne that Hutton had over-ridden "his horse a bit."[63] The departed General, he explained, had exaggerated the disloyalty of French Canada, and the degree of public corruption in the militia.[64] Friends who knew the General and all his works agreed. They, too, hoped that he had learned a lesson.[65]

Yet the lack of a clear definition of the General Officer Commanding's powers continued to trouble Minto and he determined to see it resolved. Although he temporarily enlisted Chamberlain's support, the Canadian government, entrenched in its position by the unpleasant Hutton affair, refused to budge beyond its stance outlined in Mills's constitutional counterblast. In this document Mills had described the General as a subordinate officer similar in status to any other ranking civil servant.[66] There the matter rested, at least for a time.

In retrospect, the firing of Hutton brought to a close a period of strained relations between Minto and his government. Despite what Gundy has written in his article on Minto and Laurier, during the months between the outbreak of war and Hutton's departure, Minto's behaviour toward his government had been neither correct, constitutional, nor cordial.[67] Indeed, relations came close to the breaking

[60] Laurier Papers, Strathcona to Laurier, February 13, 1900.

[61] Minto Papers, "Memo on Hutton Affair," February 3, 1900.

[62] Minto Papers, Minto to Chamberlain, April 14, 1900.

[63] Minto Papers, Minto to Lansdowne, March 2, 1900.

[64] Minto Papers, Minto to Chamberlain, February 15, 1900.

[65] George Parkin Papers, Arthur Lee to George Parkin, December 11, 1901; Minto Papers, G. Kitson to Minto, April 9, 1900.

[66] Colonial Office 42 (876), "Memo from Canadian Privy Council," June 9, 1900.

[67] See Gundy, "Sir Wilfrid Laurier and Lord Minto."

point as Minto played the self-appointed role of the exacting Pro-Consul. Yet, contrary to popular belief, Minto's actions were neither inspired nor even supported by the Colonial Office, which watched his behaviour with increasing incredulity and embarrassment. Indeed, during these months the Colonial Office, the supposed master-mind subverting Canadian autonomy, seemed much more perceptive and sympathetic toward Canadian sensitivities than its representative, the Governor-General.

Chapter Eight

The Defence of Empire

Soon after Hutton's departure Minto's relations with his government began to improve. Aware now that he had indeed overplayed his
hand and possessed the support of neither the Canadian nor imperial
government, Minto made a rapid reassessment of his situation. A new
respect for his government and its political problems and a more
realistic assessment of the nature and extent of imperial sentiment in
Canada replaced many of his old fears and misconceptions of Canadian public life. He now saw the Empire in more pragmatic and Canadian terms, as a defence against the corroding influences of American
continentalism. Since he had little faith in formal schemes for
imperial reorganization, schemes which he regarded as fragile, divisive, and largely meaningless, in his opinion the only true bonds of
Empire were self-interest and sentiment, that is to say, trade, defence,
and a commitment to common cultural values.

Several circumstances help to explain Minto's conversion to this
more practical view of Empire. The departure of General Hutton
not only removed a troublesome liability but marked the break-up of
that small imperial coterie which had done so much to insulate Minto
from Canadian public feeling. Soon after Hutton's departure, Kitson,
whose relations with the Canadian government had remained

strained, left Canada to take up an appointment in Washington as British military attaché. Two years later Parkin also left Canada, having accepted the Secretaryship of the Rhodes Scholarship Trust. There were now no more "Imperial, Anglo-American, 'Down-with-all Dagoes' pow-wows" which had characterized the former days.[1] The result was Minto's improved relations with his government, most conspicuously with the Minister of Militia, F. W. Borden. The Minister of Militia, whom Minto had previously described as corrupt, incompetent, and a nonentity, now seemed to him a thorough, pleasant, agreeable man, "a very good friend," and quite "the best min. of Militia they have had here."[2] Rumours that Borden might be replaced evoked his sincere regrets since he felt convinced that "we shall not light upon a better Min. of Militia."[3] Minto's former friends and associates must have been a little surprised to hear the Governor-General dismissing charges of patronage in the militia department as gross exaggerations. The transformation in Minto's attitudes toward Borden is suggested by his comment to Lady Minto near the close of his administration, when he confessed to his wife the hopeless impetuosities of Hutton and that "well meaning faddist" Dundonald, and noted "I can understand Borden or Parsons [the Halifax General], [since] they talk sense though we may not agree with them."[4] Although Minto's relations with his government were still far from perfect, the improvement provided a marked contrast to previous conditions.

Scarcely a month after Hutton's departure, a serious event removed another of Minto's misconceptions. A nasty, three-day riot in Montreal underlined the divisive nature of imperialism in Canada. This was a danger which Minto had often underrated, since he had been confident that given strong leadership the French Canadian would eventually "throw in his lot with the go-ahead Anglo-Saxon race."[5] Begun by McGill students celebrating the relief of Ladysmith, the riot soon spread to townsmen on both sides of the linguistic line and forced frightened civic officials to call out the militia to assist the somewhat less than dependable municipal police. Although in retrospect the event seems little more than a student prank gone sour, the incident received wide publicity at home and abroad and profoundly disturbed public leaders. In Minto's mind it would have taken "a very small spark to make a racial blaze here."[6] Throughout the tense three-day riot Minto watched events closely and reported daily to Chamberlain. Once Minto intervened directly and begged the McGill principal, William Peterson, to do nothing "to accentuate present difficulties." He explained in a later letter that "the lot of the

[1] Parkin Papers, Arthur Lee to Parkin, November 15, 1899.
[2] Minto Papers, Minto to Dundonald, March 20, 1902.
[3] Minto Papers, Minto to Brodrick, May 27, 1902.
[4] Minto Papers, Minto to Lady Minto, June 13, 1904.
[5] Minto Papers, Minto to Parkin, December 27, 1899.
[6] Minto Papers, Minto to Wolseley, March 17, 1900.

two races in Canada has been thrown together & it should be the duty of us all to assist the dual machinery."[7] Minto now realized clearly that the riot represented a much deeper cultural cleavage than he had suspected earlier.

But Minto soon discovered that French-Canadian hostility constituted only the most obvious impediment to imperial integration. The war, which Minto, like many men, initially believed would provide an impetus to imperial reorganization, had the opposite effect. It strengthened the cause of those who sought a separate Canadian political destiny. The success of the Canadian troops, combined with initial British checks and blunders, encouraged a Canadian critique of British society which went well beyond the pros and cons of tactical decisions. In countless letters-to-the-editor, Canadian returned soldiers enumerated the stupidities of British officers and compared their own martial virtues to those of the slum-born British Tommy cowed by supercilious "Piccadilly aristocrats" and wooden soldiers.[8] This letter-writing campaign reached such extravagant proportions that Minto strove to suppress it and pleaded publicly with returned soldiers to curb "their criticisms of their superior officers."[9] Yet Canadian criticism did not cease, and as it continued it turned into a full-fledged critique of British society and the imperial mission. Men began to search for the causes of British "race deterioration" and to question British fitness for imperial leadership. Altogether it created what Minto saw as an "appalling self confidence" and a serious imperial danger.[10] While convinced imperialists attempted to capitalize on this changed Canadian public mood by writing confidently of Canada's mission to regenerate the British race and become the future seat of imperial grandeur, the fact is that the war seriously compromised the old and more traditional imperial plans.

An imperial reaction had begun, a reaction which Minto himself had foreseen and forecast. Perhaps even more disturbing, it seemed to have found a voice in the reputedly most loyal formation in Canadian politics, the Conservative party. Early in April 1900 Sir Charles Tupper himself inaugurated a political campaign in Quebec to discredit Laurier's "imperial ardour." In Quebec City before a large Conservative assembly Tupper boasted that he had smashed the old Imperial Federation League and informed his audience that he found Laurier far too imperialist.[11] Despite Minto's strong affection for the venerable old leader, he deplored Sir Charles's tactics. Still, he recognized the deep undercurrent of English Canadian opposition to additional imperial commitments. As Minto explained to Queen Victoria, English Canadians, though always eager "to share in the glories of the Em-

[7] Minto Papers, Minto to William Peterson, March 7, 1900.

[8] See Fredericton *Gleaner*, December 28, 1900; Toronto *Mail and Empire*, April 1, 1903; Ottawa *Journal*, December 31, 1901.

[9] Toronto *Mail and Empire*, November 6, 1900.

[10] Minto Papers, Diary, July 31, 1900.

[11] Montreal *Gazette*, April 3, 1900.

pire," displayed "no corresponding desire to accept its responsibilities."[12]

The rapidity and clarity of Minto's reassessment of Canadian imperial possibilities had another cause. Early in March 1900 Chamberlain asked Minto to sound out Canadian public men on the possible creation of an Imperial Advisory Council. To Chamberlain a Council was a means of exploiting the imperial sentiment provoked by the war. Confident of imminent British victory in South Africa, Chamberlain planned to sweeten the proposal by inviting some form of colonial participation in the peace settlement. But in his mind the planned peace conference would serve simply as the precursor to a more permanent consultative body. The proposed new Council would be similar to the Indian Council and would consider matters of common interest, beginning with defence. Chamberlain even suggested that Councillors might hold titles and membership in the House of Lords. In short, it was part one of a larger plan.

Minto took more than a month to prepare a formal reply to Chamberlain's request. Meanwhile he consulted carefully with many prominent public men—Laurier, Tupper, Foster, Mulock, Parkin, Senator George Drummond, G. M. Grant, the respected old principal of Queen's University, and J. S. Willison, the editor of the Toronto *Globe*. He also clipped articles, studied editorials, and followed closely the curious contemporary debate on imperialism, a debate which ranged all the way from Tupper's Quebec speech and Bourassa's trenchant denunciation of Canadian participation in South Africa to Laurier's well-known delphic retort, "If you want us to help you, call us to your councils."[13]

Minto methodically worked his way through this array of contradictory material, trying to weigh its relative importance and avoid entanglement, although once he came perilously close. During the parliamentary debate on imperialism, George Drummond, the Montreal Conservative Senator, consulted Minto on a resolution he proposed to introduce in the Senate, requesting Canadian representation at any South African peace conference. This resolution, he hoped, would stimulate debate on the specifics of imperial federation. Minto wired Chamberlain at once for advice and direction, explaining the "friendly" intent of Drummond's motion. The Colonial Office, busily preparing its plans for the proposed Advisory Council, seemed delighted and instructed Minto to "strike while the iron is hot," confident that New Zealand and Australia would follow suit.[14] They warned Minto, however, that there would be no chance Canadian opinion could affect seriously the peace settlement unless, of course, it agreed with the position of the imperial government. Minto immediately communicated Chamberlain's views to Drummond and drew his attention to Chamberlain's desire for a more general wording

[12] Minto Papers, Minto to Queen Victoria, October 20, 1900.
[13] Canada, House of Commons, *Debates*, March 13, 1900, 1846.
[14] Colonial Office 42 (875), Minute, John Anderson, March 15, 1900.

of the resolution.[15] Much to Drummond's dismay, a week later Minto begged the senator to excuse him from further association with the resolution. In the interim he had spoken to Laurier and the Prime Minister made no secret of his displeasure with Minto's consultation with opposition leaders on proposed parliamentary resolutions. Then he added the gratuitous and chilling comment that "he did not want to have a Jameson Raid in this country."[16] It took no great subtlety to grasp the meaning of Laurier's words. Minto explained to Drummond that it would be wrong for him "to appear to direct opinions in anything which seems political."[17]

In mid-April Minto despatched his response to Chamberlain's March proposal. Minto's report was a thorough, perceptive analysis of Canadian public feeling which gave Chamberlain little cause for encouragement. Indeed it was so bleak a report that the Colonial Secretary felt Minto had frightened his respondents by excessive talk of military obligation. Minto warned Chamberlain that an Advisory Council, although possible in some "remote future" and altered circumstances, seemed an impractical scheme for the immediate future. Even loyal imperialists who endorsed the plan added the rider that it entail no additional material obligation. In fact, Minto continued, Canadian public men impressed upon him that extreme caution must characterize any future imperial initiative. Above all, it must involve no pecuniary burden and preferably provide some tangible benefit. He warned Chamberlain against placing too much stock in Laurier's fancy imperial oratory, particularly his double-edged slogan "if you want our aid, call us to your councils." Whatever he might say, the Prime Minister was no imperial federationist but a Canadian "independentist." On the other hand, he felt certain that Laurier would consider favourably some tariff arrangement. This was a scheme which Minto thought "far more likely to bring about Imperial unity than any joint system of Imperial defence." Anything which suggested "some practical gain to the colony" seemed to brighten the spark of imperial sentiment in Canada.

But Minto made it perfectly clear that Laurier and French Canada were not the only stumbling blocks to imperialism. He explained that in English-speaking Canada "there is ... another class who though they intensely love the old country, feel that Canada is prosperous & well-to-do ... [and] though singing 'God save the Queen' at every opportunity would hang back from closer imperial ties."[18] This was a theme he would return to on many future occasions. He felt that it was important to dispel the ignorance of the British public who seemed to suppose that Canada was "bubbling over with admiration for the Old Country & a desire to share her battles." While there were always "plenty of young bloods ready to go anywhere ... Canadian public

[15] Minto Papers, Minto to George Drummond, March 22, 1900.

[16] Minto Papers, Memo, Laurier-Minto Interview, March 23, 1900.

[17] Minto Papers, Minto to George Drummond, March 27, 1900.

[18] Minto Papers, Minto to Chamberlain, April 14, 1900.

opinion ... is not generally of such an Impl. fire-eating nature as many people seem to think."[19] Minto's final suggestion that Laurier, despite his considered reluctance, ought to be invited to attend any proposed peace conference contained small comfort since Chamberlain had no intention of encouraging any real colonial participation.

Chamberlain's request had forced Minto to make a crash study of Canadian imperial sentiment. His analysis confirmed his suspicions of formal constitutional schemes and led him to more pragmatic solutions. It also gave him an opportunity to put Chamberlain straight, to give him a lead which he felt confident the Colonial Secretary would soon take up.

Consequently, in the following months Minto confidently expected some big imperial initiative to rekindle the dying embers of imperial sentiment. What he wanted was some practical plan of action, based on trade or defence. But as the months passed nothing happened, the spirit of imperial enthusiasm engendered by the South African war seemed to die, and the Empire, Minto lamented in March 1902, seemed to be drifting with no clear destination. Then, a few weeks later, Sir Michael Hicks-Beach, the British Chancellor, and a staunch free trader, announced the first breach in Britain's sacred free trade system. Imperialists immediately regarded Hicks-Beach's tax on foreign corn as the beginning of an imperial Zollverein. As Minto had predicted, even Laurier seemed interested, and raised the issue in a House of Commons speech which was widely reported in Britain and immediately endorsed by Chamberlain's Birmingham Liberal Unionist Association. Chamberlain obviously had plans, which he would test on the colonial premiers during the imperial conference that summer.

Several months before Hicks-Beach's startling announcement Chamberlain had issued invitations to all the colonial premiers to attend a conference in London. Styled in the mould of the Diamond Jubilee conference of 1897, this meeting was to be held during the festivities celebrating the coronation of Edward VII in June of 1902. The conference, Chamberlain suggested, might consider common economic, political, and defence problems. Laurier immediately erased the last two items from the imperial agenda. In his impeccably polite but firm manner, the Prime Minister informed Chamberlain that he could see no possible reason to disturb the satisfactory political and defensive rules of Empire. He would be happy, however, to discuss at length the more important matters of trade, communications, and transportation.

To Minto, Laurier's reply to Chamberlain crippled the conference from the start. While he had no faith in "any cut and dried proposals," particularly those which called for "contributions from the colonies of men and money," still Minto felt that Laurier ought to come to the conference table in a more responsive mood. Laurier's failure to use this opportunity to work out a more satisfactory plan of mutual de-

<hr />

[19] Minto Papers, Minto to Brodrick, December 3, 1901.

fence was, Minto confided to George Parkin, "the worst thing done in an Imperial sense since I have been here."[20]

In response to this hint from Minto, Parkin began a series of public meetings to force Laurier to take a more constructive attitude toward the conference, but his campaign had little concrete effect. It simply served to illuminate the contradictions within the imperialist movement. While Parkin, conscious of the divisiveness of the tariff issue in British politics, stressed the defence question, the redoubtable Colonel G. T. Denison mounted a vociferous campaign to educate the British public to the virtues of an imperial trade policy.[21]

Meanwhile, Laurier stubbornly refused to budge beyond his publicly stated support for imperial preferential trade. Laurier's stand not only confounded his Canadian critics but forced Chamberlain into a political corner. For, despite the Chancellor of the Exchequer's temporary tax on foreign corn to pay the cost of the war in South Africa, the British Cabinet had no intention of repudiating its sacred creed of free trade for an economically dubious imperial preferential trade system. To meet Laurier's challenge Chamberlain not only had to remove a mountain of ignorance, fear, and suspicion, but answer the valid objections of the old free trade advocates. This, he discovered, could be achieved only outside the confines of the British Cabinet.

Chamberlain's decision to leave the British Cabinet over one year later to campaign for an imperial preference, however, had little or nothing to do with the wiles of the Canadian Premier.[22] Chamberlain had taken Laurier's measure long before. He had made that clear in a conversation with Lady Minto during the Coronation festivities. Laurier, he informed Lady Minto, was a "cad" who did not know his own mind.[23] He made this unflattering assessment even more explicit in a letter to his son, Austin, shortly after the colonial premiers had left London. "As you know," he wrote, "I do not entirely trust Laurier. . . . His ideal is an independent Canada."[24] Despite Minto's warnings, Chamberlain had much more confidence in Canada's "British population," particularly Canada's Finance Minister, W. S. Fielding, whom he trusted to lead the Canadian crusade.

Perhaps more than any other "Canadian," Minto helped persuade Chamberlain to stake his career on the imperial trade cause. In the year between the colonial conference and Chamberlain's resignation from the British Cabinet, Minto plied the Colonial Secretary with clippings from newspapers, journals, and speeches favourable to the cause. Over the next months Minto made a superficial survey of Canadian public opinion. He solicited trade figures from civil servants, and canvassed the opinions of politicians and public men. He

[20] J. S. Willison, Sir George Parkin (London, 1929), 235.

[21] George T. Denison, The Struggle for Imperial Unity: Recollections and Experiences (Toronto, 1909), 333-34; see also Daily News, May 27, 1902.

[22] Colvin, "Sir Wilfrid Laurier and the Imperial Problem," 375.

[23] Minto Papers, Diary, July 21, 1902.

[24] Austin Chamberlain Papers, University of Birmingham, Chamberlain to Austin Chamberlain, August 25, 1902.

even submitted a seven-point questionnaire to J. S. Willison, now editor of the Toronto News, a paper he considered "much the best in the Dominion." Then in a series of letters and reports he despatched the results to Chamberlain, analyzed and interpreted. He also sent a version of his report to his brother Arthur, an ardent opponent of Chamberlain's scheme, in an attempt to convert Arthur to Chamberlain's cause.

Minto's optimistic report, although often qualified and tentative, left little room for doubt, particularly to the converted. According to Minto the Canadian Cabinet, at least Laurier, Fielding, Mulock, Borden, and Fitzpatrick (he did not know but feared Sifton's opinions since they were far from friendly), was firmly behind Chamberlain. In his mind they had not wavered an iota from their strong stand at the colonial conference. There were, however, three possible impediments to unqualified Canadian support—the free trade West, protectionist French Canada, and the Canadian Manufacturers Association. These were three rather formidable opponents, one might have thought; but Minto disagreed. The West, he argued, could be won by exploiting its desire to become the granary of the Empire. French Canada, or the "better" part of French Canada (Israël Tarte, now safely out of office, assured Minto), would rally readily to Chamberlain's plan. There remained the Canadian Manufacturers Association, "that selfish beast," which he felt certain would give trouble. But Laurier twice told him he would "take his coat off for the cause" or, pacify the Canadian Manufacturers Association with higher duties against the United States.[25] Therefore, Canada needed only a leader to arouse its latent imperial sentiment. Nor did Chamberlain have any reason to doubt the validity of Minto's assessment, which agreed so implicitly with that of Fielding, the man he trusted to manage the Canadian campaign and with whom Chamberlain maintained a lively correspondence.

As usual, Minto took no pains to disguise his support for an imperial preference, although the issue was one of political controversy in both Britain and Canada. In August 1903, a month before Chamberlain's resignation, for example, Minto agreed to address the closing banquet of the fifth British Empire Chambers of Commerce Congress meeting in Montreal. The imperial preference debate had dominated the Congress's deliberations, and in his speech Minto decided to make it perfectly clear where he stood on the subject. Peeved by Laurier's light-hearted toast to the Empire, Minto took a more sombre view. In Minto's opinion the Empire, composed not of colonies but nations, needed ties stronger than sentiment to meet the challenge of an uncertain future. Only closer commercial relations based on preferential conditions would arrest impending imperial disintegration. What is to be your choice, he asked:

A mighty Empire, a brilliant constellation of nations, united in common interests, disseminating throughout the world the spirit

[25] Minto Papers, Minto to Arthur Elliot, September 10, 1903; Minto to Arthur Elliot, January 4, 1904; Minto to Chamberlain, August 6, 1903.

of free institutions and liberal ideas, proud of a glorious history, and confident in the promises of the future—or, the gradual estrangement of that Empire's component parts?

"This is not the time to sit down and fold one's hands," he concluded somewhat anti-climactically, "it is the time for those who believe in the future of our Empire to speak out."[26] Minto had unquestionably followed his own advice.

His speech invited the opinion of his opponents, not only on the content but the propriety of his speech. British and Canadian Liberal journals reacted immediately. Some branded Minto's speech "improper";[27] others predicted his recall;[28] while a third group dismissed his oration by ridicule.[29] Although Laurier appeared unoffended by Minto's address and even suggested printing it in pamphlet form, the Liberal press took a very lofty stand. The King, the Toronto Globe told its readers, would not have been "so ill advised, but if he ventured on such a course the great esteem in which he is held would not save him from general censure."[30]

Politically, the most devastating and virulent attack on Minto's speech came from the articulate young politician, Henri Bourassa, the hero of the recently formed Ligue Nationaliste. La Ligue immediately called an open meeting at Le Théâtre national français in Montreal, at which orator after orator recited the tedious history of Minto's reputed misdoings beginning with the South African war. It was Bourassa himself who captured the mood of the meeting in his acid denunciation of Minto, "Cet homme qui ne pourrait être dans la politique Anglaise qu'une nullité absolue, qui n'a jamais été bon là-bas, qu'à courir des chevaux sous un nom d'emprunt, joue quelque rôle ici par sa situation officielle."[31] Bourassa continued his attack on Minto in the House of Commons. And he carried his critique to such lengths that Laurier felt forced to intervene. He privately admonished Bourassa to stop, explaining to Bourassa that "whatever his opinions might be he was bound to behave like a gentleman."[32] To Minto the Prime Minister's admonition struck just the right tone.

Minto's speech and the Nationaliste reaction conjured up all the old ghosts of imperialist excess, and did nothing to make imperial preference more palatable in French Canada. Nor did it constitute an auspicious prelude to the campaign Chamberlain inaugurated the following month when he announced his resignation from the British Cabinet to begin his final campaign for imperial consolidation. Although a month before the Colonial Secretary had practically informed Minto of his imminent departure from the Cabinet, at first Minto could scarcely believe the good news.

[26] Minto Papers, "Chamber of Commerce Speech," August, 1903.

[27] Daily News, August 29, 1903; Liverpool Post, August 26, 1903.

[28] Hamilton Herald, August 29, 1903.

[29] Shipping World, August 25, 1903.

[30] Toronto Globe, September 8, 1903.

[31] La Patrie, 24 août, 1903.

[32] Minto Papers, Diary, August 31, 1903.

Minto's respect for Chamberlain rose rapidly. Only a year before, during the Coronation festivities, he had confided to his diary his less than flattering assessment of the Colonial Secretary. At that time Chamberlain seemed to him a "hard-headed man of business" bent on exploiting the colonies for imperial benefit, and devoid of "the inbred courtesy to endear him to colonial statesmen." In Minto's opinion Chamberlain was "a very strong man but not a very sympathetic one."[33] Above all, he was completely out of touch with colonial sentiment. Now Minto regarded Chamberlain as the "one" British politician willing to sacrifice place for principle, a true statesman of imperial vision whom he hoped would soon replace Balfour as Prime Minister.

Minto greeted Chamberlain's campaign with equal joy. He saw it as "a great struggle" for high stakes, the beginning of a new era. Perhaps it was the last real chance of Empire, a crusade which would decide the ultimate political destiny of Canada. A great sense of urgency pervaded Minto's letters, interviews, and speeches on the subject. He informed British friends that the people of Britain must decide and decide now if they were ready for the sacrifice and burden of imperial responsibility. On the other hand, Canada stood near "the parting of ways," one of his favourite expressions. It must choose now between independence through Empire or absorption and domination by the United States. The struggle had already begun, particularly in the West, which according to Minto was the battleground of Canadian nationality. The invasion of American men, money, and branch plants such as Westinghouse and Deering, the talk of reciprocity, rumours of Canadian writers "in the pay of American interests," and the existence of other unidentified nefarious "back door" political forces proved how tenuous the situation had become.[34] In Minto's view, Canada had no more than ten years—Israël Tarte's deadline—to determine its destiny. "If I were a Canadian," Minto told one audience, "I should object to be called a Colonist. I would be called a Canadian, but I would be an Imperial Canadian, and a very Imperial one, too."[35] To Minto the destinies of Britain, that is Greater Britain, and Canada were tied, the time was now and the price of failure high.

Given Minto's commitment to the cause it would have taken a character transformation to have restrained him from bending every effort to assist Chamberlain. His letters to Chamberlain, except for the period just prior to the Colonial Secretary's resignation, became more frequent than when Chamberlain occupied the Colonial Office. These letters assured Chamberlain that Canada was "heart and soul with you in your campaign."[36] He continued to ply Chamberlain with informa-

[33] Minto Papers, Diary, July 20, 1902.

[34] Minto Papers, Minto to Lady Minto, March 6, 1904; Minto to Chamberlain, December 14, 1903.

[35] Ottawa Citizen, January 19, 1904; Minto Papers, pamphlet, Canadian Club Speech, Ottawa, January 18, 1904.

[36] Minto Papers, Minto to Chamberlain, December 14, 1903.

tion and advice. He also served as his Canadian confidant, a role made more important owing to Fielding's growing shyness of the Chamberlain crusade. He entertained and introduced sympathetic British visitors and reporters recommended to him by Chamberlain, and in official correspondence with the British government did everything to interpret Canadian affairs to support the Chamberlain thesis. He described Canada's future as problematic and stressed the consequent need for immediate British action. In short, Minto became the faithful friend and warrior Chamberlain, a shrewd judge of men, had every reason to expect. This assumption of Minto's fidelity, more than any other, helps explain Chamberlain's decision in May 1903, four months before his resignation from the British Cabinet, to extend Minto's term an additional year, although the decision violated a precedent Chamberlain had wished previously to establish.

Initially Minto seemed optimistic. He was confident Chamberlain would quickly convince a sufficiently large segment of the British public or persuade his former Cabinet colleagues to join his courageous stand for Empire, thereby forcing his way back into the limelight of British public life. But time and circumstance slowly eroded Minto's confidence and made his role as Chamberlain's Canadian confidant more and more ambiguous. While Minto's personal relations with the former Colonial Secretary remained warm, a note of irritation bred of disappointment crept into Chamberlain's correspondence with Minto. Where was the Canadian public support? What had happened to Fielding? Why would Laurier not provide some gesture of support to dispel British fears of colonial indifference? Why did Laurier continue to tolerate reciprocity speeches from two senior Cabinet colleagues, Sifton and Cartwright? Would a change of government in Canada alter circumstances?[37]

Minto's bland replies could scarcely have proved reassuring. He explained that the Canadian public was temporarily peeved over the Alaska settlement, and did not want "to be considered beggars." Moreover, Fielding could go no farther until Britain displayed some interest, since Fielding scrupulously refused to interfere in British politics. On the other hand, Laurier had made his position perfectly clear at the colonial conference, despite his adamant refusal to have the proceedings published. As for the insidious talk of reciprocity, it simply underlined the urgency of the issue. Minto believed that a Conservative government would change nothing, particularly under its colourless new leader, R. L. Borden.[38]

As time passed even Minto began to doubt many of his own arguments, although his personal faith in the cause remained firm. Losing causes had always inspired Minto's devotion, be they the Carlist crusade, the passing social order, or the Chamberlain tariff, but soon a qualified pessimism seemed to pervade his conversations and correspondence. He confided to his diary that Chamberlain appeared to be losing touch with colonial opinion. Every day, time was "being

[37] Minto Papers, Chamberlain to Minto, August 17, 1904.
[38] Minto Papers, Minto to Chamberlain, July 10, 1904.

irretrievably lost." Perhaps Laurier had always wanted independence. Perhaps Canadian independence was possible. This was a
thought which preoccupied his mind more and more during his final
months in Canada. Minto's growing doubts about the place and fate of
Canada in the Empire can be appreciated, however, only in the larger
context of his concurrent campaign to work out a satisfactory system
of imperial defence, a campaign which followed a similar pattern and
led to a similar uncertain conclusion.

Chapter Nine

The Defence of Canada

Long before Chamberlain began his tariff campaign, Minto had launched another battle to persuade the Canadian and imperial authorities to reform and reorganize the Canadian militia. What he wanted was to provide Canada with a more efficient, dependable line of defence, not an exportable Canadian contingent to fight the Empire's wars. Behind this campaign lay a number of unspoken assumptions. In Minto's mind, military training not only guaranteed a country's territorial integrity against an external foe but constituted an important means of inculcating patriotic virtues. No nation, Minto argued, could expect to survive and flourish unless it possessed a loyal, disciplined, and physically fit citizenry, committed to public service. Properly constituted, a militia could do much to form a nation fit to meet its destiny. An efficient militia was therefore the first condition of real autonomy, or "the proper price of larger dignities."[1]

Canada's defence policy, insofar as it existed beyond the broad commitment to protection against foreign invasion and aid to the civil power, depended largely upon the priorities and initiative of the Minister of Militia. Contrary to popular belief, Borden's ideas, or at least his rhetoric, differed little from that of the Governor-General. For

[1] C. P. Stacey, "Defence," *Canadian Defence Quarterly* (April, 1931), 321.

example, both frequently made common cause against the War Office's attempts to subordinate the Canadian militia to imperial control. Conscious of General Leach's recent recommendation that the General Officer Commanding the Canadian militia be placed under the Halifax General's jurisdiction, Minto himself never tired of reminding the War Office that the Canadian militia constituted a separate force under Canadian control. As long as the War Office treated the Canadian militia as a dependent subordinate command, it would continue to remain a weak and ineffectual force, a liability rather than an asset to imperial defence.

Minto's most explicit statement on the separation of commands occurred during the Seymour-Hutton dispute. Then he had reminded the Halifax General that Canada's militia was an autonomous command governed by an Act passed by the Canadian Parliament. Even before this exchange of correspondence Minto had rejected the notion that the imperial government could move the Canadian militia outside the country's borders.

During the visit to Canada of the Duke of Cornwall and York in 1901 the issue re-emerged in the guise of military protocol. In Halifax British regulars from the imperial garrison and Canadian militiamen from the city had planned to form a joint guard of honour for the Duke. Immediately the question of command arose. Should the British or Canadian General Officer Commanding assume command? To Minto there was no question. The Canadian General must be in command.[2] The militia "must be the servant of the Dominion," he explained in a later letter to Lord Roberts.[3] Nor did Minto let the matter rest. On other occasions he requested the War Office to cease corresponding directly with Canadian officers, including the General Officer Commanding the Canadian militia, since these communications undermined the authority of the local force.[4]

However, the War Office learned slowly if at all, and during Minto's administration the War Office promoted several schemes to bring Canada more closely under its control. Their most conspicuous proposals included regimental exchanges, linked battalions, "repatriation" of the 100th Regiment (Royal Canadians), not to mention outright recruitment. On each occasion Minto, the vigilant defender of Canadian military autonomy, firmly resisted them.

During the heady days of the 1897 Colonial Conference Laurier had actually approved a plan for the exchange of regiments. The plan's purpose was to improve the quality of the Canadian militia through association with the British regular troops in Canada. While Minto and Hutton opposed the scheme from the start, and couched their objections in practical language, their real motives may have been more jurisdictional. The exchanges themselves benefited the Canadian militia little since they took place during the summer and

[2] Colonial Office 42 (886), Minto to War Office, September 2, 1901; Colonial Office 42 (883), Minto to Chamberlain, October 9, 1901.

[3] Minto Papers, Minto to Roberts, October 11, 1901.

[4] Colonial Office 42 (865), Minute, "C.D.," May 18, 1901.

hence deprived it of the permanent unit's valuable service at a crucial training period. However, the real objection to the exchanges in the eyes of Minto and Hutton was that they were simply a devious War Office device to erode the authority of the Canadian General Officer Commanding and to bring his command under the control of the Halifax General. Through Minto's persistence and with Borden's consent the exchanges ceased after two summers, much to the disappointment of both the War and Colonial offices.[5]

Captain M. Nathan, secretary to the Colonial Defence Committee, had another scheme to gain control over the Canadian militia, but it failed to get beyond the administrative drawing board. In 1898 Nathan suggested to his superiors in the War Office a linked battalion system which he felt would raise some 6,000 men in Canada for the British army. According to his plan certain Canadian militia regiments would bear the more illustrious names of British regular regiments and serve as a recruitment depot for the main line regiment on active service. Even if one subtracted the 1,400,000 French Canadians and 120,000 Indians from Canada's population, Nathan explained, the War Office would have "no difficulty" raising at least six battalions in Canada.[6] The plan, however, found no favour with Laurier and little support elsewhere. Minto himself saw no hope for the plan. Not only would it prove impossible to attract Canadians into the British army at the prevailing British pay rates, but it would also destroy the Canadian militia's own recruiting ground. Worst of all, it would increase Canada's unhealthy military dependence upon Britain and foster a false sense of Canadian self-satisfaction rather than force Canada to face the responsibility for the defence of its own territory. In Minto's mind, Canada's greatest service to itself and the Empire was self defence, not token contributions to the British army. Any nation with pretensions to autonomy must be capable of protecting its own territory.

Minto did not oppose cooperation or the retention and cultivation of sentimental ties between the Canadian militia and the British regulars. Indeed, the idea of a system of linked battalions appealed to him, but not in the form Nathan had suggested. Two years later, Minto proposed his own plan for linked battalions. In contrast to Nathan's blueprint, Minto's proposal was based solely on sentimental and voluntary principles and would have benefited the Canadian militia as much or more than the British army. He also insisted on complete Canadian control of the participating militia units and rejected any hint of formal, administrative, or jurisdictional ties to the British equivalents. According to Minto's plan, Canadian militia regiments would simply adopt the designations of British regular regiments. They would be encouraged to retain close fraternal ties and to exchange men, officers, and ideas, but these exchanges would be tailored exclusively to the needs and circumstances of each regiment.

[5] Colonial Office 42 (865), Minute, John Anderson, December 20, 1898; Colonial Office 42 (895), Minto to Alfred Lyttleton, January 29, 1904.

[6] War Office 32 (427), Minute, Lansdowne, May 13, 1898.

Although Minto rejected the idea of any legal obligation to serve in time of war he felt completely confident that sentimental ties cultivated in peacetime would be sufficient to rally the linked Canadian battalion "as one man" in wartime.[7] The War Office had no use whatever for Minto's seemingly impractical project; to them it would become a needless administrative nuisance and provide no obvious benefit. Minto's plan, therefore, met the same ignominious administrative fate as Nathan's earlier scheme.

The idea of repatriation of the 100th Regiment (Royal Canadian), unlike most War Office schemes, possessed as many Canadian supporters as War Office advocates. The Royal Canadian Regiment, although raised in Canada during the Indian Mutiny and despite its name, had long lost its original Canadian character and was now composed largely of Irish recruits. Repatriation, of course, never meant making the regiment part of the Canadian permanent militia establishment, but simply inducing Britain to move the regimental depot from Ireland to a Canadian location. This proposal attracted the interest of practical politicians as well as military glory seekers. In 1896, for example, the City of Toronto, anticipating an annual depot income of some $100,000, petitioned the War Office to relocate the regiment within its precincts. Although the War Office displayed interest, seeing it as a means to "keep the Army full upon present rates of pay," at the time reasons of economy prevented further action.[8] Two years later, however, the War Office revived the idea by despatching the 100th Regiment to the Halifax garrison, accompanied by a request to the Canadian government to maintain the regiment's numerical strength through recruitment in Canada. Much to everyone's surprise the Canadian government not only welcomed the idea, since they saw it as a means to avoid sending more troops to South Africa, but suggested the creation of two battalions, one stationed permanently in Canada, the other stationed in the British Isles or elsewhere, but both staffed by Canadian officers from the Royal Military College or the Canadian militia.[9] The British decision to send the Royal Canadians to South Africa, however, temporarily blocked the plan and led to a Canadian counter offer to garrison Halifax with Canadian militia for the duration of the war. The British lost no time accepting the offer. But by the end of the war Canadian military enthusiasm had waned and with it, much to Minto's relief, any serious talk of repatriation. According to Minto, the perennial problem of low British pay rates, the depot's distance from the main prospective manpower pool in central Canada, and Halifax's bad initial impression of the Regiment doomed the project to failure from the start.[10] Nor could he see that it would improve the state of the Canadian militia.

[7] Colonial Office 42 (896), Minto to Brodrick, November 19, 1900.

[8] War Office 32 (427), Minute, Wolseley, January 4, 1899.

[9] Colonial Office 42 (875), Privy Council Order, January 17, 1900; Minto to Chamberlain, January 18, 1900.

[10] Colonial Office 42 (875), Minto to Chamberlain, January 24, 1900.

British recruitment in Canada constituted a particularly difficult problem. While Minto never contested the British government's right to recruit, he considered it a peculiar form of folly. Talk of the formation of a battalion of Canadian Guards in London, the establishment of an imperial infantry regimental headquarters in Western Canada, and even the New Zealand Premier's War Office-inspired plan unveiled at the 1902 Colonial Conference to create a mobile imperial regiment composed of colonial units received a cool reception at Rideau Hall. All failed to solve the more important problem of making the Canadian militia a more dependable, efficient fighting unit. Minto felt that the British government would do better to press the Canadian militia to assume full responsibility for the defence of its own territory rather than devise dubious schemes to sap or circumvent the Canadian militia. In each case these schemes could be twisted all too easily into a grievance. In Western Canada they were seen as a senseless drain of settlers and in French Canada as a dangerous legal obligation. It is "the greatest mistake," Minto informed his brother, for "the ultra imperialists at home to talk of recognized contributions from the colonies of men or money. [They] simply don't know the feeling of the colonies."[11]

Yet Minto's preaching converted few. Time and again, particularly during the South African war, the British government requested permission to recruit troops in Canada, despite Minto's attempts to discourage the British authorities.[12] Ironically, Laurier readily consented to these requests, regardless of protests from the Governor-General and some members of his Cabinet.[13] Obviously, compliance constituted a rather clever political ploy consistent with the Prime Minister's South African policy. In English Canada it could be represented as proof of Laurier's imperial zeal. In French Canada, British recruitment in Canada could be shrugged off as the exercise of an imperial right beyond the control and concern of the Canadian government. Above all, it made no claim on the public purse. In this way the War Office's shortsighted, selfish policy played directly into Laurier's hands. Meanwhile, the Canadian militia and the cause of reform languished unheard and unheeded by either the British or Canadian governments.

Although Minto and Borden made common cause in defence of Canadian military autonomy, their support was based on quite different assumptions. On his part, Minto possessed a perception of his own position in military administration which the Minister of Militia did not endorse. He also envisaged a comprehensive programme of imperial military cooperation which, however laudable, was consid-

[11] Minto Papers, Minto to Arthur Elliot, October 17, 1902; also Laurier-Minto interview, March 19, 1902. Minto opposed any "red tape obligation on the part of Canada to supply military aid."

[12] Minto Papers, Minto to Brodrick, February 18, February 21, December 3, 1901; Colonial Office 42 (882), Minto to Brodrick, March 30, 1901.

[13] Borden Papers, Borden to Laurier, January 21, 1901; Toronto *Globe*, October 15, 1902.

ered impractical by both the British and Canadian governments. Finally, the Hutton dispute demonstrated Minto's peculiar view of the relative position of the military and civilian authority in Canada, but this view had been denied and rejected by the Canadian government. Yet this rejection did not appear to deter Minto.

Minto's claim to a larger role in the military affairs of the country grew out of two important viceregal functions. Both were related to his role of imperial representative in Canada. First, Minto believed that whatever the Canadian Militia Act said or failed to say, Canadian military autonomy had been qualified by the British government's ultimate responsibility for Canadian defence. As long as Britain assumed this responsibility, Canada had a moral obligation to keep its land force in a satisfactory state of readiness and he, as the representative of the imperial government, possessed a duty to see that Canadian defences remained in order. Minto also believed that in his capacity of Commander-in-Chief of the Canadian militia he possessed direct and personal authority over military affairs, not through Cabinet—"for purposes of command not of administration"—a perception he used to justify his interference in militia affairs and his direct communications with the General Officer Commanding.[14] Certain "promotions & appts. besides the ordinary ones," he explained to Lord Dundonald, the General Officer Commanding, "bear in themselves imperial importance, & as regards these I consider the entire control is in my own hands as regards final approval."[15] Two examples will demonstrate Minto's peculiar concept of his office.

The first grew out of Minto's obsession with the anomalous position of General Officer Commanding. Convinced that the undefined position of the Canadian General Officer Commanding constituted the root cause of the perennial conflict between ministers and generals, a year after the Hutton crisis Minto devised a plan to overcome this difficulty. Minto's plan was designed to appeal to Canada's autonomous aspirations by tying Canadian control of the British garrisons at Halifax and Esquimault to a redefinition of the position of the General Officer Commanding. Since the existing system was a proven failure, he explained to the War Office, there remained only two possible alternatives. The first meant subordinating the militia to the Halifax Command (the Leach Report's suggestion), but this was unacceptable to the Canadian government. The second, which Minto endorsed, was a complicated plan placing all Canadian and British troops in Canada under one General Officer Commanding residing in Ottawa. Although commanding two separate forces, the new General Officer Commanding would be responsible to both the Canadian and British governments and report to the latter through the Governor-General's secretary. This plan reveals the parameters of Minto's own pretensions. The War Office itself had tried to explain to Minto during the Seymour dispute that a similar proposed system of communica-

[14] Minto Papers, Minto to Borden, July 12, 1904.
[15] Minto Papers, Minto to Dundonald, September 22, 1902.

tion would prove unacceptable to the Canadian government, but obviously Minto had not been persuaded.

The second example involved a dispute over patronage, and as such it belongs to the traditional battleground of ministerial responsibility. The quarrel began in March 1900 when Chamberlain informed Minto that the War Office would provide forty-four commissions in the regular army to qualified Canadian militia officers who were either serving in South Africa or graduates of the Royal Military College. Determined to keep these awards in his own hands, Minto immediately wrote to Chamberlain protesting the Colonial Secretary's proposal that the commissions be granted on the recommendation of the new General Officer Commanding the militia who was due to arrive in Canada in July. Minto argued that the new General Officer Commanding would be unfamiliar with the militia and consequently he, as Governor-General, ought to be entrusted with the selection. Accordingly, he would accept advice from a board composed of three senior imperial officers serving the Canadian militia in order to remove any possibility of "personal feeling" or "political pressure."[16] The three officers Minto suggested were his friends Kitson and Foster, and "for appearances sake," Colonel M. Aylmer, a close friend of Borden.[17]

Meanwhile, Minto sent Borden Chamberlain's despatch. The Minister published the notice immediately and instructed candidates to report at designated places for medical examination. Determined to keep these appointments in his own hands, Minto objected to Borden's notice and the government withdrew the militia order. At the same time, it made clear in a Minute of Council its opposition to Minto's selection procedure. All militia officers recommended for commissions, it insisted, must pass through the Militia Department. Moreover, the government could not tolerate the creation of a selection board composed of subordinate officers in the employ of the Canadian government who reported directly to the British government.[18] Minto appeared unmoved by the Council Minute and claimed that the War Office would never consent to their procedure, despite the fact that the War Office originally suggested that the recommendations pass through the Militia Department. The government therefore appealed directly to Chamberlain, insisting that it did not contest the War Office's right to recruit in Canada but if that were its intention it ought to appoint its own agents. Minto immediately seized upon the point and put himself forward as an appropriate imperial agent to nominate candidates.

Public disclosure of the dispute brought the predictable Canadian grumbling about Downing Street domination.[19] However, Downing Street, judged by the Colonial Office's reaction, seemed equally

[16] Colonial Office 42 (875), Minto to Chamberlain, March 24, 1900.

[17] Minto Papers, Minto to Kitson, April 10, 1900.

[18] Colonial Office 42 (875), Minto to Chamberlain, April 7, 1900.

[19] *Saturday Night*, May 14, 1900; Montreal *Herald*, May 4, 1900; Toronto *Globe*, May 3, 1900.

alarmed by Minto's pretensions. "The anxiety of Ld. Minto to eliminate his Ministers completely from this matter," John Anderson
wrote, "is a bad sign." Ministers, he continued, "must have more
knowledge of the several candidates than either the Gov. Genl. or the
imperial authorities . . . we cannot treat ministers as if they were
totally unfit to be trusted. They are the Queen's Ministers in Canada &
we cannot ignore them."[20]

The Colonial Office then suggested that the commissions be
treated as honours recommendations and that Minto submit the
names of candidates suggested by his ministers together with his own
comments, but the point seemed utterly lost on Minto. He immediately informed Laurier that the imperial government had asked
him as Governor-General to recommend candidates for commission.[21]
He was shrewd enough to realize, however, that without the administrative assistance of the Militia Department his victory would be
compromised. Consequently, he asked Laurier if he could count upon
the aid of the Militia Department. Laurier restated his objections to the
proposed selection procedures but agreed that the Department might
assist unofficially and as a courtesy. Convinced that he had won "a
valuable principle as regards appointments," Minto saw his victory as
a clear vindication of his claim to a greater role in military administration.[22] Canadian military autonomy held few terrors for Minto so long
as he retained his right to interfere directly.

Minto's demand for an enlarged viceregal role in military affairs
had a pragmatic purpose, too. In his opinion, Canadian access to
British military men and resources was a prerequisite to reform, and
no one was better placed than he to initiate plans and see that they
followed proper lines. He knew the War Office and the British military establishment. He also possessed ideas.

According to Minto, the proper place to begin was with Canada's
South African war veterans. These men who had seen active service,
who had learned the grim lessons of war and appreciated the value of
thorough training, became the white hope of all Canadian military
reform. But how best could their experience be utilized, their competence maintained and their training broadened?

Canada, Minto argued, provided too small and limited a field for
competent Canadian talent. Good men left in Canada would become
stale, complacent, out of touch and of little real use to their country.
Only positions of command in the British army, even temporary ones,
would give Canadians the opportunities they deserved and required.
Throughout the South African war Minto repeatedly begged Chamberlain, Lord Roberts, and other senior officers to assist Canadians to
gain more and better staff positions.[23] "It is impossible," he explained

[20] Colonial Office 42 (875), Minute, John Anderson, April 7, 1900.

[21] Minto Papers, Minto to Laurier, April 11, 1900.

[22] Colonial Office 42 (875), Minto to Chamberlain, May 12, 1900.

[23] Minto Papers, Minto to Chamberlain, November 24, 1900; Colonial Office 42
(888), Minto to Chamberlain, April 22, 1902; Governor-General's Numbered Files, 350,
Chamberlain to Minto, June 27, 1902.

to George Parkin, "to expect Canadian officers to go on fighting for us in Impl. wars unless they share in Impl. professional awards."[24] In the case of Colonel Otter, the respected Commanding Officer of Canada's first contingent, Minto interceded directly with the Colonial and War offices and extracted the promise of a British position worthy of Otter's abilities and reputation. With their permission he announced the offer at Otter's home-coming reception. But the War Office failed to honour its promise despite Minto's repeated reminders.[25]

Discouraged but not deterred, Minto continued his campaign to persuade the War Office to take a more active interest in Canadian military reform. In 1903 he proposed a more comprehensive peace-time package. He tried to convince the War Office to establish short-term staff officer exchanges, to reserve two annual staff college positions for capable Canadian officers and to offer a brigade command in the regular army to a Canadian militia officer every two or three years. No one knew better than he how jealously these plums were guarded and how many applicants there were for how few places, and he made little headway. Despite his disappointment Minto, when faced by the War Office's reluctance, devised another plan. He suggested that the War Office turn over its two remaining Canadian garrisons at Halifax and Esquimault to the Canadian government, on the condition that its commanding officer and senior staff be appointed by the imperial government but open to all Canadian militia officers.[26] Although the failure of his larger reform plans later forced him to withdraw this recommendation, he still insisted that Canadian officers be eligible for all positions in the gift of the Halifax Garrison. Yet he elicited no enthusiastic response from the War Office.

Minto could not understand the indifference of the War Office to Canadian military reform. It seemed utterly immune to advice and suggestion. Then, during his 1902 visit to Britain for the coronation of Edward VII, he believed he had discovered the reason why. The War Office was in a state of utter confusion. Lord Roberts was Commander-in-Chief, and as much as Minto liked Roberts he realized that one could expect only tinkering from him. Surrounded by his entourage of favourites, Roberts presided over the chaos with a dignity which belied the true state of affairs. Viscount Kitchener sarcastically informed Minto that conditions were so bad that "one could run a W.O. elsewhere for a year without the W.O. finding one out."[27] And that seemed to be the size of it. From the Canadian perspective this was a sorry state indeed.

Meanwhile things were far from quiet on the home front. Borden obviously had plans, too, but in Minto's eyes they tended to be the wrong sort of plans. They were essentially patchwork and parochial and behind them one could usually detect some powerful political motive. These had to be stalled, stayed, or sabotaged, or they would

[24] Minto Papers, Minto to Parkin, September 26, 1904.
[25] Minto Papers, Minto to Chamberlain, December 5, 1900.
[26] Colonial Office 42 (896), Minto to Brodrick, November 19, 1900.
[27] Minto Papers, Diary, July 23, 1902.

pre-empt Minto's larger programme. More serious still, in Minto's opinion, Borden misunderstood the proper lines which ought to govern relations between the military and civilian authorities. Over the last quarter-century or more, Britain had brought the military under the control of a civilian minister, but not without a struggle. The Wolseley gang had never really accepted the fact and had tried frequently to institute a restoration. Borden's attempts to imitate the British civilian example revived the contentious issue in a colonial setting. Determined to block Borden, Minto and Hutton and others were convinced that a successful Canadian settlement of the issue might assist a restoration of the military's proper place in Britain itself. This issue had assumed a central place in the Hutton dispute but it had not been resolved, nor did it remain dormant over the next few years. In various guises it continued to haunt the debate on military reform. In Minto's view, without a proper settlement of this issue Canadian military autonomy constituted a real danger. It meant turning over Canadian defence to the mercy of venial, colonial politicians.

This issue arose again soon after Hutton's departure. Anxious to exploit his temporary advantage, Borden attempted a number of administrative and legislative reforms designed to re-assert ministerial control. In Hutton's day, the Militia Department operated like a British military district. All section heads reported to the General through the chief staff clerk, Hutton's friend Hubert Foster. Section heads were forbidden to speak directly to the Minister; only the General possessed that right. Borden's discovery of Hutton's deliberate distortion of a ministerial instruction during the dying days of the General's administration convinced the Minister of the need to alter the system. Borden immediately abolished the post of chief clerk and ordered all section heads to report directly to him through the Deputy Minister. This enhanced his own control over the department and strengthened the role of the civilian authority. Not surprisingly, Minto disapproved of the measure. He saw it as an attack on the General's authority. But after some consideration, even he conceded that there was "a good deal to be said for Borden's desire to be directly informed."[28] Minto was not always so generous.

However, Minto faced a tactical difficulty in objecting to many of Borden's reforms. Since the Minister cleverly cloaked his reforms in Canadian nationalism, Minto's objections could easily be construed as a lack of Canadian sympathy. On the surface Borden's motives were unimpeachable. No one could deny the need for more and better places for returned Canadian South African war officers. How best to achieve that end was another matter. Borden had made his intentions perfectly clear in his abortive attempt to designate a successor to Hutton, when he had tried to name a Canadian officer to the post. The desire for a Canadian General Officer Commanding was as old as the post itself, which according to the Militia Act must be held by an officer of the British army. As a half-way measure Borden attempted to name

[28] Colonial Office 42 (896) Minto to Brodrick, November 19, 1900.

Colonel the Honourable Matthew Aylmer, an imperial officer resident in Canada, to the vacant post of General Officer Commanding. Minto considered Aylmer too weak a candidate, and completely under the Minister's influence, and he quickly vetoed the attempt. Conscious of the growing public demand for a Canadian General Officer Commanding, Borden retaliated with a draft amendment to the Militia Act which would have granted Canadian militia officers access to the position of General Officer Commanding.

The proposed amendment never got beyond the Governor-General's desk. His objections persuaded the Colonial and War Offices to request its withdrawal. Some of his objections, however, tell us more about Minto than the real problem of naming a Canadian to this post. According to Minto, a Canadian would simply be the servile puppet of the party in power. He also believed that the post would invite political logrolling and destroy cultural harmony since, in his opinion, French Canadians would not tolerate an English Canadian officer. Moreover, in Minto's eyes, there existed no suitable Canadian of sufficiently exalted social standing for the position. More to the point, he felt that the appointment of a Canadian would cut Canada off from the professional training and experience necessary for a modern military force. To Minto, there were better ways of providing competent Canadian officers with the challenge and experience they deserved and required. He also pointed to the fact that Canadians, like Percy Girouard, who had done their service with the British army were scarcely debarred by the existing regulations.[29] So successfully did Minto block this project that Laurier later even denied the existence of the proposed amendment.[30]

Some of Borden's other ideas were more difficult to frustrate, given the War Office's reluctance to satisfy the needs of Canada's South African war veterans. Therefore, Minto wavered in December 1900 when Borden, pushed on by Cabinet colleagues like Mulock, moved to replace three senior imperial staff officers, namely Foster, Kitson, and Stone, to make places for three of Canada's South African war veterans, Pelletier, Otter, and Cartwright. Minto recognized the need to provide these men and others with better, more responsible administrative positions, but he saw a better solution in another larger scheme of imperial cooperation. However, Borden's problem was immediate and the need real; consequently Minto agreed to the limited staff shuffle.

Minto also agreed to meet Borden half-way on another minor matter. Basically, Minto disliked Borden's proposal to amend the Militia Act in order to raise the highest militia rank from Lieutenant-Colonel to Colonel, but with a little pressure he persuaded Borden to restrict its use to honorary colonels. It thereby became a political rather than a military award and something of a standing joke. Soon Colonels, many of whom had never seen a day's military service, blossomed forth with more gold braid than Lord Roberts. Perhaps the

[29] Colonial Office 42 (875), Minto to Chamberlain, March 26, 1900.
[30] Colonial Office 42 (879), Minto to Chamberlain, April 15, 1900.

incident which best exposed the whole ludicrous affair occurred while Minto was pinning a Fenian Raid medal on the new Colonel, Sir Wilfrid Laurier, and in a stage whisper Cartwright asked the Colonel on which side he had fought.[31]

But these were relatively minor matters. Some of Borden's other proposals were of a more serious nature and threatened to eliminate the imperial presence in the Canadian militia. These must be stopped at all costs; otherwise Canada would lose any chance of imperial aid. In this respect, no measure seemed more unfortunate than Borden's decision to restore paragraphs 68 and 69 of the militia Orders and Regulations. These paragraphs had defined the place of imperial officers on loan to the Canadian militia. According to these paragraphs, which had existed since 1879, command of Canadian militia troops was limited to those imperial officers holding Canadian commissions. They also stipulated that seniority in rank be determined by the date of an officer's Canadian commission. Since most imperial officers loaned to the Canadian militia received a Canadian commission which granted them a one-step promotion, this regulation had caused little difficulty in the past. But when Hutton appointed Lieutenant-Colonel F. G. Stone to command the Canadian artillery with no advance in rank (since a lieutenant-colonel was the highest rank permitted any Canadian officer other than General Officer Commanding), Stone not only failed to gain rank but he lost his British seniority by accepting a Canadian commission. To solve this problem Hutton simply suppressed paragraphs 68 and 69 of the militia Orders and Regulations. In remedying Stone's grievance, however, Hutton created a host of others.[32] The problem was accentuated, too, by Hutton's invocation of the Queen's Regulations which gave regular army officers precedence over colonial officers.

Borden's restoration of paragraphs 68 and 69 aroused howls of protests from more junior British officers at the Royal Military College. These men enjoyed not only their recently acquired preferential status but an exalted rank and seniority within it. Convinced of this group's importance to military reform, Minto espoused their cause and insisted on strict adherence to the Queen's Regulations. The War Office needed no prodding. It asked the Canadian government to rescind the offending regulation "without delay."[33] But when the Canadian government refused and contended that their militia Orders and Regulations were simply declaratory of an Act which lay within their jurisdiction, the Colonial Office backed the Canadian contention. In their opinion, the Canadian case was "a perfectly reasonable one" and they suggested that the question go before the Law Officers of the Crown for a legal opinion.[34]

[31] Minto Papers, Diary, January 1, 1904.
[32] Even Kitson thought Hutton's measure unwise. Minto Papers, Kitson to Minto, April 9, 1900.
[33] Colonial Office 42 (886), G. Fleetwood Wilson to C.O., August 31, 1900.
[34] Colonial Office 42 (886), Minute, G. W. Johnston, May 19, 1901.

With the War Office's consent, the Law Officers received the case and reported in February 1901, completely upholding the Canadian contention.[35] Accepting the Law Officers' opinion with ill grace, the War Office countered peevishly that in future Canada must refrain from depriving imperial officers of "the attributes of the rank . . . given . . . by the Crown."[36] Aware that the War Office response emanated from a "purely military Dept . . . unaccustomed to considering questions from a colonial point of view," the Colonial Office, espousing the Canadian case as its own, decided to press its advantage.[37] They not only rejected the War Office contention but demanded that it repeal the section of the Queen's Regulations giving imperial colonels in Canada precedence and command over Canadian officers. The Colonial Office even refused to consider the War Office's final request, not an unreasonable one, that all imperial officers loaned to the colonies receive an advance in rank.

Minto profoundly regretted the Law Officers' decision and could not accept the Colonial Office's attitude. Obviously, they did not appreciate the need to maintain an imperial presence in Canadian military affairs, but that was understandable given the fact that it was run by civilians. The War Office might be more amenable. Some six weeks after the final settlement Minto decided to reopen the case. Recently, a Captain Andrews had been loaned to the Canadian militia with no advance in rank. What, Minto inquired, did the Colonial Office propose to do? Although the Colonial Office expressed its sympathy for Andrews and recommended an advance in rank, it firmly refused to reopen the affair.[38] In despair, Minto appealed to Lansdowne to take up the matter, but Lansdowne had already capitulated, and there the matter stood.[39]

But this was only the beginning of Minto's problems. Early in 1903 Borden, confident of Cabinet and public support, began another major reform offensive. He announced his intention of undertaking a thorough revision of the Militia Act which would alter substantially the existing military establishment. Minto immediately sounded the alarm. He asked Borden and Laurier to delay proceedings until he could consult the imperial authorities. Borden's proposed amendments, he wrote Brodrick, contained three provisions detrimental to imperial interests. First, the proposed new Act, section 3, vested the position of Commander-in-Chief in the King, whereas presently it read the Governor-General—an obvious attempt to curb Minto's pretensions. Second, Borden intended to omit section 37 of the present Act which restricted command of the Canadian militia to an officer of the regular army, thereby reopening an old contention between him and the Governor-General. Third, and much to Minto's annoyance,

[35] Colonial Office 42 (886), Minute, R. B. Finlay, February 16, 1901.
[36] Colonial Office 42 (886), War Office to Colonial Office, March 9, 1901.
[37] Colonial Office 42 (886), Minute, C. T. Davies, May 17, 1901.
[38] Colonial Office 42 (883), Minute, Davies, August 28, 1901.
[39] Minto Papers, Minto to Lansdowne, August 31, 1901.

Borden had refused to make provision in the proposed new Act for placing the militia under the King's Regulations in the event of Canadian and imperial forces serving together. Given the unreformed state of Canadian defences, "it seems to be culpable," he concluded, "to give up an iota of any little Imperial military control we possess."[40]

The Colonial Office was at first sympathetic. It was particularly unhappy with the Minister's failure to preserve the position of General Officer Commanding for an imperial officer. On the other hand, it seemed undisturbed by Borden's other proposed amendments. Section 3 "simply agrees with Sec. 15 of the B.N. Act [sic]," noted A. B. Keith, the Colonial Office's constitutional expert.[41] But in view of Minto's objections it agreed that the Canadian government ought to withhold the bill until Borden could consult the War Office and the Commander-in-Chief of the British army. Borden, too, agreed to Minto's proposal, and his meeting with the War Office was scheduled for December 1903. By this stratagem Minto hoped to delay matters until the imperial government forbade the changes or Canadian common sense intervened.

Meanwhile, Minto and the new General Officer Commanding the militia, Lord Dundonald, who shared Minto's objections to the new Act, bombarded the Colonial and War Office and any other influential friend who would listen with warnings, counsel, and advice. Borden's pet proposal to open the position of General Officer Commanding to Canadian officers, of course, received greatest attention. A lively transatlantic discussion ensued, Minto pushing his cure-all two-master plan and the Colonial Office insisting on some more effective system of surveillance and control.[42] The present system, the Colonial Office reasoned, was so inadequate that it mattered little whether a Canadian or an imperial officer commanded the militia. Moreover, it thought that any new system would prove worthless unless it guaranteed "a right to get openly at the truth and a right of remonstrance and appeal to the Colonial public."[43] Finally, it proposed that the Committee of Imperial Defence be asked to suggest a better arrangement, but its proposal that Canada accept a British Inspector-General who would submit an annual report to the War Office which it could publish found no favour with the Canadian government.

Nevertheless, Minto could scarcely disguise his delight with the Colonial Office's sudden interest in military affairs. He thought that he had finally found an imperial ally whom he could exploit to help him fight against the bill. In a twelve-page, typescript letter to Chamberlain, once again Minto outlined his views on the whole spectrum

---

[40] Minto Papers, Minto to Brodrick, April 10, 1903.

[41] Colonial Office 42 (892), Minute, Keith, April 14, 1903.

[42] Colonial Office 42 (895), Minto to Chamberlain, April 15, May 28, September 15, 1903; Chamberlain to Minto, May 14, 1903.

[43] Colonial Office 42 (895), Minute, John Anderson, May 8, 1903; Minto Papers, Chamberlain to Minto, May ?, 1903.

of Canadian defence. It was largely a rehash of all his old tired nostrums, his two-master plan for the office of General Officer Commanding, his opposition to Canadian control of the British garrisons, and his demand for greater recognition of Canadian military talent within the British army. He still opposed British recruitment in Canada and Dundonald's recent call for the return of British regulars to Canadian soil. Yet a recent visit to Toronto had persuaded him of the possibility of placing a large imperial force in Western Canada "not many hours from the Pacific ports," which might serve as an example of military efficiency to the Canadian militia.[44] Above all, he impressed Chamberlain with the folly of following Borden's scheme, which he believed would only enlarge the Canadian government's field of patronage and corruption, an argument to which he returned when all else failed. But it was ceasing to have much effect on the Colonial Office. "We know," one Colonial Office official noted, "that he is inclined to state a very unfavourable view of everything the Militia Dept. does. The Admiralty & W.O. are not so dissatisfied."[45]

The Committee of Imperial Defence had been well prepared for its December rendezvous with the Minister of Militia. Scarcely a month before the proposed conference between Borden and the Committee of Imperial Defence, Dundonald sent Sir William Nicholson, Director of Military Intelligence and a member of the Committee's "fixed nucleus," a detailed nine-page typescript memorandum outlining the arguments against the Canadian position, points for compromise, and other confidential material useful to the British government.[46] In view of Minto's and Dundonald's frequent and extensive communications with the British government, Minto's subsequent charge that the War Office sold the pass because it was insufficiently informed seems scarcely credible.

The fact is that Minto's delaying tactics backfired, largely because Balfour's Cabinet reconstruction in September which followed Chamberlain's resignation altered the political power balance in the British Cabinet, and reduced Minto's chances of persuading it to reject Borden's plans. The loss of Chamberlain, a sympathetic powerful ally who occupied a position in the Cabinet second only to the Prime Minister, and his replacement as Colonial Secretary by Alfred Lyttleton, a weak, ineffectual, and inexperienced politician, diminished the Colonial Office's influence in British Cabinet deliberations. The move of Minto's friend Brodrick from the War Office to the India Office and the promotion to the War Office of H. O. Arnold-Forster, an energetic, ambitious man with little tolerance for traditional court interference, further reduced Minto's chances of influencing Cabinet decisions.

In larger terms, the Cabinet reconstruction permitted the settlement of an old argument over imperial military strategy in North

[44] Colonial Office 42 (895), Minto to Chamberlain, May 28, 1903.

[45] Colonial Office 42 (883), Minute, E. Wingfield, June 8, 1901.

[46] Colonial Office 42 (896), Dundonald to Nicholson, November, 1903.

America. In the past Selborne, the first Lord of the Admiralty, had tried to persuade the Committee of Imperial Defence to reconsider Britain's colonial defence commitments in North America. Selborne and Balfour, both strong advocates of Anglo-American friendship and War Office retrenchment, favoured a withdrawal of the imperial garrisons from North America. Moreover, the Admiralty, rejecting the idea of opposing the United States' navy in the Caribbean and the Atlantic, wished to bring home the Atlantic squadron and concentrate its full strength in European waters.[47] According to Selborne, their two greatest Cabinet opponents to a withdrawal of the garrisons were Brodrick, who was "too sticky & not sufficiently resourceful," and Chamberlain, who "doesn't know all the facts & is impatient of those he doesn't like."[48] The Cabinet changes tipped the balance in favour of the Selborne-Balfour thesis since the new War Secretary, Arnold-Forster, agreed entirely with Balfour that a fight with the United States, "our cousins across the Atlantic is perhaps the most improbable."[49]

A week before their conference with Borden, the Committee of Imperial Defence gathered to discuss Canadian defences. Balfour had now no difficulty persuading the Committee to abandon the idea of defending Canada against an unlikely American attack and "to place the whole responsibility for the Militia upon the Canadian govnt."[50] Once fear of an American front ceased to occupy the minds of serious imperial strategists, the Canadian militia's inefficiency no longer seemed the nightmare it had been. Consequently, Borden had won his battle by default.

Unaware of the imperial strategists' changed plans, Minto confidently expected Borden, once in London, to fall under the imperial spell and capitulate. But three days before the Committee's December 11 meeting, Borden met Arnold-Forster, explained his plans, and agreed upon a settlement.[51] The Committee of Imperial Defence's meeting, however, proved more than a pleasant formality to rubber-stamp the Arnold-Forster-Borden agreement. Members of the Committee seized the opportunity to discuss the whole range of Canadian-imperial defence problems, which they embodied in an eight-point résumé.

The imperial government readily conceded Canada's right to name a Canadian militia officer to the post of General Officer Commanding subject to the Crown's right to appoint, in time of war, "a Senior General Officer of the Regular Army to the supreme joint command." In turn, the Committee suggested that an imperial officer might, at the invitation of the Canadian government, make an "occa-

[47] War Office 32 (266), Admiralty to War Office, April 19, 1902.

[48] Balfour Papers, British Museum, Selborne to Balfour, April 5, 1903.

[49] Samuel F. Wells, Jr., "British Strategic Withdrawal from the Western Hemisphere," Canadian Historical Review (December, 1968), 340.

[50] Cabinet 38/31 no. 79, "Minutes of 25th Meeting of the Committee of Imperial Defence, December 4, 1903.

[51] Arnold Forster Papers, British Museum, Diary, December 8, 1903.

sional inspection of the Militia." It agreed, too, that the "Governor-General of Canada should continue to be c-in-chief of the forces." One of its most controversial suggestions was that Canada ought to consider raising two infantry battalions, one to serve in Canada and the other in India at the Indian government's expense. It also agreed to reserve two annual staff college positions for Canadian officers and to appoint selected Canadians to short-term staff posts in the regular army. Some of these concessions ought to have delighted Minto. However, contrary to Minto's explicit instructions it also offered to turn over the Halifax and Esquimault garrisons to the Canadian government. Finally, at Minto's request, the Committee raised the question of the relative rank of militia and regular army officers on joint manoeuvres, but it rejected his insistence that imperial officers possessed "powers of executive command over Canadian troops by virtue of their Imperial Commissions." Instead, it concluded an agreement granting recognition of the imperial commissions of British officers serving in the Canadian militia in exchange for the recognition of the Canadian commissions of militia officers serving with regular troops in North America.[52]

When Minto received a detailed account of the conference's proceedings he could scarcely believe his eyes. He could not see how the imperial government had been so shortsighted and stupid, and for a long time he used every petty pretext possible in order to upset the agreement. "H. M. Govnt. by sheer idiocy," he wrote in his diary, "are ruining the military position here."[53] He placed much of the blame, of course, on Lyttleton who, friends told him, "behaved more stupidly even than I had imagined."[54]

When Borden returned Minto, much to his delight, found that the Minister's version of the meeting contrasted substantially with the War Office's memorandum which Lyttleton had sent. Properly exploited, he might still be able to use this fact to sabotage this insidious agreement. Borden had denied the War Office's affirmation that he had agreed to take over the Halifax and Esquimault garrisons and send an infantry battalion to India. The Minister insisted that he had given no such assurances. Moreover, he understood that the War Office had consented to reserve six, not two, imperial staff positions a year for Canadian officers.[55] Above all, he rejected Minto's assumption that he had bought a package plan, since the War Office had attached no pre-conditions to his proposed amendment of the Militia Act.[56]

An appeal to Lyttleton confirmed Borden's version of the meeting. The Colonial Secretary regretted that the War Office's Secretary should have "composed the minutes on the theory that what he

[52] Cabinet 38/d/ no. 82, "Minutes of the 26th Meeting of the Committee of Imperial Defence," December 11, 1903.

[53] Minto Papers, Diary, January 3, 1904.

[54] Minto Papers, Diary, March 2, 1904.

[55] Colonial Office 42 (896), Minto to Colonial Office, January 6, 1904.

[56] Colonial Office 42 (896), Borden to Minto, March 1, 1904; Borden Papers, Borden to Lyttleton, March 1, 1904.

conceives ought to have been arranged was arranged."[57] Still, Minto remained unconvinced until he received an official copy of the Committee meeting's minutes. This took four months to complete. Meanwhile, he showered the Colonial Office with letters in which he objected to the appointment of a Canadian to the position of General Officer Commanding, claimed wide public support for his opinion, and described the terrible morass of Canadian public life.[58] However, his letters convinced no one and the Colonial Office soon grew tired of his persistence. "Lord Minto will not understand," John Anderson complained, "that a quasi-independent Commander-in-Chief is incompatible with complete Ministerial responsibility."[59] Another official added, "Lord Minto is evidently annoyed that his views have not been accepted and implies that H. M. G. are acting in ignorance."[60] Still Minto persisted.

Borden's parliamentary presentation of the amended Militia Act provided another opportunity to renew the crusade. In Minto's opinion, Borden's bill violated the December agreement. It had omitted two important imperial items, provision for the Crown to appoint a regular officer to the joint command in the event of war and the right of regular officers to command Canadian troops during joint manoeuvres. Although Borden promised to insert the Crown's right to appoint a supreme Commander during the bill's second reading and to amend the militia Orders and Regulations, giving regular officers the right to command Canadian troops during joint manoeuvres, Minto advised Lyttleton to insist on their inclusion in the Militia Act.[61]

The Colonial Office shared Minto's concern that Borden had failed to provide for the Crown's right to name a supreme commander during war and instructed Minto to insist on its inclusion in the new Act. But it was also tiring of Minto's quibbling. "I do not see how we can proceed on the assumption that Sir F. Borden is lying," one official noted. "Lord Minto seems to be trying to force our hand."[62] It decided, therefore, to trust Borden to honour his promise on the question of relative rank.

Still Minto fought on, stimulated by Borden's decision to press for an even more radical reform. He had decided to replace the position of General Officer Commanding with an advisory committee composed of military and civilian experts along the lines suggested by Lord Esher's War Office (reconstruction) Committee. The Minister's relations with Dundonald were close to the breaking point, particularly over the Militia Bill, and Borden saw the Council as a means of ridding himself of the General, reinforcing civilian control, and creating a more adequate source of information, continuity, and

[57] Colonial Office 42 (896), Minute, Lyttleton, January 12, 1904.
[58] Colonial Office 42 (896), Minto to Lyttleton, January 5, 8, 10, 22, 1904.
[59] Colonial Office 42 (896), John Anderson to M. F. Ommanney, February 2, 1904.
[60] Colonial Office 42 (896), "A.F." to H. B. Cox, March 23, 1904.
[61] Colonial Office 42 (896), Minto to Lyttleton, March 21, 1904.
[62] Colonial Office 42 (896), "A.F." to H. B. Cox, March 23, 1904.

coordination in military affairs. Borden had finally revealed his full hand.

Anticipating a storm, Borden broached the subject of a Militia Council gently. He informed Minto of his interest in the system but suggested that the present did not seem the most appropriate moment. Some time before, however, he had informed a friend that his "mind was made up to take the plunge, as I have all I can stand of the existing system and absurd condition of things."[63] Much to Borden's surprise, Minto greeted the idea with relative calm. He expressed his approval of the Esher report's proposal, although he confessed he was not entirely convinced it would work well in Canada. Yet he agreed to consider the possibility seriously despite concerted opposition in his viceregal entourage, particularly from his Military Secretary.

Behind Minto's apparent equanimity lay a subtler motive. He saw in Borden's scheme a means of retrieving lost ground and of persuading both the imperial and Canadian government to buy his famous two-master plan. During a March conversation with Charles Parsons, the General Officer Commanding regular troops in Halifax, Parsons had suggested making the Halifax General the Inspector-General of the Canadian militia. This position was an important new post in Borden's proposed Militia Council,[64] and Minto saw at once how Parson's plan could be tailored to fit present exigencies. The Inspector-General could serve as the first member of the proposed Militia Council, appointed by the imperial government and responsible to it and the Canadian government and invested with almost the identical powers presently possessed by the General Officer Commanding the militia. The Colonial Office, however, had no interest in the plan, and it did not even bother to reply to Minto's suggestion. Nor did Minto prod them, since a new crisis had broken and it preoccupied most of his remaining time in Canada.

It was the Dundonald affair which finally killed Minto's will to fight the new Militia Act. From the start he had taken an active interest in Dundonald's appointment and had begged Chamberlain to send a man of "repute, presence, capacity, wealth," tact, and a wife with "social qualities"—all for £800 a year![65] But contrary to popular belief Minto held no brief for Dundonald. He disliked Dundonald from the beginning. Indeed, Minto's first encounter with the General Officer Commanding, the twelfth Earl of Dundonald, the hero of Ladysmith, proved most inauspicious. During the interview Dundonald spent most of his time complaining about the precedence table in Canada which placed him, the scion of a distinguished Scottish aristocratic family, after ministers of the Crown rather than after the Governor-General. Despite Minto's initial unfavourable impression he strove to assist the new General at every turn. He offered to find him a house in Ottawa and invited him to discuss militia matters any time at the General's convenience.

[63] Borden Papers, Borden to T. D. R. Evans, April 12, 1904.
[64] Colonial Office 42 (896), Charles Parsons to Minto, March 16, 1904.
[65] Joseph Chamberlain Papers, Brodrick to Chamberlain, December 26, 1901.

But the General's personal quirks could scarcely be ignored and were often the cause of much merriment at Rideau Hall. Although Dundonald was reputed to possess popular qualities, charm, imagination, and eloquence, Minto considered him egotistical, unbalanced, vindictive, and theatrical. In the privacy of his diary and personal correspondence, he referred to him as "Dundoodle," that "dangerous demagogue," that "awful stick," that "vain, unreasonable creature," that "petulant baby," and "that crank with a brain the size of a fruit head."[66] Minto also regarded him as a poor administrator, who let stores rot for want of care. He also thought of him as a faddist who engaged in expensive, dubious experiments, and a man generally indifferent to the slovenly, undisciplined state of the Canadian militia.

Long before Dundonald arrived Minto had tried to warn him "not to ride the horse too hard." There were other ways of handling Borden, who was "very sensitive to a little butter."[67] But it took the General little time to compile a three-point case against the Minister. Two of his grievances, the alleged suppression of Dundonald's first annual report and the government's parsimonious attitude toward militia expenditures, were minor matters which only assumed greater importance after Dundonald's dismissal. His third grievance, Borden's Militia Bill, the precursor to the Militia Council, proved too much for the General, and as early as January 1904, the date he first learned of the imperial government's capitulation to Borden's demands, Dundonald sought a way of warning the Canadian people of "certain dangers before it was too late."[68] He had even considered resigning his post at that time to contest a Canadian constituency.

According to Minto, Borden's alleged suppression of Dundonald's first report was simply a figment of the General's lively imagination. The "suppression," more precisely Borden's request that the General transfer a defence scheme from Part I to Part II, which would not be presented to Parliament, could scarcely have constituted a serious grievance. At the time, at least, Dundonald seemed willing to live with the indignity. The reason for Borden's request, security, though not entirely credible, seemed no more preposterous than Dundonald's charge that the Minister wished to suppress criticism of the militia. For Borden offered to include in Part I any comments from the deleted sections Dundonald thought appropriate.[69] Moreover, he could not have considered Dundonald's "suppressed" report too damaging since he agreed to open the unrevised controversial Part II to any committee struck by Parliament or to any other interested member.[70] Dundonald, however, rejected Borden's offer and took the case to Sam Hughes, the opposition military critic, and

[66] Minto Papers, Minto to Lady Minto, July 2, 1904; Diary, April 20, 1903; Minto to Arthur Elliot, August 13, 1904.

[67] Minto Papers, Minto to Dundonald, March 26, 1902.

[68] Minto Papers, Diary, January 3, 1904.

[69] Borden Papers, Borden to Dundonald, February 21, 1903.

[70] Canada, House of Commons Debates, March 30, 1903, 209.

Hughes raised the question in the House, an action which scandalized Minto.

Dundonald's second grievance, inadequate funding, had plagued the militia from its birth. Few ministers had done more than Sir Frederick Borden to improve conditions—raise pay and wring larger supplies from a reluctant government. Twice the Minister threatened to resign rather than reduce his estimates. Yet it is true that neither Laurier, Borden, or indeed the imperial government shared Dundonald's inordinate concern that there existed a danger of an imminent American invasion and consequently, they refused to endorse the expensive line of land defences which the General prescribed. According to Dundonald, their rejection of his plans constituted a standing grievance, a dangerous dereliction of duty which demanded public attention.[71]

It was Borden's proposed Militia Council which precipitated the final explosion, not that relations had been particularly cordial for the past months. The Militia Bill, however, had deeply divided the Minister and the General. Borden had refused to take Dundonald to London with him for the understandable reason that the General had made no secret of his disapproval of Borden's case. Borden's victory, of course, did nothing to improve relations and from that time on he "seemed to think," Minto explained to George Parkin, "he could upset the decision of the W.O. or render it ineffectual."[72] Borden's decision to create a Militia Council, construed by Dundonald, and rightly so, as an overt attack on the office of General Office Commanding, made the break inevitable. Dundonald simply sought the appropriate occasion.

On June 3, during a Montreal militia officers' banquet, Dundonald decided to launch his campaign. Before a large audience and in the presence of a press reporter, he accused the government of gross political interference in militia affairs. An example of flagrant interference, he explained to a slightly embarrassed audience, occurred recently while raising a cavalry regiment in the Eastern Townships, the Scottish Light Dragoons. Sydney Fisher, the Minister of Agriculture, whose constituency was in that area, had objected to the number of Conservatives on the officer list and while he was Acting Minister of Militia had stricken some names from the list, notably that of Dr. Wilfred Pickles, a well-known political partisan. The facts, though carefully selected, were essentially as Dundonald had described them, although perhaps not as Sydney Fisher might have told them.

A vigilant politician, anxious to retain political patronage in the hands of the faithful, Sydney Fisher might have been more discreet had he not been embroiled in a heated contest to re-elect the Quebec Provincial Secretary. But Dundonald's own actions were not above reproach. He had appointed Colonel Charles A. Smart, a man who knew little of the area and had depended upon the advice of the Conservative Senator G. B. Baker, Fisher's chief local opponent.

[71] Colonial Office 42 (893), "Dundonald's Memorandum on the State of the Militia," n.d.

[72] Minto Papers, Minto to Parkin, September 26, 1904.

When Smart submitted his proposed list of regimental officers, three names on it were relatives of the Conservative Senator and another, Dr. Pickles, was Baker's chief political henchman and mayor of Sweetsburg. Although the proprietor of a rifle range, Pickles was without any particular qualification for a senior military position, a fact even he himself recognized. Moreover, given Dundonald's open flirtation with the Conservative party, Fisher had reason to be suspicious. Consequently Borden, urged on by Fisher, continued to delay approval of Smart's list of officers. Then just before June camp, Borden informed Smart he was leaving Ottawa for a month and entrusting the Department to his old friend and colleague, Sydney Fisher. This gesture needed no interpretation. Aware of the familiar rules of political patronage, Pickles withdrew his name, not wishing to sabotage Smart's plan to get his men into camp before June. When Fisher learned of Pickles' decision he approved the list immediately, erasing Pickles' name.[73] Fisher, however, foolishly failed to inform Dundonald of Pickles' request, and left the General to draw his own conclusion. Nevertheless, Fisher's conduct constituted a flagrant example of political intimidation and one which opponents might construe as a much greater offence, particularly on the eve of a general election—a consideration not lost on Dundonald.

Although Minto deplored Fisher's behaviour, he held no brief for Dundonald. At Borden's request Minto spoke to the General and told him no government "could possibly approve of an officer in his position publicly criticizing the actions of Ministers" and suggested three possible courses: resignation, apology, or bluff. Dundonald, however, offered no satisfactory justification for his action. He simply said that "he hated Laurier & wanted to do him all the harm he could."[74] He also asked Minto not to take too constitutional a line against him. Generally Dundonald seemed amused at the predicament of the government and clearly planned a large campaign, a possibility which caused Minto endless apprehension, since Dundonald was so unpredictable.

Minto insisted on seeing Fisher too. Although he tried to maintain an absolutely impartial position, this interview aroused more viceregal sympathy than anger. Minto had always liked Fisher, and considered him a sound, sensible, able Minister; and during their conversation Fisher, full of gratitude and contrition, almost wept on the Governor-General's shoulder. Convinced by Fisher's act, Minto contented himself with lecturing him on the need for purity in militia affairs, remarking that Fisher's conduct "was more the action of a busy-body than having anything politically corrupt in it."[75]

Minto's position was not easy, for Rideau Hall was divided. Many members of his staff supported Dundonald and urged Minto to take a

[73] Canada, House of Commons Debates, June 10, 1904, 4583; Minto Papers, Borden-Minto interview, June 9, 1904.

[74] Minto Papers, Dundonald-Minto interview, June 10, 11, 1904.

[75] Minto Papers, Minto to Lady Minto, July 2, 1904.

harder line with his ministers.[76] Yet Minto resisted their advice and his relations with his government remained correct, indeed cordial, throughout. The government, however, lost no time determining its reaction to Dundonald's speech. A sub-committee of the Cabinet, consisting of Borden, Sifton, and Fielding, met at once and announced its decision to dismiss Dundonald. When Laurier informed Minto of the Cabinet's decision, Minto put up only a paper resistance. If the government insisted on Dundonald's dismissal, Minto asked, would it not be correct form to request Fisher's resignation too? Laurier would not hear of it, nor would he agree to retain the General and await his inevitable recall. In view of the General's public criticism, Laurier felt that no government "could do so with any sense of dignity" even if it were defeated in the House or at the polls.[77]

Later that same afternoon Borden arrived with the Order-in-Council dismissing Dundonald which Minto signed without protest, even though he scarcely approved the Council Order's exaggerated justification of Fisher's actions. He made that sufficiently clear in a memorandum he composed after he had affixed his signature to the Cabinet's order. This was the only concession he made to his more hot-headed friends and staff. Nevertheless, in writing the memorandum, Minto, mindful of the Hutton affair, was careful not to contest the government's constitutional position. Even so, when Laurier took exception to the document, solemnly asking Minto if he intended to dismiss his advisers, the Governor-General capitulated immediately, and agreed to withdraw the memo lest his actions be considered partisan. He did so, he explained later, because he feared making "myself become a centre around which the political storm would rage."[78] Minto's hasty retreat may have been caused by more than Laurier's weighty words. The night before, seeking guidance from Todd's constitutional works, Minto had read how Dufferin, during the Pacific Scandal, had refused to censure his ministers while he retained their advice, leaving it to Parliament and the people to decide for or against the government. He felt he ought to be guided by Dufferin's example. Whatever the cause, Minto's behaviour offers a stark contrast to his conduct during the Hutton affair. Minto had become a very constitutional viceroy.

From the start, Minto knew that dismissal would not silence the aggrieved General. And as he heard reports of the distraught General pacing his lawn, muttering to himself amidst a menagerie of "endless dogs and cats" which he kept "tied by separate chains to pegs on the grass," Minto wondered what late May madness had seized the General's troubled mind.[79] The General, however, soon made his intentions clear. With his usual dramatic flair he announced his decision to

[76] Minto Papers, Arthur Guise to Lady Minto, June 26, 1904; Douglas M. B. H. Cochrane, Earl of Dundonald, My Army Life (London, 1926), 226-27 and 258.
[77] Colonial Office 42 (896), Minto to Lyttleton, June 14, 1904.
[78] Minto Papers, Laurier-Minto interview, June 17, 1904.
[79] Minto Papers, Minto to Lady Minto, June 5, 1904.

contest a Canadian constituency and shortly published a manifesto condemning the government in no uncertain terms. The manifesto called upon all true citizens to keep both hands on the Union Jack, a direct attempt to trade on the "racial" conflict which had entered the controversy by Laurier's inadvertent use of the word "foreigner" (étranger) to describe Dundonald.

Dundonald's decision to contest a constituency destroyed any vestige of viceregal sympathy for him. Minto had always deplored Dundonald's open flirtation with the opposition, particularly his use of Sam Hughes as "his henchman," but now he had become simply the cat's paw of the Conservative party. Such behaviour was scarcely designed to enhance the reputation of imperial officers. Dundonald's popular reception in English Canada, a section of which pictured him as a self-sacrificing hero, a mixture of Robert Bruce, Napoleon, and Wellington, made Minto wonder if the General's madness had become a national contagion. During Minto's own last interview with the General he found Dundonald "hopeless to deal with—mad—& abusive & a hard job to keep my temper."[80] Nothing, he felt, not even the undoubted political corruption in the country, could justify Dundonald's subsequent language and behaviour. The time had come to put an end to his mischief. Although previously Minto had cautioned the British government not to do anything which might be construed as interference, he now advised recall.

Much to Minto's relief, the War Office ordered Dundonald to return at once. "I daresay," Arnold-Forster recorded in his diary after an interview with Dundonald upon his return, "he is quite right, but if he talked there as he talks here I do not wonder that he got into trouble."[81] The Colonial Office's reaction was less equivocal. The "line taken by the Canadian Ministers in this O-in-C. & their justification of Mr. Fisher's actions" was, according to the Permanent Under Secretary, "perfectly sound & unobjectionable."[82]

Ironically, Dundonald's actions hastened rather than retarded the creation of Borden's Militia Council, the crowning victory of the Minister's reform campaign. Appropriately, the Order-in-Council authorizing the establishment of the Militia Council was the last order Minto signed as Governor-General and, although its creation represented the defeat of his own prescription for military reform, he performed the act graciously and informed Borden he supported the idea and would do everything possible to make it work. Minto proved as good as his word and went to great pains before he left Canada and after, to try to persuade the British government to release Colonel Percy Lake, a former Quartermaster General of the Militia and the man the government felt best suited to give the Council a sound start.

In Minto's opinion, the defeat of his reform strategy had been caused by War Office indifference as much as by Borden's aggressive autonomy campaign. This, together with the flagging interest in

[80] Minto Papers, Diary, 22 July, 1904.

[81] Arnold-Forster Papers, Diary, August 11, 1904.

[82] Colonial Office 42 (897), M. F. Ommanney to H. B. Cox, June 16, 1904.

Chamberlain's tariff crusade, created in him a curious sense of uncertainty which he tried to resolve during his final days in Canada. Although Canadian independence as such held few terrors for him, he still felt that Canada's best chance for real autonomy and independence rested on some imperial solution. Indeed, given British indifference, independence sometimes seemed the only option open, but for the nagging doubts caused by the overwhelming power of Canada's southern neighbour.

Chapter Ten

The Pursuit of Continental Concord

No Canadian Governor-General in the early twentieth century could remain indifferent to the imperatives of Canadian-American relations. Like a long shadow the American presence coloured Minto's perceptions of Canada. As British Americans, Canadians shared a continent with an affluent neighbour ten times more populous than themselves. For well over a century and more this long, poorly defended border had produced strife and controversy. Twice it had brought war, and its continuing perils had enhanced the importance of the imperial factor in Canadian life. Consequently many Canadians had been in no hurry to attain greater autonomy in external relations. For without the presence or promise of British military support Canadian autonomy would have constituted a very shallow claim.

When Minto arrived in Canada in the autumn of 1898 Canadian-American relations seemed in a particularly precarious condition. The accumulated disputes of over a decade remained unsettled, and the United States was riding the crest of one of its waves of imperial ambition. Yet, on the larger world scene, Britain and the United States seemed to be moving toward an uncertain understanding or entente. Geography and history, too, had made Canada an indispensable party to any general settlement. No permanent

Anglo-American rapprochement was possible while serious Canadian-American disputes remained outstanding. Nor could Canadian-American goodwill be assured without a general settlement.

Minto fully appreciated the importance of an Anglo-American understanding, and shortly after he received news of his appointment as Governor-General he met with his old friend Harry White, the first Secretary of the American Embassy in London, to discuss "the possibility of my assisting the better feeling that now exists" between Canada and the United States.[1] Before he left Britain in 1898 he also publicly pledged to do what he could to achieve a rapprochement, the only public policy commitment he made prior to his assumption of office.[2] To Minto these words were more than a rhetorical gesture. In his opinion, friendship based on secure, recognized physical, economic, and cultural boundaries constituted Canada's best form of security. It was also the safest form of imperial defence.

Although Alvin Gluek has seen Minto's views on American society as an impediment to better Canadian-American relations, in fact they consisted of nothing more than the conventional platitudes of patrician society on both sides of the Atlantic.[3] Many American public men, notably Lodge, Hay, Olney, and Roosevelt, shared Minto's disdain for the new plutocracy and the gaudy display of the nouveau riche. They, too, feared the effects of unregulated immigration on American political and social institutions and deplored the growth of violence and anarchy represented by the assassination of McKinley. Still, Minto never doubted that American "thinking people" and the "best society are as anxious as we are" to maintain Anglo-American friendship. And he felt that together they could achieve an equitable settlement of Canadian-American differences though there remained the danger, inherent in any democratic system, that some day "the tail might possibly wag the head."[4] Far from offending American public men (and usually Minto had the good sense to keep his ideas to himself and British correspondents), these same views were frequently pressed upon him during visits to the United States by men like Lloyd Bryce, the former editor of the North American Review, or by Roosevelt.[5]

Minto's criticisms of American democracy, plutocracy, and social habits were motivated more by class than national bias, nor were they limited to American society. He regretted the absence of courtly manners, "chivalry or codes of honour," in Canada as well as the United States and condemned "the self-satisfied luxury" on both

[1] Minto Papers, Diary, July 31, 1898.

[2] The Times, October 29, 1898.

[3] Alvin C. Gluek, Jr., "Pilgrimages to Ottawa: Canadian-American Diplomacy, 1903-13," Canadian Historical Association Papers, 1968, 70; "The Passamaquoddy Bay Treaty, 1910: A Diplomatic Side Show in Canadian-American Relations," Canadian Historical Review (March, 1966), 7.

[4] Minto Papers, Minto to Colonel Arthur Lee, January 3, 1900.

[5] Minto Papers, Minto to Lansdowne, March 8, 1903.

sides of the Atlantic. The abrasive manners of Joseph Chamberlain were no more attractive to Minto than American or Canadian equivalents. "A man either is or is not a gentleman. He is clever but a gentleman he never will be," Henry Labouchere said of Chamberlain.[6] To Minto, it was important to be a gentleman, and when Minto condemned American duchesses "immersed in cigarettes and bridge," both of which he detested, he did so not because they were American but because they were new. In the same manner, he also lamented the desecration of the Canadian prairies by railroads, the "passing of the red man," the frivolous court of Edward VII, the introduction of motor cars, and the changes in women's dress.[7]

Still, Minto was far from blind to the virtues of American society. He admired its vitality, adaptability, and practicality, and he felt that Canada had much to learn from its example. He also welcomed American immigrants to Canada "with money, energy and knowledge of the requirements of life" and preferred them to British settlers.[8] But he was not blind to the faults of American life nor oblivious to their imperial ambitions. Only a fool or a man of great foresight could ignore the signs of the times. When Minto arrived in Canada the expansionists of 1898, McKinley, Hay, Roosevelt, Mahan, and Lodge, were in the ascendancy, and Cuba, the Philippines, Puerto Rico, Hawaii, and Panama soon fell to their ambitions. Minto also lacked that sense of Anglo-Saxon kinship which moved Balfour and Chamberlain and permitted them to see these American colonial conquests as part of a larger racial burden. "It's all very well for people in England to romance about the sentimental love of his Anglo-Saxon Race on either side of the Atlantic," Minto explained to his brother, "but mercifully England had an ocean between him and his love."[9]

Minto's fears were not entirely unfounded, since American imperial ambitions were not confined to the "inferior races." Moreover, the Venezuelan scare and President Cleveland's blustering message to Congress were still fresh in many men's minds, and the growth of American military strength, General Nelson Miles's gratuitous public comments on Canada's indefensibility, rumours of impending Fenian border raids, congressional Boer sympathy during the South African war, American threats to end unilaterally the Clayton-Bulwer Treaty, and violence on the Klondike all served as stern reminders that Anglo-American friendship remained far from secure. And this fact was readily recognized by many pragmatic Anglo-American well-wishers.

Yet, contrary to what Alvin Gluek has written, throughout his Canadian years Minto went out of his way to foster friendship between the two peoples. He was, as he told the British Ambassador in Washington, M. Herbert, "a believer in the value of personal contact from both sides of the Border." His close friendship with Henry

[6] George Curzon Papers, H. Labouchere to George Curzon, April 6, 1898.

[7] Minto Papers, Diary, June 11, July 23, 1902; September 16, 1904; May 3, 1905.

[8] Minto Papers, Minto to Arthur Elliot, September 10, 1903.

[9] Minto Papers, Minto to Arthur Elliot, February 26, 1899.

White, the first secretary at the American embassy in London, gave him easy access to American public men which he and Lady Minto, who made frequent social visits to Washington, readily exploited. In public speeches and in private correspondence with American public men he stressed his belief in "the immense value of our political friendship," and made it clear that he would prefer to "have a U.S. ship alongside one or a U.S. regiment, than that of any other nation in the world."[10] Nor is it true that he failed to seek "occasions that fate bestowed to improve relations."[11] For example, he encouraged E. T. H. Hutton to invite the popular New York Governor, Theodore Roosevelt—whom Minto liked and admired, particularly after his visit to New York in the autumn of 1899—to attend the Queen's birthday honours parade in Ottawa. Minto saw this as a friendly gesture and one which the American Governor appreciated and reciprocated. On another occasion, in Rossland, a British Columbian mining town with a large American population, Minto went out of his way to praise "our cousins" and their contribution to the development of the town.[12] And when Minto visited the Yukon in 1900 he asked Pauncefote, the British Ambassador in Washington, to arrange an official reception for him at Skagway, the "American" port on the Lynn Canal. The reception proved a great success and Minto and the American Commanding Officer in charge of the honour guard remained fast friends long after the tour. In Dawson Minto did everything in his power to soothe American sensitivities. The American Consul, J. C. McCook, "a pompous, ill-conditioned Irishman inclined to stand on his dignity,"[13] had been slighted by the Canadian welcoming committee in charge of Minto's tour. Minto immediately asked to see him, invited him to dinner, and sent him away happy. On another occasion Minto interrupted a tour of southwestern Ontario to accept a hasty invitation to visit Detroit. The American response seemed overwhelming. Approximately 150,000 people lined the streets and the "one continuous roar of applause," he informed the British Ambassador in Washington, made a joke of the Diamond Jubilee. He also consented to a military guard and a civic banquet, which he had forbidden on his Ontario tour because he hated banquets, and recieved the freedom of the city, all of which he interpreted as "a genuine indication of friendship."[14] Judged by their press comment, American opinion also appeared to have approved of Minto's excursions into social diplomacy.

Similarly, Minto's failure to attend three important American ceremonies was motivated by no ill-will or desire to slight American

[10] Minto Papers, Minto to Herbert, May 5, 1903; Diary, November 10, 1898; July 31, 1898. See also Toronto Mail and Empire, December 15, 1898; Minto Papers, Minto to Colonel Arthur Lee, January 3, 1900; Minto to Roosevelt, September 2, 1902.

[11] See Gluek, Jr., "Pilgrimages to Ottawa," 70.

[12] Rossland Miner, September 11, 1900.

[13] Minto Papers, Diary, August 18, 1900.

[14] Minto Papers, Minto to Michael Herbert, May 17, 1903; Minto to Chamberlain, May 17, 1903.

feeling. For each occasion he possessed a convincing explanation. The first, an invitation to attend the opening of a Chicago federal building in 1899, had been billed as a great international event bringing together the heads of state of Canada, the United States, and Mexico. Although it conflicted with his long-planned trip to New York, Minto agreed to cut short his New York plans and go to Chicago if indeed the President of Mexico attended. The publicity, of course, had been overdone, and when Minto learned that the vice-president, Ignatio Mariscal, would represent the Mexican President, he declined the invitation, convinced that Laurier's presence would prove sufficient.

The second, Minto's absence from President McKinley's second inaugural ceremonies, was caused by nothing more sinister than a technicality beyond his control. According to Minto's instructions he could leave Canadian territory only if he obtained Colonial Office approval and appointed a Deputy. By law the General Officer Commanding at Halifax served as his Deputy and received £30 a day from the Governor-General's own salary. "They make it very difficult for me to get away," Minto complained to the British Ambassador in Washington, "I may go to the North Pole but not to the U.S. except under more difficult conditions."[15] Nevertheless Minto had every intention of attending the McKinley inaugural, though he possessed some initial qualms about the propriety of his presence at a public ceremony only one month after Queen Victoria's death. However, as soon as he received Colonial Office permission, he prepared to leave. He informed Laurier that he had written to the General Officer at Halifax and that the General had agreed to act as Administrator in his absence. But after close consultation with his Cabinet, Laurier refused to accept the Halifax General, since his rank and status had recently been reduced.[16] Laurier then suggested that Minto appoint the Chief Justice of the Supreme Court of Canada instead. The Colonial Office agreed that the Chief Justice would be a more appropriate and convenient officer than the Halifax General and wrote the King requesting his approval of the proposed change. Several months later the King approved the change, but his approval came too late to permit Minto to attend the inaugural.

McKinley's assassination in September 1901 provided another occasion to visit Washington. Unfortunately the assassination occurred only a few days before the Duke of Cornwall and York was due to arrive at Quebec. This posed a number of practical problems, particularly given Minto's inordinately large role in the detailed preparations. Reluctantly, Minto consented to go, but when a rearrangement of the funeral schedule advanced the official ceremonies one day, Minto could not again alter his plans and he wrote Roosevelt at once regretting his absence. To atone for his failure to go to Washington, Minto persuaded Laurier to proclaim a national day of mourning. The American Embassy in London interpreted this as a

[15] Minto Papers, Minto to Michael Herbert, October 22, 1902.
[16] Colonial Office 42 (881), Minto to Chamberlain, February 20, 1901.

very friendly gesture and thanked Minto personally for his efforts.[17] No evidence seems to exist suggesting private or public pique at Minto's absence at this or other occasions. Indeed, a year later the rumour that Minto would replace Pauncefote as British Ambassador in Washington elicited a flattering chorus of American press approval, although Minto himself did not relish the prospect.[18] He already had his sights set on India.

Nor does a closer examination of Minto's record in the more practical realm of formal diplomacy suggest a man anxious to impede Canadian-American settlements. His interventions in the three great Canadian-American diplomatic events of his career, the International Joint High Commission meetings, the Alaska boundary settlement, and the pelagic sealing negotiations reveal an image which is quite the contrary. In the first instance, there was little Minto could do, since the International Joint High Commission, convened to settle the whole slate of Canadian-American differences, had terminated its Quebec meetings and was about to move to Washington when Minto arrived in Canada. Yet, despite his ignorance of the diplomatic particulars, Minto wrote at once to Pauncefote, the British Ambassador, expressing his desire to see "as great a flourish of trumpets as possible over a successful issue even to one of the minor subjects of discussion," a suggestion which ran counter to the Canadian strategy.[19] Given Minto's ignorance of the complexity of the issues at this point it was difficult to go beyond platitudes and generalities. But at Christmas, Laurier returned to Ottawa accompanied by Lord Herschell, the able leader of the British delegation, who had been invited to Rideau Hall for the recess. Both gave Minto an opportunity to learn first hand the problems facing the Commission, particularly the Canadian refusal to settle a single item unless they received a favourable agreement on the Alaska boundary or a liberal reciprocal trade treaty. Yet, despite his sympathy for the Canadian position, Minto remained unconvinced of the wisdom of Laurier's strategy, and wrote him in Washington just before negotiations ended, lamenting "that owing to public attention being so much fixed on reciprocity other issues which may be obtained may be undervalued by the public of Canada."[20] He did not press the point, since he realized that the Americans were difficult negotiators and that the Canadian public would never tolerate the surrender of Canadian rights, real or perceived, without adequate compensation. He also recognized that the Canadians still possessed some trump cards, particularly the British government's promised refusal to abrogate the Clayton-Bulwer Treaty of 1850 which forbade unilateral construction of an inter-oceanic canal in

[17] Governor General's Numbered Files, Public Archives of Canada, Henry White to Lansdowne, October 24, 1901.

[18] New York Evening Journal, May 31, 1902; New York Mail and Express, May 31, 1902.

[19] Minto Papers, Minto to Julian Pauncefote, November 23, 1898; Minto to Lord Herschell, November 23, 1898.

[20] Minto Papers, Minto to Laurier, February 10, 1899.

Central America, until the United States became more reasonable on the Alaska dispute. He felt that the Americans would respect a strong position and urged the British government to hold firm against American pressure, confident that the February break in negotiations constituted a recess or a cooling period rather than a termination.

A glance at the causes of the Commission's failure, causes which transcend the opinions or actions of a colonial governor, suggest the real factors which impeded better Canadian-American relations during Minto's administration. First, despite frequent protests of goodwill, the American administration could not or would not control its delegation, particularly John W. Foster, the "crusty," "cranky" old veteran pelagic sealing diplomat,[21] who never recovered from his defeat in Paris in 1893 at the hands of the Canadians and who drove the Chairman of the American delegation to despair.[22] Nor were the American delegates themselves free agents but captives of public interests and pressures hostile to an equitable settlement. For example, when news of the American offer to lease Canadians a port on the Lynn Canal together with a land corridor linking it to Canadian territory became public, the American West-Coast press reaction forced the delegation to withdraw the offer. Similar forces prevented a more reasonable Canadian position. Although the Canadian delegates—Laurier, Cartwright, Davies, and John Charlton— represented the most friendly, pro-American elements in the Liberal party, public pressures seemed bent on preventing a serious settlement. Even "old Commercial Union Liberals were against concessions to Washington," a feeling which became so persistent that a Cabinet delegation consisting of Blair, Mills, Sifton, Fielding, and Tarte, all the strongest Ministers, went to Washington to persuade Laurier to terminate negotiations at once and come home.[23] Laurier reluctantly agreed and came home, a prisoner of a growing nationalist movement, and declared that he would make no more pilgrimages to Washington.

Nothing was more symbolic of Canada's new prosperity and self-confidence than the northern gold fields, and even after the disputed Alaska boundary area had lost its commercial value, any attempt to compromise even a faulty claim met stiff resistance. Laurier had used the emotive issue to break off negotiations and had refused to settle any issue until the Americans agreed on an Alaskan boundary. "If it were a private matter," Minto explained to Colonel Gerald Kitson, the British military attaché in Washington, "two reasonable individuals would settle it in 5 minutes."[24] Yet the dispute was neither private nor rational, and while it remained unsolved it blocked the road to a more general settlement.

[21] Saywell, ed., The Canadian Journal of Lady Aberdeen, 475.

[22] Salisbury Papers, Christ Church Library, Oxford, Julian Pauncefote to Salisbury, December 23, 1898; Foreign Office 5/2421, Herschell to Salisbury, October 11, 1898.

[23] Laurier Papers, J. S. Willison to Laurier, December 27, 1898.

[24] Minto Papers, Minto to Kitson, May 17, 1902.

Although British and American diplomats, anxious to secure a more permanent Anglo-American understanding, made several unsuccessful attempts at settlement, they accomplished little or nothing until the late spring of 1902. Meanwhile, Canada's bargaining position grew increasingly weaker. Initially, Canada's strategy of breaking off talks until the Americans became more reasonable on Alaska seemed vindicated. Soon after the International Joint High Commission's discussions terminated in February 1899, John Hay, the American Secretary of State, informed the British chargé d'affaires in Washington that President McKinley "was so anxious for a settlement" that he "would be prepared to agree to arbitration for the whole frontier, even at the risk of possible objection from Congress."[25] But when the Senate learned of Hay's discussions it protested and McKinley displayed none of the courage Hay had predicted. Later that year, however, British involvement with war in South Africa gave the advantage to the United States. Just before war began the Colonial Office asked the Canadian government to send a Cabinet minister to London to present the Canadian case to the British government. Once in London, Louis Davies, the Canadian Cabinet spokesman, received a stern lecture from John Anderson on the untenable nature of the Canadian case and the importance of "coming to some settlement before further bad blood had been excited." He impressed upon Davies that Canada must assume responsibility if "any trouble ensues."[26] He also informed the Canadian Minister that the British government could no longer postpone abrogation of the Clayton-Bulwer Treaty, despite its earlier promise, "even if concessions are not granted on Alaska."[27]

The sincerity of the British warning soon became painfully apparent. Just after the South African war began, Chamberlain wrote Minto appealing to the Canadian government to consent to a temporary boundary line since "in view of present circumstances it is very imp. to ensure friendly relationship between the two countries."[28] Laurier gave in at once, but he soon discovered that this represented only the first instalment in a larger settlement. Three months later, during the darkest days of the war, the British government, faced with American threats to abrogate unilaterally the Clayton-Bulwer Treaty, agreed to sign an agreement, the Hay-Pauncefote convention, which freed the Americans from the Clayton-Bulwer Treaty's restriction. Before the British signed the convention, Chamberlain sought the Canadian government's consent to relieve the British government of their previous promise, which the Canadians could scarcely have withheld under the circumstances. The American Senate's rejection of the new convention in December 1900 granted Canada only a temporary reprieve. Canada, however, had lost its strongest card, and the Americans, having gained their point, were content, in the words of Presi-

[25] Colonial Office 42 (871), Reginald Towers to Salisbury, May 4, 1899.

[26] Colonial Office 42 (874), John Anderson to Chamberlain, October 4, 1899.

[27] Colonial Office 42 (868), Minute, John Anderson, June 15, 1898.

[28] Colonial Office 42 (874), Chamberlain to Minto, October ?, 1899.

dent Roosevelt, to let "sleeping dogs lie," that is until the spring of 1902.[29]

In the spring of 1902 it was Minto who took the initiative on the Canadian front to press for a final settlement. Several things explain his desire for an immediate settlement. Ever since his visit there in the summer of 1900, Minto feared violence in the Yukon, a fear fed by rumours which gained wide credence in the autumn of 1901 of an attempted American coup d'état. Although Minto's friend, the American Commanding Officer at Skagway, assured him that there existed no cause for apprehension, Minto felt the rumours contained some foundation. He was all too conscious that it would take little to provoke an unpleasant incident there. Minto also knew that John Anderson, during the Duke of Cornwall and York's visit, had almost persuaded Laurier to abandon Canada's claims on the northern Lynn Canal. According to Anderson, Canada possessed a much stronger case along the southern border, near the Portland Canal. Anderson's argument interested Laurier immensely, not simply because the commercial value of the Yukon trade had declined, but because Canadian interest had shifted from the Lynn to the Portland Canal, the proposed terminus of two trans-continental railways. Finally, in May 1902 Minto's Washington informant, Colonel Kitson, warned him that an ugly mood was growing in the American capital which spelled trouble.[30] Roosevelt had already sent more troops to the disputed area and in a mid-term election year the President seemed to mean business. It was not unlikely that he would attempt to appease a strong anti-British sentiment with a show of strength on the Alaskan boundary. Minto knew the new President and knew that he was a stronger, tougher, and more difficult man than his predecessor, a man who would take "some holding to say the least of it."[31]

Conscious of Laurier's weakening position, Minto decided to approach the Prime Minister directly. During the interview he tried to impress Laurier with the seriousness of the matter, explaining that should some local disturbance arise "it might lead to grave consequences."[32] Laurier needed no persuasion and, given the Cabinet's harder line, probably appreciated the viceregal prodding. He agreed with Minto that something must be done and promised to discuss the subject with the American Ambassador to London, Joseph Choate, during his proposed visit to London to attend the Coronation of Edward VII in June 1902. Meanwhile, Minto wrote to Lansdowne, the Foreign Secretary, describing the seriousness of the outstanding boundary dispute.[33]

Laurier's London Conference constituted an important turning point in the tortuous Alaskan negotiations. First, Minto arranged an

[29] Allan Nevins, Henry White: Thirty Years of American Diplomacy (New York, 1930), 192.

[30] Minto Papers, Kitson to Minto, May 17, 1902.

[31] Minto Papers, Diary, August 15, 1902.

[32] Minto Papers, Minto to Laurier, May 17, 1902.

[33] Minto Papers, Minto to Lansdowne, June 4, 1902.

interview at the Foreign Office with Lansdowne, Laurier, and Mulock, at which Laurier appeared both concerned and conciliatory. During the discussion he agreed to meet Choate, White, and Whitelaw Reid, if a conference could be arranged. While Choate himself hesitated to meet Laurier, given Roosevelt's recent instructions to "let sleeping dogs lie," Minto arranged an informal meeting between Laurier and Henry White which paved the way for a meeting with the Ambassador. At this meeting Laurier demonstrated his desire to make several important concessions which the Colonial Office described as "an abject surrender to the United States."[34] In the past, Canada had insisted that the boundary be drawn by a court of arbitration charged with adjudicating the entire area in dispute, a court consisting of an unequal number of jurists. This was to assure finality. On the other hand, the Americans demanded a court of arbitration composed of an equal number of jurists. They also insisted on the exclusion of Dyea and Skagway, the two "American" ports on the Lynn Canal, from the court's consideration. Despite his Cabinet's parting warning to hold firmly to the Canadian position, Laurier agreed to accept the proposed American composition of the court and to return Dyea and Skagway to American control, for a monetary consideration, should the tribunal find they lay within Canadian territory. Later that year, Laurier, supported by Minto, even agreed to exclude Dyea and Skagway from the proposed court's jurisdiction.[35] Essentially it was Laurier's London concessions which paved the way to the subsequent settlement, although his difficulties were far from finished.

The Canadian Cabinet was still unconvinced of the wisdom of Laurier's concessions, and in January Laurier had great difficulty persuading his Cabinet to accept the terms of the Herbert-Hay Treaty concluded the previous month, embodying the London concessions. Minto himself worked on some ministers and tried to persuade them of the necessity of Laurier's earlier concessions. But the Cabinet, particularly Sifton, Fielding, Davies, and Fitzpatrick, put up a stiff opposition, stubbornly insisting on a return to the original Canadian position.[36] Finally the Cabinet capitulated, but only on the condition that Laurier try once more to alter the composition of the proposed tribunal. Throughout the tense Cabinet controversy Minto attempted to strengthen Laurier's resolve and he shared his relief with the final outcome.[37] "For the sake of good feeling between the two countries," Minto wrote Herbert, the British Ambassador in Washington, "we ought not to grudge even getting the worst of it—if it is at all within reason." But agreement was far from secure.[38]

The premature public announcement of the American composition of the proposed tribunal created a storm of protest which threatened to sabotage the entire treaty. To secure Senate approval,

[34] Colonial Office 42 (890), Minute, John Anderson, September 1, 1902.
[35] Minto Papers, Minto to Michael Herbert, October 21, 1902.
[36] Minto Papers, Minto to Lansdowne, January 23, 1903.
[37] Minto Papers, Diary, January 24, 1903.
[38] Minto Papers, Minto to Michael Herbert, January 3, 1903.

Roosevelt named three partial politicians, Henry Cabot Lodge, Elihu Root, and George Turner, all of whom had previously pronounced against the Canadian case. This was a flagrant violation of the treaty's terms calling for "impartial jurists of repute."

At first Minto refused to believe the press reports announcing Roosevelt's appointments. Herbert had assured both him and Laurier that the American president would name Supreme Court judges.[39] Even with all the best will in the world, Laurier could not accept them without raising a ferocious storm in Parliament, not to mention his Cabinet. Moreover, Minto thought that it would be wrong to acquiesce in the nominations. If, he explained to Laurier, "we once show ourselves willing to accept this manner of doing business with the United States we shall establish a dangerous precedent in regard to future negotiations."[40] There were obviously limits to the concessions and humiliations Canada could accept to secure better Canadian-American relations, and something had to be done.

After careful consideration Laurier and Minto decided to protest the American appointments to the Colonial Office on the grounds that they were "a violation of an important article of the treaty."[41] The Colonial Office agreed and wondered if Roosevelt had deliberately tried to sabotage the Herbert-Hay Treaty. Given the circumstances they asked the Foreign Office if it were wise to "proceed with the rtfn of the Treaty."[42]

Determined to force a settlement, the Foreign Office refused to consider the suggestion. Under Lansdowne's direction, the Foreign Office, with Balfour's blessing, had worked assiduously to secure American friendship. They had pushed for the Herbert-Hay treaty during Chamberlain's absence in South Africa, November 1902 to March 1903, while the Colonial Office, Canada's strongest defender, lacked a voice in the British Cabinet, and they refused to countenance any delay or controversy, particularly at this stage. The Foreign Office, therefore, rejected Canada's protest and warned the Canadian government against "sowing the seeds of lasting ill-will between the two countries." Its only solution was the suggestion that Canada appoint delegates "appropriate to the altered circumstances."[43] However, Minto persuaded Laurier to reject this proposal, arguing in his best schoolboy style that Canada would gain much "in the eyes of the world . . . by adhering to our bargain."[44] In this way Minto felt that Canada might shame the Americans into more decent diplomatic behaviour.

Meanwhile, Minto and Laurier tried their hand at direct, though informal, negotiations with Washington. Laurier's "secret agent" in

[39] Colonial Office 42 (892), Ommanney to Minto, January 12, 1903.

[40] Minto Papers, Minto to Laurier, February 23, 1903.

[41] Colonial Office 42 (892), Minto to Onslow, February 20, 1903.

[42] Colonial Office 42 (892), Minute, John Anderson, March 21, 1903.

[43] Colonial Office 42 (894), F. H. Villiers to Colonial Office, February 25, 1903; Onslow to Minto, February 26, 1903.

[44] Minto Papers, Minto to Michael Herbert, February 27, 1903.

Washington, Edward Farrer, had informed him that Lodge, conscious of his own partiality, might be induced to withdraw. Minto wrote at once to Herbert, asking him to persuade Hay to reconsider the appointment of Lodge and Turner. Minto also informed the Colonial Office of his negotiations and confidently expected the British to stay ratification until it heard from the Canadian government.

Afraid Canadian meddling might sabotage the treaty, the Foreign Office, however, decided to ratify the treaty immediately. Minto was furious and wrote at once to the Colonial Office. He reminded it of Herbert's repeated assurance which had induced the Canadian Cabinet to accept the treaty. Roosevelt's violation of the treaty's stipulation, he argued, had now freed Canada from all previous obligation to accept it. The Foreign Office's ratification while negotiations were proceeding simply added insult to injury.[45]

The Colonial Office once again endorsed Minto's protest entirely. The Foreign Office had disregarded its advice and the Colonial Office saw no reason to defend the blunder. John Anderson wrote, "The F.O. should have delayed ratification.... The thing has been badly conducted all through.... The result will be most deplorable, and it will cause more mischief in Canada than anything that has happened for years. It is no use attempting any further explanation or defence and the sooner we get to business the better."[46]

The Canadian press reacted as Anderson had predicted. *Saturday Night* condemned British diplomacy. Another journal described the American side of the tribunal as "made up like a backwoods jury in a murder case."[47] Several other papers accurately predicted the outcome: "The British member of the commission will give Canada away," an attitude Minto deplored but a result he, too, feared.[48]

The Canadian government, fearing the worst and wishing to clear itself of the whole affair, requested the Colonial Office's permission to publish all correspondence leading up to ratification, including Herbert's assurance that the American members would be impartial jurists of repute. Herbert himself offered no objection. Still the Colonial Office was embarrassed by the request. "If published," A. B. Keith, a Colonial Office clerk noted, "they will show that Canada was fooled into accepting the Treaty."[49] Quite understandably, the Foreign Office refused to sanction publication. However, Chamberlain was now back in Britain and in full command. He sternly lectured Henry White on Roosevelt's crude diplomatic behaviour.[50] He also demanded an explanation of the Foreign Office's actions and promised that if after the proposed tribunal's deliberations the Canadian

[45] Minto Papers, Minto to Chamberlain, March 2, 1903; Colonial Office 42 (892), Minto to Chamberlain, March 7, 1903.

[46] Colonial Office 42 (892), Minute, John Anderson, March 7, 1903.

[47] Toronto News, March 2, 1903.

[48] Montreal Star, January 27, 1903; Toronto Globe, January 28, 1903.

[49] Colonial Office 42 (892), Minute, A. B. Keith, March 19, 1903.

[50] Nevins, Henry White, 195.

government wished to publish the correspondence, "H. M. G. will raise no objections."[51]

Despite American duplicity and Herbert's blundering, Minto managed to retain confidence in the tribunal's outcome. The Canadian members, Louis Jetté and Allan Aylesworth, were prominent members of the Canadian Bar and Clifford Sifton, the chief Canadian legal agent, was "the ablest man" in the Canadian Cabinet. The only English representative, Lord Alverstone, England's Lord Chief Justice, inspired a similar confidence. In Minto's mind, the Canadian case itself, though weak on several points, seemed strong on others, particularly on the important southern border. These were points which any court must recognize.

But the final decision was not the result of adjudication but diplomacy, shirt-sleeve diplomacy. Months before the tribunal met, Roosevelt began his diplomatic offensive by feeding Herbert with scare stories about Yankee Jingoes forcing him to mark out a frontier should the tribunal fail. Lodge, who arrived in London a month before the meetings, canvassed Alverston, Balfour, and Chamberlain and extracted a promise from them "to work on the Canadians."[52] The American Embassy received similar instructions to impress upon Balfour, Chamberlain, and Lansdowne the possible price of failure. Balfour wrote immediately to Alverstone and suggested the need for conciliation. Lansdowne, too, spoke to the Chief Justice and made no secret of his "great desire for a settlement."[53] Alverstone agreed and left Lansdowne with no doubt of his resolve not to let the tribunal adjourn without effecting a final settlement. Both the British and American governments had conveniently ignored the judicial nature of the tribunal.

Alverstone himself made no secret of the fact that the final decision constituted a negotiated compromise, not a judicial decision, a confession confirmed by a brief glance at the results.[54] Alverstone first agreed with the Americans that the boundary line ought to run around the inlets of the coast rather than cut across them, a perfectly justifiable interpretation given the ambiguous wording of the original treaty. Moreover, his persistence forced the Americans to concede a compromise eastern boundary line giving Canada more territory than it might otherwise have received. The Canadians took no particular exception to this diplomatic feat! His final decision, however, to draw the southern boundary line between four islands, created great surprise and a storm of Canadian criticism, since both sides had argued previously that the channel ran either north or south of the four islands, not between them. Moreover, only a few days before this

[51] Colonial Office 42 (892), Chamberlain to Lansdowne, March 27, 1903; Colonial Office 42 (892), Chamberlain to Minto, April 2, 1903.

[52] John A. Garraty, Henry Cabot Lodge (New York, 1953), 247.

[53] Balfour Papers, Lansdowne to Balfour, August 8, 1903.

[54] Balfour Papers, Alverstone to Balfour, October 20, 1903; Lansdowne to Balfour, October 20, 1903.

surprise decision Alverstone had stated categorically that he preferred the Canadian argument that the channel ran north.

The Canadian members of the tribunal, who felt betrayed by
Alverstone, refused to sign the final award. Their chief counsel,
Clifford Sifton, wrote a strong letter to The Times, describing Alverstone's actions as "a travesty of justice." Canadian newspaper
opinion at home reacted in a predictable manner.

At first Minto tried to stem the tide of criticism, since the Canadian accusation impugned the honour and reputation of England's
Chief Justice. He also regretted that Canada felt England had sacrificed Canadian interests for American friendship. He worried lest
the tribunal's decision might lead, as Laurier threatened, to demands
for greater Canadian diplomatic autonomy. Therefore, he decided to
defend the imperial government and his friend Alverstone from any
accusations.

As soon as the Canadian delegates returned from London, Minto
sought an interview with them and with Laurier and Cartwright. He
tried to persuade them of the award's justice, taking a very practical
line. He reminded them that Canada had received a better settlement
than it might have had Canada been independent. He pointed to
Canada's vulnerable military position in North America and stressed
its dependence upon British protection. Although Minto himself had
emphasized previously the strategic importance of the four islands in
the Portland Canal, he now argued that they were strategically worthless.[55]

Much to Minto's surprise, the Canadians admitted the validity of
many of his arguments. Then Sir Richard Cartwright informed Minto
that Canadians did not object to the award so much as the manner in
which it had been determined, a point the press stressed continu-
ally.[56] Others backed Cartwright's contention and attempted to demonstrate the injudicious nature of Alverstone's decision. Finally,
Minto conceded that there must have been some serious misunderstanding, which he resolved to clear up.

Determined that England's Chief Justice should receive a fair
hearing, he suggested to the Colonial Office that Alverstone ought to
make a public defence of his actions to counter the disagreeable
Canadian press criticism. But the Colonial Office refused to hear of the
proposition, since it considered the whole matter

> most unfortunate but it is distinctly a case in which the least said
> the soonest ended. The C. J. mistook the men he was dealing with
> and the correspondence which I understand he has been carrying
> on with Aylesworth about that gentleman's public utterances is
> not from what I have gathered, likely to improve his position if it
> should ever see the light.[57]

[55] Colonial Office 42 (893), Memorandum of Laurier-Minto interview, December 3,
1903.

[56] Colonial Office 42 (893), Memorandum of Cartwright-Minto interview,
November 13, 1903.

[57] Colonial Office 42 (893), Minute, John Anderson, December 2, 1903.

The more Alverstone explained, the more he convinced people that his decision had been a diplomatic rather than a judicial one. Still Minto remained unsatisfied. He was convinced Alverstone must possess a better defence than he had hitherto revealed. In this spirit he decided to write the Chief Justice a private, friendly letter and solicit a reply which he could show confidentially to people, which might help to still the uproar. Alverstone readily agreed and penned Minto a fulsome report, but one which confirmed rather than contradicted Minto's worst fears. In reply, Minto made no secret of his indignation. "Your Lordship's arguments," Minto wrote, "fail to remove the suggestion against which you contend, and I still persist in believing that, on these points, the decision rendered cannot be supported on judicial grounds." Minto did not mince his words. "I would not speak my whole mind," he continued, "if I did not state to Your Lordship my conviction that, in this part of Your Lordship's decision [the islands in the Portland Canal] there is an injustice to Canada which nothing in the case can justify and no language can explain."[58]

The Alaska settlement, which Minto had worked so hard to secure, appeared to undermine his imperial argument that Canada's survival on the North American continent depended upon British military, diplomatic, and economic assistance. It seemed to strengthen the cause of the anti-imperialists and confirm their worst predictions about imperial perfidy. Nor, in Minto's eyes, could it have happened at a worse time, just as Chamberlain commenced his imperial preferential campaign. Their confidence in British diplomacy eroded, Canadians might now turn more toward the United States. His fear was confirmed by a rash of press articles on the favourable prospects of a reciprocal trade agreement and a speech by Cartwright endorsing closer trade ties with the United States as a constructive step toward the "reunion" of the Anglo-Saxon race. To Minto this sentiment was, in Macdonald's words, "veiled treason."

Still, even the Alaskan award failed to shake Minto's conviction that a reasonable settlement of Canadian-American differences constituted Canada's safest security against American intrusion. And soon after the Alaskan decision, and despite Laurier's opposition, or, more precisely, his Cabinet's opposition, Minto backed British-American efforts to solve the longstanding Pacific fur-sealing dispute. At first, neither the Americans nor the Canadians displayed any sign of altering their traditional arguments. The Americans continued to claim that Canadian slaughter of seals on the high seas, rather than their slaughter on the islands which they owned, threatened to exterminate the herd. On the other hand, the Canadians denied the charge and refused to prohibit deep sea sealing unless their fishermen received compensation for the loss of a lucrative livelihood. Stung by his Alaskan experience, Laurier proved most stubborn. On the other hand Minto, while recognizing Canada's claim for compensation, pressed Laurier to come to an early and reasonable settlement, even a

---

[58] Colonial Office 42 (893), Minto to Alverstone, December 22, 1903.

temporary settlement, to save the herd which he, like the Americans, believed to be endangered.[59] Minto did not remain in Canada long enough to see a settlement. But in the wake of the bitter Alaskan award, on this subject Minto provided a stronger voice for conciliation and concord than his advisors.

Minto's Canadian administration has sometimes been considered a poor period of Canadian-American relations, but given the importance of the issues at stake its accomplishments ought not to be underrated. It was during these years that an Anglo-American rapprochement was reached, of which the Alaska boundary settlement was the first instalment.[60] Without this larger understanding the important subsequent settlements would not only have been more difficult but much less significant. There is nothing to suggest that further diplomatic achievements would have been retarded by Minto's retention of the Governor-Generalship. Nor is there any reason to believe that the settlement of these disputes would have been accomplished more rapidly had another person than Minto held the viceregal office between the years 1898 and 1904. For settlement depended upon people and circumstances beyond the control of a colonial Governor. Yet in the area open to him, Minto worked consciously to clean the slate which he had inherited. Perhaps in no other area did he display more clearly his reputed qualities of sound common sense than in dealing with Canadian-American relations.

[59] Minto Papers, Laurier-Minto interview, January 9, 1904; Minto to Durand, May 11, 12, and July 13, 1904.

[60] For example, the International Waterways Commission was set up in 1903 before Minto left Canada. See Peter Neary, "Grey, Bryce, and the Settlement of Canadian-American Differences, 1905-1911," *Canadian Historical Review* (December, 1968).

Chapter Eleven

The Shadow of Monarchy

Canada had come to mean something very special for Minto, something more than a vast physical territory or a stepping-stone to greater glory. He seemed to see it as a commitment to a new way of life or an idealized emerging "New Britain," imbued with American vitality but tempered by British social and political institutions. Twice Canada had given Minto a chance to fulfill his potential; such challenges had not been possible in the Old Country. And as he travelled the breadth of the new land he saw a similar transformation repeated hundreds of times over, particularly in the Canadian West. There he found what he called "the vanguard of the best of our people, refined, full of ideas, full of energy, splendid people." In his mind they offered a striking contrast to those "stupid duchesses one might be honored to meet in the old country" where faddism, frivolity, self-satisfied luxury, and decadence suggested a society in decline.[1] Often he had even toyed with the idea of remaining in Canada after the expiry of his term of office, and on the eve of his departure he had still not abandoned the idea of settling in Canada, building a house at the

[1] Minto Papers, Diary, September 15, 1904.

foothills of the Rockies in sight of the Bow River, and making this his home.[2]

By 1904 Minto had obviously caught the contagion of Canada's "last best west." Despite his reflex disdain for progress, settlement, and the railway's desecration of the prairie and its primitive society, Minto could not disguise his pride in the sheer growth and physical expansion of the country. Tiny settlements he remembered from his 1885 days had by 1904 grown into towns, and towns into cities. It seemed to him like "a fairy tale." The growth of a city like Winnipeg provided him with an excellent example of the West's spectacular development. He remembered it in 1880 as a town with a population of some 25,000 and a main street which was still a quagmire, but by 1904 it boasted a population of 95,000 with "high buildings, banks and warehouses rivalling London and New York."[3] Like so many of his Canadian contemporaries he could see no end to Canadian prosperity and confidently predicted the profitable exploitation of at least four transcontinental railroads. Still he wondered what this would mean to Canada? Certainly western expansion would alter irretrievably the nature of Canada, and might even change the power structure of the Empire itself. But a nation's development depended upon more than physical expansion and vitality; it required values, direction, and leadership.

Already this prosperity which held such promise aroused in Minto certain forebodings. According to Minto, the South African war had sparked a curious sense of Canadian confidence and self-congratulation which the country's subsequent material prosperity seemed to feed and justify.[4] Although Minto shared this pride and confidence, he feared that Canadian success in the arts of war and peace had created a restless, unpredictable self-assurance and an impatience with discipline, restraint, and authority, and this unsettled him. Everywhere commercialism appeared rampant and a deadening materialism left time for money-making but little else. And unfortunately, for Minto, Canada lacked a leisured class which might have provided social leadership, standards, and direction. Some people said that all this would come with time; Canada was still a raw country with a society in the making. Nevertheless there were distress signals which Minto felt could not be dismissed lightly. English Canada seemed particularly deficient and in need of firmer cultural moorings. It possessed no sense of time, tradition, and continuity, or deference to the claims consecrated by history. Where, he wondered, would it all end? Already Canada seemed close to a parting of the ways. If positive action were not taken now, tomorrow might be too late. Canada would lose its distinctive character and fail to fulfill its true potential. With a sense of purpose and urgency Minto determined to do what he could to reverse the unfavourable tide.

[2] Minto Papers, Diary, September 21, 1900; Minto to Lady Minto, September 9, 1904.

[3] Minto Papers, Diary, September 23, 1904.

[4] Minto Papers, Diary, July 31, 1900.

There were several things he decided to do. The monarchy was Canada's oldest and perhaps most distinctive political institution. While politically non-partisan, it remained a central institution uniting region, creed, and culture, and at no time did the monarchy command higher Canadian esteem than in the closing years of Queen Victoria's reign, particularly after her spectacular Diamond Jubilee. As the man who moved as the shadow of monarchy, Minto decided to use his position and the respect and influence it commanded to create the social leadership and direction which Canada required.

Minto possessed a broad view of his viceregal powers, to say the least. A proponent of strong monarchy, he believed that the monarch ought to be a sort of patriot king, a man who never hesitated to question the inordinate power of the Commons and who protected the people, particularly minorities, from the arbitrary decrees of their elected rulers. Minto saw himself as much more than a respectable national social convenor. He regarded himself as a type of self-appointed national ombudsman and social *animateur* who could reach beyond the limited range of the partisan politician. Through his good offices individuals and groups, alienated and ostracized by the capricious hand of partisan authority, might be restored to their proper place in society.

His 1900 Yukon tour provides one good example of Minto's concept of his viceregal responsibilities. This tour, more than any other action, earned him the enmity of Laurier's powerful Minister of the Interior, Clifford Sifton, "the villain," as Sifton was privately called at Rideau Hall.[5] As soon as Minto announced his decision to visit the Yukon goldfields, the Dawson Citizen Committee began preparing a petition, exposing territorial mismanagement and corruption and calling for specific political and administrative reforms. Despite Sifton's agent's best efforts to dissuade him, Minto received the controversial petition and insisted that it be read publicly. He himself cross-examined the Committee's spokesman and replied to the petition. In his reply he agreed with particular points and volunteered to intercede with the government on the Committee's behalf. Almost immediately people hailed Minto as a liberator, "the possessor of a magician's wand before whom all grievances were to vanish."[6] Sifton's announcement of extensive political and administrative reforms the day of Minto's arrival did nothing to diminish his reputation. It created the illusion that Minto had accomplished in one stroke what countless pleas and petitions had failed to achieve. Had the Governor-General decided to resign, the Klondike Nugget wrote, he would have had no difficulty winning a Commons seat.[7]

Minto enjoyed his popularity immensely and determined to justify the northern community's faith as soon as he returned to Ottawa. Meanwhile, he ordered his secretary, A. F. Sladen, to compile a report on Yukon affairs gleaned from the oral and written testimony of a host

[5] Minto Papers, Louise Grey to Lady Minto, May 21, 1903.

[6] Minto Papers, Minto to Laurier, September 5, 1900.

[7] Klondike Nugget, August 18, 1900.

of willing witnesses. Minto's political views, had they been publicized, would scarcely have endeared him to a true democrat, since he felt that the Yukon had no need of a municipal government or a legislative council owing to the restless population. What he would have preferred was "a strong administrator," not more representation.[8]

The unbridled, enervating, political corruption so evident in the north profoundly shocked the Governor-General. The Yukon Commissioner, William Ogilvie, "an honest but weak" administrator, painted a bleak picture of Sifton's political wrongdoings, things which "would utterly condemn the Minister."[9] According to Ogilvie, Sifton traded liquor licences openly to party friends. He had heard that one licence sold in Toronto to political partisans brought $20,000 in the Yukon. The Minister also surrounded himself with men of dubious reputation. His chief liquor licence purveyor, J. D. McGregor, for example, had been rejected by the Yukon Council because he had served a jail sentence for horse stealing. W. H. P. Clement, Sifton's legal adviser to the Yukon Council, had been placed under arrest for corruption. Moreover, the charge continued, Sifton did all in his power to impede prosecution. He had also done everything possible to get the vigilant North West Mounted Police commissioner, S. B. Steele, sent to South Africa during the war.[10] Minto's opinion of the Minister was unequivocal. Sifton, Minto wrote his brother, "is a thorough rascal rolling in the plunder of the Yukon," a man who had risen from a small surveyor "to the position of a rich man with a house on the St. Lawrence & one of the finest steam yachts on the Lakes."[11] The Governor-General's meddling in Sifton's lucrative Yukon kingdom created considerable Cabinet embarrassment and unease, but Minto was neither repentant nor ready to retreat.

The northern miners might have grievances, but no group suffered more from prejudice, neglect, and maladministration than the Canadian Indian under Sifton's administrative jurisdiction, and Minto did not hesitate to tackle the Minister on this question, too. Minto's attitude toward the Canadian Indian, "once the ruler of the soil," combined a romantic concept of the noble savage untainted by civilization with a distaste for philistine evangelical religion and nineteenth-century progress. During his administration, Minto worked closely with the Indian peoples, whom he respected, and as Governor-General he maintained an active interest in their welfare. In November 1900, for example, the Chiefs and Warriors of the Caughnawaga Reserve, a group Minto knew from his Nile voyageur days, petitioned him to exempt the reserve from the Indian Advancement Act, which required all bands to elect councillors. Minto immediately endorsed their request and sent it to his government. On

[8] Minto Papers, Minto to Chamberlain, August 19, 1900.

[9] Minto Papers, "Memorandum re Yukon Affairs," October 31, 1900; G. Lynch to A. F. Sladen, August 17, 1900.

[10] Minto Papers, "Memorandum re Yukon Affairs," October 31, 1900.

[11] Minto Papers, Minto to Arthur Elliot, April 12, 1903.

another occasion the Mohawk Indians on the Bay of Quinte Reserve complained to Minto that Sifton had dismissed their old doctor for political reasons, leaving them without competent medical aid. Again, Minto wrote directly to Sifton protesting the Minister's action and refused to accept Sifton's facile explanation.[12]

Minto enjoyed visiting reserves and insisted they be placed on his viceregal itinerary. Minto had never forgotten or forgiven Lansdowne's cavalier treatment of Poundmaker in 1885. On that occasion Lansdowne had treated the Great Chief as a ludicrous spectacle. In contrast, Minto used official occasions to solicit Indian opinion and complaints on a variety of subjects: civil liberties, education, supplies or undue interference in Indian affairs. Minto not only conveyed these messages to his government, but pleaded for a more realistic treatment, and followed up on his requests to make sure they were not merely acknowledged and then forgotten.[13] Not content to depend for information on occasional visits to reserves, he asked sympathetic North West Mounted Police friends to keep a close eye on reserves and to report miscarriages of justice directly to him. He also insisted on entertaining chiefs or their spokesmen during their official visits to Ottawa.[14] In 1902, for example, when Minto found the Qu'Appelle Sioux Indians in an unusually sullen mood during his visit, he refused to be satisfied until he discovered the cause. As he soon discovered, the Commissioner, David Laird, "a tall cadaverous looking Scotsman more like an elder of the Kirk than anything else," had forbidden all Indian dances.[15] Minto was furious, and he informed the Indians in Laird's presence that he saw no harm in their dances and invited them to dance in the Commissioner's presence. "I suppose I shall be reported as usual as in violent opposition to my ministers," he confided to his diary, but "I do not care a d---."[16] He considered Laird's petty tyranny typical of missionaries' "narrowminded" attempts to civilize the Indian and, he added, "I have long grudged my substance when the plate goes round."[17] He deplored Indian agents' attempts to put the Indian into "a black coat & tall hat (probably with what feathers he can collect around the brim) a costume in my opinion more derogatory to his dignity & far from stamping him as a good Indian."[18] His traditional dress, he wrote Laurier regarding the Laird incident, is far less barbaric than that of the popular highlander's kilt.

This philistine, levelling tendency seemed characteristic of so much of English-Canadian society, and it appeared to be poisoning

[12] Minto Papers, Minto to Sifton, May 1, 15, 1899.

[13] Minto Papers, Minto to Laurier, February 17, 1903.

[14] Minto Papers, Minto to Fred. White, May 19, 1903; Minto to Laurier, May 19, 1903; Minto to Lieutenant-Governor of the North West Territories, June 9, 1903; E. Malony to Minto, January 13, 1903; Minto to Sitting Bull, December 16, 1903.

[15] Minto Papers, Minto to Laurier, February 17, 1903.

[16] Minto Papers, Diary, September 30, 1902.

[17] Minto Papers, Diary, August 7, 1900.

[18] Minto Papers, Minto to Laurier, February 17, 1903.

French-English relations, too. Like many of his predecessors, Minto tried to breach this growing cultural gap. He himself had no difficulty accepting a two-nation concept, and felt more at home with conservative, Anglophilic French Canadians like S.-N. Parent, Sir Henri-Gustave Joly de Lotbinière, and Louis Lavergne than with many of the English elite. Indeed, these old aristocratic French-Canadian families seemed natural allies against the worst effects of democracy, materialism, and the creeping vulgarization of society, and he held the Montreal "nouveau rich English" responsible for the erosion of this natural conservative alliance.[19] Their conduct during the South African war, arousing "racial hatred," "has been positively wicked," and the "conversation of English society here repeated to me is foolish in the extreme," he wrote Chamberlain.[20] The Montreal riot and stories of Ontario farmers going to bed with guns at their heads fearing a French-Canadian invasion, were simply symptomatic of this deep national malaise.

In Quebec, but more particularly in Montreal, Minto tried to ameliorate the situation. He was naïvely confident that more frequent social encounters between the cultural elites would produce beneficial effects in society generally. At least, he wrote to Laurier, viceregal efforts would indicate how deeply he deplored the existing state of cultural division. Then, in December 1902, Minto decided to tackle the problem directly. He called to his office several prominent Montreal citizens—Dr. William Peterson, Senator George Drummond, and Louis Lavergne, to ask them to help him to improve French-English relations. Thereafter the Mintos themselves devoted much of their annual Montreal season to bicultural soirées in which Lady Minto's excellent command of French and Lord Minto's brave efforts received favourable press commendation and set a pace for the Montreal English community who sought viceregal recognition.[21] But despite their obvious good intentions, their efforts had only an ephemeral effect.

Minto felt that part of the general cultural misunderstanding stemmed from English Canada's lack of a sense of time, tradition, and continuity and their disregard for claims consecrated by history. English Canadians, Minto complained, failed to value their historical monuments and to collect and preserve the records of their past. To Minto, a people without a past was a people without a future. Though never extensive or deep, Minto's own reading contained a good portion of history, particularly Canadian history. He patronized and encouraged historical societies and is still remembered for his aid to the Quebec Literary and Historical Society, the Canadian Landmark Association, and the Montreal Antiquarian and Numismatic Society, all of which he commended to his successor as projects worthy of active viceregal support. In Quebec Minto spent endless hours in the

[19] Minto Papers, Diary, December 9, 1902.

[20] Minto Papers, Minto to Chamberlain, November 24, 1900.

[21] Montreal *Star*, December 8, 1902; Minto Papers, Minto to Laurier, December 18, 1902.

company of William Wood, a soldier and historian, examining the old fortress and reconstituting in his mind the battle scenes of the French régime. In 1901 the highlight of his uneventful Nova Scotian tour was a visit to the Louisburg ruins, where he infuriated local officials by bringing his own historical guide. One can imagine his horror, therefore, when Laurier sent him a Privy Council Order in 1903 which authorized the construction of a road across the Plains of Abraham, an order the Prime Minister later claimed to have signed without examining it carefully. Minto returned the Order unsigned to protest the destruction of this historic site.[22] Laurier agreed with Minto and the Cabinet dropped the issue at once. Minto, noting the irony, explained to his brother that Laurier and all the prominent Quebec French-speaking families commended him for preventing this "vandalism on the Plains,"[23] while the English papers accused him of blocking progress and the will of his advisers. But Minto had spoken a little too soon, for several months later he, F. G. Scott, and William Wood met to draw up a larger plan for the defence of the Plains, a plan taken up with great enthusiasm by Minto's successor.[24] Indeed, Minto felt so strongly on this subject that he made preservation the topic of his farewell speech to the citizens of Quebec City. Never, he warned, permit modern ideas to "improve away the charm of this old city."[25]

That same year, 1903, Minto's timely intervention helped secure an appropriate "permanent" home for Canada's public records. Although Canada possessed an archivist as early as 1872, he lacked authority to collect public documents or to secure a suitable storage place. In 1897 the government had created a commission of enquiry into the state of Canada's public records, but its report had been tabled and ignored. Meanwhile, Minto had heard of "large assignments of unsorted papers some of which I know to be valuable, being removed from the Privy Council Office for benefit of the paper factories."[26] Minto also learned that General Herbert had ordered all papers in the Militia Department dated prior to 1882 to be burnt. Minto wrote at once to Laurier to describe the chaos, and suggested the construction of a fireproof building and the appointment of an official records keeper who would not only conserve government papers, but collect "all documents across Canada of interest to the history of the nation." Minto himself had spent over two years in the 1890s sorting and putting his own family's papers in order. Laurier readily accepted Minto's suggestion and agreed to erect an archives building and to appoint a Dominion Archivist with wider powers. Minto's action doubtlessly saved important historical records from destruction.

[22] Minto Papers, Diary, March 24, 1903.

[23] Minto Papers, Minto to Arthur Elliot, September 2, 1904.

[24] Minto Papers, Minto to F. G. Scott, October 5, 1904. In 1899 there had been a great uproar over the proposed sale of building lots on the Plains, a number of protests coming from the United States and Britain. Then Minto had suggested buying part of the Plains from the Ursuline Order.

[25] Montreal Star, September 1, 1904.

[26] Minto Papers, Minto to Laurier, January 19, 1903.

Another attempt, this time to save a valuable collection of Canadian Indian objects, achieved only a partial victory. When Minto learned from his Montreal banker that the Bank of Montreal possessed a large Indian collection acquired from the estate of a Mrs. F. D. Freeman which the Bank proposed to sell on the open market piecemeal, he decided to try to persuade a Canadian museum to buy it all to avoid the eventual loss and scattering of the collection. Although he failed to convince a Canadian museum to take the collection, he did persuade the British Museum to purchase it. Nevertheless, Minto regretted this loss to Canada, and he wished that Canada possessed a national museum to complement its public archives; had he remained in Canada longer he would have pressed his government to create one.[27]

Minto's attempt to encourage the development of social leadership in Canada proved much less successful. Underlying Minto's efforts were certain social assumptions shared by few Canadians. Minto, of course, was no democrat. In his opinion, leadership and direction ought to come from men of independence, training, and experience, which were usually the attributes of birth but not necessarily so. Typically, he lamented the absence of "sound leadership" in Canada and blamed it on the country's lack of a leisured class which would provide direction and example for those beneath their social station.[28] Even so, there were, he thought, men of wealth and attainment who ought to be induced to take a more active part in the country's public life and might be encouraged to do so if given some official recognition or mark of esteem, such as titles or honours.

These assumptions help to explain some of the bitterness which characterized Minto's quarrel with Laurier over honours recommendations. On the surface, the controversy appeared as a simple disagreement over the mechanics of honours recommendations. In other words, the debate centred around the question of whether the Governor-General or the Prime Minister possessed effective control over honours recommendations. More basically, Minto and Laurier also disagreed on the question of the place and purpose of honours in Canadian society. Although titled himself, Sir Wilfrid remained embarrassed by his own title and was determined never to accept another. Ironically, only Minto's timely intervention saved Laurier from that fate in 1902. To commemorate the Coronation of Edward VII, the Prime Minister had been offered an advancement in the peerage, but he had declined it. A Colonial Office clerk's error in deciphering the coded cable, however, distorted Laurier's reply. Minto detected the error immediately and assured the Colonial Secretary that the Prime Minister would not accept the honour. Titles, Laurier felt, were "unsuited to a democratic country."[29] They encouraged transatlantic loyalties and constituted a general political nui-

[27] Minto Papers, Diary, February 4, March 24, 1903.

[28] Minto Papers, Minto to Chamberlain, November 7, 1900; Parkin Papers, Minto to Parkin, November 4, 1900.

[29] Joseph Chamberlain Papers, Minto to Laurier, August 31, 1901.

sance since they simply created and fed petty party quarrels among Cabinet colleagues. Party title seekers hounded him relentlessly and were disappointed and resentful when their claims were not met. Indeed, Laurier himself might well have been willing to surrender any claim to honours recommendations save for Aberdeen's habit of considering honours essentially party patronage. This precedent had given the impression among the party faithful that all honours awards were politically inspired. Considerable confusion might ensue, therefore, if a Governor-General recommended for honours the president of the Canadian Pacific Railway in the wake of an exposé on discriminatory western freight rates and a bitter labour dispute, to cite one practical case which arose in 1901.

On the other hand, Minto possessed a curious view of his own function in the honours recommendations, a view consisting of a mélange of constitutional objections and practical considerations. He rejected the Aberdeen precedent as an aberration from accepted constitutional practice, an interpretation confirmed by correspondence with Lord Stanley, Aberdeen's predecessor. Honours recommendations, Stanley replied, remained the exclusive right of the Governor-General, though political claims ought not to be excluded from consideration. While Minto acknowledged the desirability of consulting Laurier, he made a strange distinction between Laurier's personal advice as Prime Minister and his recommendations as the official spokesman of the Cabinet. Determined to reject out of hand those recommendations made in Laurier's latter capacity, he reserved the right to decide which mask Laurier wore on what occasion.[30] To Laurier, Minto insisted that honours remained a royal prerogative, a claim which Laurier never contested, although the Prime Minister might have added that neither had the royal prerogative been delegated to Minto since his own suggestion reached the Crown only as recommendations from the Colonial Office.[31]

Nor were Minto's recommendations any more impartial and free from personal considerations than those made by Laurier. Minto might fret much about the folly of Cabinet consultation and the unsavoury influence emanating from that source and insist on his desire to see honours bestowed on artists, writers, doctors, military officers, and not simply politicians. But a wide gap frequently separated principle from practice. In 1901, for example, Minto recommended for honours two imperial officer friends, Lieutenant-Colonel De la C. T. Irwin and Lieutenant-Colonel G. C. Kitson, and only Cabinet opposition prevented him from adding a third, Lieutenant-Colonel F. G. Stone. This seemed a somewhat excessive representation of imperial officers given the limited number of places available to Canadian candidates. The next year he submitted the names of two more imperial officers serving in Canada, Colonel W. H. Cotton and Lieutenant-Colonel M. Aylmer, and omitted the Canadian Deputy Minister of Militia, Lieutenant-Colonel L. F. Pinault. Moreover, his

---

[30] Joseph Chamberlain Papers, Minto to Chamberlain, April 22, 1901.
[31] Joseph Chamberlain Papers, Minto to Laurier, December 23, 1900.

decision to press the claims of Edward Clouston, his Montreal banker, Montague Allan, whose Montreal house he sometimes occupied, and the Conservative Senator George Drummond, a close friend and companion, might easily be interpreted as a payment for personal services rendered. This was scarcely an example of the lofty impartiality he endorsed in imperial communications on the honours controversy.

Minto's honours recommendations worried Laurier very little so long as they were confined to innocuous imperial officers, many of whom would return to Britain taking their titles with them. But Minto's attempt to honour the Canadian Pacific Railway president, Thomas Shaughnessey, during the Duke of Cornwall and York's visit in 1901, aroused a storm of Cabinet protest which forced Laurier to raise the contentious issue of responsibility for Canadian honours recommendations. On the surface Minto's case for Shaughnessey seemed sound. The Canadian Pacific Railway had built five special rail cars for the royal couple and placed the "Empress of India" at their disposal on the west coast. It had also acted as host during stages of their journey across Canada. In Minto's mind neither the recent bitter rail strike nor western farmers' abhorrence of the Canadian Pacific Railway constituted sufficient grounds to deny Shaughnessey recognition. And any reference to his close association with the Conservative party simply enhanced Minto's sense of outraged righteousness and his determination to eliminate politics from honours recommendations. Anticipating trouble, Minto had written Chamberlain privately in April 1901, explaining his version of the controversy and asking for clarification.

Chamberlain's response ought to have settled the affair. At least it ought to have satisfied Laurier, had the Prime Minister seen the communication. For Chamberlain's suggested solution bears all the marks of a seasoned pragmatic politician. While supporting Minto's contention that honours recommendations continue to be made on viceregal responsibility, Chamberlain reminded Minto that political considerations could scarcely be excluded. He explained that in Britain "honours are always given on the advice or at least assent, of the Prime Minister or the Minister specially responsible," and these recommendations were, he confessed, often "made on party considerations."[32] According to Chamberlain, Minto ought always to consult Laurier and if the Prime Minister objected to the Governor-General's proposals, these objections ought to be communicated to the Colonial Office. In most cases, particularly politically sensitive cases, Laurier's objections would be sufficient cause for the Colonial Office to refuse to recommend the disputed candidate's name to the King. In effect, Chamberlain proposed giving the Canadian Cabinet a veto power, which is all Laurier ever requested.

Although leaving Minto considerable power, Chamberlain's formula required a degree of understanding and cooperation between the Governor-General and Prime Minister. But this was sadly lacking as the ensuing feud, the first test case, amply demonstrated. To mark

[32] Joseph Chamberlain Papers, Chamberlain to Minto, May 18, 1901.

the Royal visit to Canada in the late summer and early autumn of 1901, the Colonial Office informed Minto that the Duke of Cornwall and York would confer two K.C.M.G.s and six, later seven, C.M.G.s on suitable Canadian candidates. Minto immediately wrote Laurier proposing the names of Muloch and Fielding for the two higher awards. When Fielding declined, Minto suggested the name of Frederick Borden, whom he had come to like and respect for his military zeal and stout British sympathies, but Laurier rejected both candidates, and Minto was forced to find alternatives. Then Minto proposed the name of S.-N. Parent, the Quebec mayor and Prime Minister, whom Minto felt would be a very suitable and worthy recipient. Conscious of political and regional rivalry, Laurier agreed but on the condition that the Toronto and Montreal mayors receive a similar award. Yet there were only two K.C.M.G.s and Minto refused to ask for a third. After considerable negotiation Minto and Laurier finally disposed of the K.C.M.G.s. They went to Louis-Amable Jetté, Lieutenant-Governor of Quebec, and John A. Boyd, Chancellor of the High Court of Justice of Ontario. Then they attempted to mollify Parent and Préfontaine, the Montreal mayor, with C.M.G.s, but the latter two refused to consider the humbler award. George Drummond, the Montreal Conservative Senator, then followed suit, also feeling himself entitled to the higher distinction. The Toronto mayor, A. O. Howland, possessed no such scruple, and was happy enough to take what he had been offered. The rectors of Laval and McGill universities displayed similar gratitude. So, too, did Joseph Pope, Septimus Denison, Lawrence Buchan, and F. S. Maude, Minto's Military Secretary. The horse trading which preceded the designation of honours, the frayed tempers, wounded egos, and subsequent rancorous public debate, sullied Minto's efforts to buttress the Canadian social order. It is true that Laurier and his Cabinet colleagues had been unnecessarily difficult, but Minto himself had been scarcely blameless. When the Duke and his entourage learned of the dispute they felt Minto had been far too rigid and uncooperative and offered to reopen the case. The Duke had no objection to making more K.C.M.G.s available, but Minto remained adamant and refused to discuss the matter further.

Much of the Cabinet's rancour had been caused by Minto's insistence on Shaughnessey's honour. In Minto's opinion Shaughnessey must have the Knight Bachelor, a claim which he pressed despite Laurier's objections. Faithful to Chamberlain's instructions, Minto informed the Colonial Secretary of Laurier's objections as he saw them, but assigned his own explanation and interpretation. Fearing that Minto might misconstrue his objections, Laurier also wrote directly to the Colonial Secretary, but his letter arrived too late; otherwise, Chamberlain suggested in reply, he might have blocked the award.[33]

Anxious to absolve its leader, the Liberal press displayed appropriate fury. Was Shaughnessey's knighthood given, the Toronto Star

[33] Joseph Chamberlain Papers, Laurier to Chamberlain, September 17, 1901; Chamberlain to Laurier, October 6, 1901.

asked bitterly, "because the C.P.R. charges more and higher rates on Canadian freight than the U.S.?" The Toronto *Telegram*, an independent Conservative journal with a chronic case of "Mintomania," described the affair as "an outrageous distribution of royal honours," and blamed Minto for the outrage.[34] Although many Tory papers were elated by this "Disorder Among The Democrats," the dispute transcended party lines.[35] The Hamilton *Herald* and the Ottawa *Citizen* were also unhappy with Minto's honours recommendations. Other papers, inspired by a London report, predicted Minto's recall and began speculation on his successors. Lords Strathcona, Jersey, De Blaquere, Curzon, and Milner were all suggested as possible candidates.

The most virulent and searing assault on Minto came from the pen of J. W. Dafoe, the editor of the Manitoba *Free Press*, whose owner, Clifford Sifton, had ordered the attack. Dafoe used the occasion to launch a major assault on Rideau Hall pretensions, this insidious "military, political and social power with roots beyond the sea."[36] In his trenchant denunciation Dafoe resurrected all Minto's alleged constitutional offences beginning with his reputed attempt to force the government to send troops to South Africa. Minto resented Dafoe's attack most, knowing that it had been inspired by a minister of the Crown. Consequently, he asked Laurier to speak to Dafoe and explain the substance of their honours dispute. Laurier complied and Dafoe desisted, at least temporarily.[37] Laurier himself seemed somewhat surprised by the vehemence of the press attack and tried to draw its fire. He branded as "sheer nonsense" the story that he had requested Minto's recall.[38] Ironically, Israël Tarte, Laurier's volatile Minister of Public Works, who had crossed Minto's path many times previously but who possessed a strange affection for the Governor-General, an affection frequently reciprocated, did most to break the vicious rumour cycle. In a public statement he branded Minto "the soul of honor and loyalty to his ministers" and deplored the shameful and false "way in which his name is being dragged into the press," since he was a man "who has no means of answering his accusers."[39]

Minto's actions seemed to have created a great deal of fuss about very little. However, the acerbic press reaction to the honours controversy can be understood best in the context of a much larger event, the Duke of Cornwall and York's 1901 Canadian visit, for this event, too, provoked widespread bitterness and recrimination. As with the subject of honours bestowal, Minto's attempts to foster royalist sentiments in Canada were based on certain political and social assumptions. Convinced of the monarchy's importance both as a central unifying national symbol and a model of a well-ordered social struc-

[34] Toronto *Telegram*, September 26, 1901; Ottawa *Journal*, September 23, 1901.
[35] Toronto *Mail and Empire*, September 25, 1901.
[36] Manitoba *Free Press*, October 22, 1901.
[37] Minto Papers, Laurier to Dafoe, November 15, 1901.
[38] *Standard*, October 17, 1901.
[39] Toronto *Mail and Empire*, October 15, 1901.

ture based on order, authority, and continuity, Minto sought occasions to permit popular celebration and re-affirmation of Canadians' loyalty to the Crown. The successful example of the Diamond Jubilee had not been lost on Minto, who had participated in its preparation, and possessed first-hand knowledge of its infectious effect upon colonial opinion. However his strict insistence upon protocol and his refusal to make concessions to local differences did little to advance the cause, as a brief glance at the acrimonious public controversy surrounding the 1901 Royal tour will suggest.

Inspired by the Colonial Secretary, the tour had begun in Australia and South Africa and had been extended to Canada largely at Chamberlain's behest. He had not only requested the Canadian government to extend a "spontaneous" invitation but had persuaded, by subtle means, the reluctant, apprehensive old Queen to consent to the Duke's prolonged absence. Minto regarded the proposed tour as a great imperial opportunity and decided to make it a great occasion. On the other hand, the Canadian government, whose loyalty always contained a generous portion of pragmatism, saw the visit as an opportunity to "boom" the country in Britain and insisted that the Duke's entourage, which contained a host of English journalists, pass through the Canadian wheat fields during the rich harvest. Minto himself was anxious to please the Colonial Secretary and convince the Royal party that the Aberdeen confusion and irregularities, which had both amused and offended the Court, had been put to flight. He also determined that the tour be conducted decently and in an orderly fashion and that it obey the strict rules of protocol, precedent, and court etiquette. To assure absolute success he placed effective control in the hands of his new Military Secretary, Major F. S. Maude, a competent, exacting, experienced administrator who had helped stage the Diamond Jubilee celebrations, but a man whose knowledge of Canada left much to be desired.

Given the potential conflict of interests, Royal, personal, public, and political, only an inordinately gifted diplomat, able to trade on a reservoir of goodwill, could emerge unscathed. The potential pitfalls were endless. The Canadian government, which saw the visit as means to promote Western Canada, fretted lest the lateness of the season and a fit of cold weather discourage immigration. In the end they wanted the tour postponed. When this could not be obtained Liberal politicians were peeved by the shortness of the tour and the Duke's inability to pass through their constituency. Laurier himself wanted the Duke to arrive at Quebec rather than Halifax, despite the lateness of the season. Sabbatarians opposed the Duke's arrival in Quebec on Sunday. The Duke insisted on seeing Niagara Falls and on reserving at least one day for duck shooting. The Clan-na-Gael threatened to assassinate the Duke, a threat which assumed greater significance following the death of the American President, McKinley. A Canadian Pacific Railway strike forced Minto to consider possible alternate travel plans. Moreover, Queen Victoria's death earlier in the year placed severe restrictions on entertainment. Court mourning forbade balls or banquets and permitted only official dinners, concerts, receptions, and reviews. There was no way to escape giving offence to some quarter, and the resultant disappointments and frustrations were tallied against Minto's account.

He, of course, had his own personal problems. Increased vice-regal costs threatened to cripple his personal budget, and he pressed Chamberlain to speak to Laurier on his behalf. After much prodding, Chamberlain complied and Laurier agreed that the government would bear all expenses, but Minto's persistence annoyed the Colonial Office which thought that the Governor-General had been unduly troublesome on this matter. The problem of personal precedence also preoccupied Minto's attentions. Ought he, as the King's representative, to take public precedence over the Duke? When the King, at the Colonial Office's request, decided against Minto's view he remained unconvinced and unconsoled and decided, rather peevishly, to restrict the number of public occasions in which they appeared together. He met the Duke at Quebec, accompanied him to Montreal and Ottawa, then left the party. The provincial Lieutenant-Governor's quarters, he explained to Chamberlain, were too small for the Governor-General and his staff. Lady Minto, however, joined the Royal party, thereby avoiding any sense of personal pique. Minto met the party again at Montreal and accompanied the Duke to Halifax where the Royal party sailed for England on October 21, aboard the *Ophir*.

Organization and public relations proved to be Minto's most difficult problems, and his rigidity and inability to get around people without going through them did nothing to ease the burden. Initially Minto, following Chamberlain's instructions to plan with the Canadian government, worked through a planning committee consisting of himself and Fielding. Then in May he replaced this by a more elaborate structure. The new organization possessed a central committee, composed of himself and Laurier, which vetted all plans and proposals. It also possessed provincial committees presided over by Lieutenant-Governors. Soon Laurier and Minto delegated much of their executive authority to Joseph Pope and Major Maude respectively. But whereas Minto's interest never lagged, Laurier, preoccupied with more pressing problems, began to stay a safe distance from the Committee's affairs. Pope, a quiet, self-effacing civil servant, became overwhelmed by Maude's knowledge of protocol and left effective control in the hands of Minto and Maude. There is no question that they planned efficiently and well, and deserved credit for the tour's organizational success. But immersed in the inevitable petty administrative details, they lost touch with public feeling and provoked an unenviable hostile press reaction which cut across party lines.

Annoyed by the Central Committee's insistence that all proposed addresses be submitted in advance, the Ottawa *Journal* suggested a boycott as the "one easy way to escape the impertinence."[40] Recep-

[40] Ottawa *Journal*, August 12, 1901.

tions in this country, the Vancouver World informed Minto, "where all men are free and equal, should be open to all, regardless of rank and clothing."[41] The Toronto Star wrote a bitingly sarcastic article entitled "Canadians Would Make A Mess Of It."[42] Nor did the London News mince words: "Canadians may be crude when it comes to courtly ways. They are quite willing to learn where their knowledge is deficient, but they do not intend to be fashioned into apes of English aristocracy, as Lord Minto would have them."[43] Papers across the country accused Minto of one, some, or all of the following offences: planning the tour to pass through the wheat fields at night, discrimination against Protestant denominations, suppressing the French language in Montreal, ejecting a dying Lieutenant-Governor, Oliver Mowat, from his official residence, and, as usual, a gross failure to understand his correct constitutional position. Even papers usually friendly to Minto joined the growing chorus of criticism. Few papers went to the extremes of Les Débats, which called for Minto's recall, but most would have agreed with the Toronto World that the Duke's visit had made Minto the most unpopular man in Canada.

Minto stoically bore the brunt of press criticism, seemingly immune to Canadian public feeling. But being more sensitive to British official reaction, he refused to leave his vindication to chance or Providence. He wrote at once to his friend George Parkin, conscious of Parkin's close connection with the press, particularly the "better" section, by which he meant The Times, and for which Parkin served as Canadian correspondent. The cuts in programme, he explained, were not his suggestions but the Duke's, who "is cutting more than a healthy young man ought." The line to take, he continued, is "(a) he is tired, (b) made special effort to come to Canada, (c) tries to meet most people." Minto concluded that it would be preferable that "I should be considered obstructive & I am quite ready to stand the shot."[44] However, Minto knew full well that Parkin's magic pen would work its spell and would clear both the Duke and the viceroy in the eyes of the British public.

Despite appearances, Minto did not remain entirely indifferent to Canadian criticism, but he had burned his fingers earlier that year preparing a "state" funeral for Queen Victoria and had become inured to Canadian public opinion. To Minto the death of the old Queen in January 1901 seemed an appropriate occasion to express the respect and affection she inspired among Canadians generally. Her reign had begun before the birth of most Canadians and she herself had come to symbolize an age. Minto began immediately to make plans and arouse sensitivities. First he objected to Laurier's letter of condolence to the Royal family which he considered stiff and cold and unrepresentative of the deep sorrow felt by the Canadian people, and he altered it to

[41] Vancouver World, August 16, 1901.
[42] Toronto Star, August 13, 1901.
[43] London News, August 18, 1901.
[44] Minto Papers, Minto to Parkin, August 25, 1901.

coincide with his own reading of the general will.[45] The next day he met Laurier and announced plans for an Ottawa "state" ceremony to commemorate the Queen's death. At the time, Laurier raised no objections. Two days later, on second thought, Minto asked Laurier if he wished to name a Cabinet representative to assist with preparations. But Laurier declined, since he thought that Joseph Pope, the Under Secretary of State, could serve as a sufficient liaison officer between Rideau Hall and the Cabinet. Richard Scott, Pope's ministerial superior, seemed equally indifferent to Minto's plans but agreed to let Pope assist.

Meanwhile, Minto consulted the Christ Church Anglican Cathedral authorities, set the date for February 2, and invited the Anglican Primate, Robert Machray, to officiate. F. W. Borden, too, agreed to assist and even offered to provide a small contingent of militia. Programmes were printed, a seating plan arranged, and costs rose. Only at this point did Minto request government financial assistance.

When Laurier summoned the Cabinet to approve the expenditure he encountered bitter opposition to Minto's plans. Although it is difficult to identify precisely the ministers with particular objections, the newspapers which they controlled or influenced provide some indication. Richard Scott, a passionate Irish Catholic, disapproved of the service being held in the Anglican cathedral, "calculated to give offence to other denominations than the Church of England."[46] The presence of Machray, though perfectly reasonable given his position and the occasion, did nothing to allay suspicions, owing to that prelate's earlier efforts to annul Catholic school rights in Manitoba. Nor was Scott alone in his complaints. W. S. Fielding, the proficient Minister of Finance, a strict Baptist and a man who was immune to viceregal favours, failed to attend Minto's service, and his paper, the Halifax *Chronicle*, carried its opposition to the point of insult. It charged that Minto had made plans without consulting his ministers. This was a particularly bitter blow since Minto liked and respected Fielding. Laurier's Minister of the Interior, Clifford Sifton, however, detested the Governor-General, so his opposition was predictable. Not only did he refuse to attend the Christ Church service but his paper, the Manitoba *Free Press*, gave its reasons. It accused Minto of trying to impose a state church on Canada, he "being a member of the Church of England," and of failing to consult his ministers.[47] In the face of this opposition Laurier withdrew his support for the service and informed Minto immediately of the Cabinet's refusal.

The Cabinet's position astounded Minto and he tried to defend himself. Laurier's suggestion that government aid would be tantamount to recognizing the existence of a state church in Canada seemed absurd. Had not the Canadian government paid for the state

[45] Minto Papers, Minto to Chamberlain, February 15, 1901.

[46] Ottawa *Free Press*, February 15, 1901; Ottawa *Journal*, January 29, 1901.

[47] Manitoba *Free Press*, January 31, 1901. See also Ramsay Cook, *The Politics of John W. Dafoe and the Free Press* (Toronto, 1963), 22-23.

funerals of John A. Macdonald and John S. D. Thompson in the Church to which they belonged? Was not the Queen entitled to similar treatment? Laurier replied, somewhat tendentiously, that the Thompson and Macdonald cases were different since they were proper burial services, the body being present, whereas the Queen's service, being a memorial service, could be held in any Church. Moreover, the Queen in Scotland belonged to the Church of Scotland and since the Ottawa Presbyterian Churches as well as other denominations planned similar memorial services, the government could not favour one over another. Reluctantly, but still mystified, Minto accepted Laurier's clever explanation although he remained unconvinced.[48]

Still Minto attempted to meet some of Laurier's objections. He changed the service's name from "state" to memorial, but there seemed little more he could do short of admitting the sectarian nature of his plans. Once again he tried to persuade Laurier to provide funds. Through some research he discovered that the government had indeed paid for memorial services in Kingston and Ottawa for Macdonald and Thompson, but Laurier denied the claim.[49] Minto's information was quite right, but by the time he found proper documentation for his point the service was over and paid for, probably out of his own pocket.

Meanwhile, the party press continued carping. Its course and content were predictable. It charged Minto with a variety of petty slights and irregularities. They said he had insisted that Cabinet Ministers wear windsor uniforms, which was not an unreasonable demand. They also claimed that he had allowed himself to become the cat's paw of the Anglican cathedral's presumptions. But the charge which annoyed Minto most and which was repeated with irritating regularity was the assertion that Minto had acted without Cabinet approval or authority. Conservative journals, however, effectively punctured this cry by calling upon the Cabinet to resign or accept responsibility for the Governor-General's actions. And this time, Minto might have left his defence in their hands.[50]

But Minto could never leave well enough alone. Instead, he decided to defend himself by distributing a press statement signed by his secretary, A. F. Sladen, denying that he had acted independently of his ministers. The arrangements, he insisted, "were considered by His Excellency together with his advisers and approved by them."[51]

Minto's public defence, quite apart from its propriety, lacked a degree of credibility. While he had in fact consulted Laurier and Scott, he had not received the Cabinet's approval, unless he mistook silence and indifference for consent. Laurier, too, may well have regarded Minto's preparations as a function of his jealously guarded viceregal or imperial prerogatives beyond the pale of Cabinet consent. Scott

[48] Minto Papers, Minto to Chamberlain, February 15, 1901.
[49] Minto Papers, Minto to Laurier, January 30, 1901.
[50] Toronto Mail and Empire, January 30, 1901.
[51] Ottawa Journal, January 30, 1901.

was particularly stung by Minto's public charge and he wrote Minto a strong note rejecting Minto's assumption that their conversations constituted Cabinet consent.[52] More seriously, Minto's public intervention simply invited extended and insulting press replies which clouded rather than clarified the issue. The Governor-General, the Halifax *Chronicle* replied, displayed

> neither wisdom nor good form. He is here, as he ought to know, mainly to do just what he is advised by those who understand both his duties and their own very much better than he does or is likely to. Canadians neither desire nor will they tolerate, from him or any one else in his position, any such interference in the purely internal affairs of this country as indicated in the despatches which have come from Ottawa concerning this matter.[53]

Given all this indecently petty bickering, the memorial service seemed ludicrously anti-climactic. When Minto arrived on Parliament Hill to lead the procession to Christ Church he met a motley array of militiamen and Cabinet ministers. The government's refusal to provide funds prevented a full muster of the militia. Four Cabinet ministers—Mulock, Borden, Fisher, and Cartwright—arrived attired in full windsor uniform and another, Israël Tarte, Laurier's maverick Minister of Public Works, attended in civilian clothes, according to Minto, "a machiavellian attempt to undermine Sir Wilfrid's authority by an excess of loyalty."[54] Laurier himself went to the service at the Catholic basilica and the other Cabinet Ministers attended the church of their choice. Meanwhile, in Quebec City, the Quebec Prime Minister, S.-N. Parent, led a united provincial Cabinet to the Anglican cathedral to attend a similar "memorial service."

Canadian reaction, particularly English-Canadian reaction, baffled Minto. Every attempt he made to foster royalist sentiment seemed to turn sour. The old, easy anti-French cry, used so frequently and carelessly to explain all, did not seem to apply here. Something more basic, general, and disturbing seemed to be at work. This feeling was confirmed by many of Minto's other loyal endeavours. His efforts to erect a national monument to Queen Victoria, obtain a commissioned portrait of the new King, or have the North West Mounted Police designated the Royal North West Mounted Police, to name only a few, met a similar fate. Moreover, Fielding displayed no more interest than Laurier in these projects. What Minto failed to understand was that Canadians objected more to the form than the substance of his actions.

In less conventional areas Minto's viceregal efforts knew some success. In 1901 Guglielmo Marconi visited Canada to complete his experiments with wireless telegraphy. Minto entertained Marconi at Rideau Hall, endorsed his project, and provided useful letters of introduction to Canadian capitalists interested in trans-Atlantic wireless communication. In December 1902, as a gesture of appreciation

[52] Minto Papers, Minto to Richard Scott, February 4, 1901.
[53] Halifax *Chronicle*, February 5, 1901.
[54] Minto Papers, Minto to Chamberlain, February 15, 1901.

as well as advertisement, Marconi asked Minto to send the first official message across the new wireless system.[55]

Captain Joseph-Elzear Bernier, the Canadian Arctic explorer, also won Minto's valuable support. Minto not only subscribed $500 to help Bernier to finance a polar expedition as an effort to assert Canadian Arctic sovereignty, but persuaded other influential people to endorse the project, notably Edward VII, Lord Strathcona, and S.-N. Parent.[56]

Finally, Minto organized the Canadian Association for the Prevention of Tuberculosis, a body devoted to a massive public health education and the creation of more and better public sanitoriums. Minto backed and fought for the Association, reputed to be the first national organization of its kind on the continent, despite the concerted opposition of Canadian medical entrepreneurs. Given the powerful influence of the initial opposition, no politician wanted to take the lead. More insulated from public pressures, a Governor-General could walk where politicians feared to tread.[57]

In the more conventional realm of viceregal influence, Minto's record is far from illustrious. He had neither the passion nor pretence to pose as a patron of the arts and letters, although he always performed his duties. Like his predecessors he opened Royal Society meetings, attended art exhibitions, concerts, and convocations, but the arts and letters owe nothing to his intervention or initiative beyond a rather mundane moral support for practical education, household science, industrial arts, and agriculture. He seemed more at home at horse shows or warning farmers to avoid docking their horses' tails, or again, providing helpful hints on horse breeding, which he encouraged with cups, medals, and prizes.[58] One reporter noted that on these occasions he spoke "as if it was meant. . . . There was a ring of sincerity in his voice, and a gleam of enthusiasm in his eye, and though there was no attempt at oratory, everyone was convinced that he was glad to be there and that he was a great lover of horses."[59]

Minto's patronage naturally reflected his personal tastes and interests, but his sporting passion created considerable consternation among the less athletic who were seeking social recognition. The more democratic complained of his preoccupation with that aristocratic sport, horse racing. Yet Minto felt that "manly sports" produced a variety of virtues such as courage, self-restraint, health, patriotism, and national character. Consequently he sought to promote them by building a skating rink and donating cups for figure-skating, curling, and lacrosse. Unlike his predecessor, Lord Stanley,

[55] Montreal Star, December 22, 1902.

[56] Minto Papers, Minto to Strathcona, May 17, 1902; Minto to S.-N. Parent, August 26, 1902; Colonial Office 42 (888), Minto to Chamberlain, February 7, 1902.

[57] Ottawa Citizen, February 15, 1901; Montreal Gazette, December 1, 1902; Minto Papers, Minto to Sir Charles Tupper, 31 May, 1901.

[58] Evening Sun, April 18, 1899; Toronto Globe, April 14, 1899.

[59] Montreal Star, May 4, 1900.

or his successor, Lord Grey, both of whom provided cups to promote a growing sporting interest, Minto's quite typical attempt to revive lacrosse, a declining national sport, met relatively little popular success.

In Canada the prestige of monarchy depended largely upon the person who held the royal proxy. Minto's character, interests, and concerns temporarily stamped the royal presence, and on this score his actions left much to be desired. His presumption, inexperience, and personal sensitivity reaped a harvest of ill-will which did little to enhance the prestige of the monarchy in Canada. Yet the score-sheet contains another side. Probably his most positive contribution to public life grew out of his activist concept of his public function. For his insistence upon meddling in affairs of substance often produced positive results, too. Once convinced of the necessity of action he did not hesitate to beard the medical entrepreneurs, block the developers, defend the Canadian Indian, or plead the cause of the northern miner. Together these activities, although scarcely of critical importance, reveal a more positive side of Minto's controversial Canadian career.

Conclusion

On the bitterly cold morning of November 18, 1904, Minto boarded the S.S. *Tunisian* at Quebec to begin his return voyage home. The thermometer read five degrees Fahrenheit and "the banks of the St. Lawrence were white & wintry and ice was forming along the shores."[1] It had been only six years and one day since he had arrived in Canada full of determination and apprehension to assume his viceregal duties. His term of office had been longer than he had anticipated and considerably longer than all of his post-Confederation predecessors, save Lord Dufferin. Twice his departure had been delayed, once at the request of Chamberlain, who had extended his term by one year, and once at the request of Laurier, who had wanted him to remain until after the November federal election. Now, as the ship left the shore, Minto felt a great sense of sadness and nostalgia or, as he wrote, "a dreadful pang."

Minto was now fifty-nine, and he was leaving Canada with no promise of future employment abroad. His service in Canada, then, might well remain his sole claim to some historical distinction. As the *Tunisian* made its slow progress down the St. Lawrence, Minto reviewed the chief events of his Canadian career and wondered what place he would occupy in the annals of Canadian history. The flattering final remarks showered upon him as he passed from town to town

[1] Minto Papers, Diary, November 18, 1904.

during his last months in Canada seemed to suggest that he had succeeded far beyond his most sanguine expectations. Yet Minto was not entirely deceived by the inevitable flattery of these parting vice-regal occasions. He knew there were those who still regarded him as an imperial busybody, an autocrat, a militarist who was out of touch with Canadian life outside Rideau Hall. They had accused him of desecrating the sabbath, indulging in aristocratic sports, and casting aspersions on Canada's climate by allowing himself and his family to be photographed wearing furs. He knew, too, that many of these epithets, complaints, and petty charges were little more than the inevitable complaints of cranks. Yet he was not quite prepared to leave his vindication to the precarious fate of history.

Even before he left Canada he tried to put the record straight. In August 1904 his old friend George Parkin gave Minto the opportunity he sought. Parkin had secured a column and a half in The Times to review Minto's Canadian career and he wrote the Governor-General for a few brief notes to make certain that he wrote "some fairly adequate review of your term of office."[2] Minto eagerly accepted the offer. In a thirty-six page, hand-written letter supplemented with key speeches, press cuttings, and reports related to his career, Minto described and assessed his Canadian administration, confident that Parkin would do the rest.

Minto saw himself as a strong, impartial, imperial arbiter, who had exacted honesty and fair play from his government regardless of the consequences, always reserving the right "to put my foot down if I suspected anything detrimental to Imperial interests."[3] According to Minto's own testimony, the four most important events of his career had been the despatch of Canadian troops to South Africa, Queen Victoria's memorial service, the Alaskan boundary settlement, and the Dundonald affair. Although a somewhat curious assortment, they were all subjects where his record had been more or less defensible. He reminded Parkin, too, of his firm stand on the honours controversy and the viceregal right to recommend Canadian candidates for commissions in the regular army. And in the privacy of his correspondence he recounted in each case how he had triumphed in the end. He also told Parkin that he had played an important part in Canadian militia reform and reorganization and could not "call to mind a single case of objection on my part on which I have not gained my point."[4] Minto's attempt to block Borden's amendments to the Militia Act, his opposition to the Minister's reinstatement of paragraphs 68 and 69 of the militia Orders and Regulations, and his efforts to impose his two-master plan to remedy the anomalous position of the Canadian General Officer Commanding had all conveniently been forgotten. Nor was Minto particularly proud of his abortive efforts to save Hutton in the early years of his administration.

[2] Minto Papers, Minto to Parkin, September 26, 1904.
[3] Minto Papers, Minto to Parkin, September 26, 1904.
[4] Minto Papers, Minto to Parkin, September 26, 1904.

Whatever Minto might like to think, the fact is that he had had little discernible effect on the formation of high policy. To a certain extent his failure was inherent in the itinerant nature of his office. Yet his own character and inexperience did nothing to obviate this disability. Save for his modest contribution to the resolution of Canadian-American differences, it is difficult to cite one example where his initiative or intervention altered the nature or direction of Canadian or imperial affairs. His propensity for lost or losing causes, his avid support for imperial defence cooperation and imperial trade reorganization moved neither the Canadian nor imperial governments, despite his ceaseless prodding and his prodigious expenditure of time and paper. Nor does evidence support the claim of both his friends and opponents that he dragooned Canada into participation in the South African war. Plagued by inexperience and the inability to distinguish the important from the trivial, Minto's initial bungling created the indelible image of himself as the high-handed, imperious pro-Consul manipulated by Downing Street, and these were images, constantly reinforced by his numerous critics, which the ritual of parting addresses, illuminated or otherwise, could not erase. It mattered little to his critics that there was another side. They did not care to admit that as time went on Minto found subtler means of exercising influence, of persuading men and solving problems. His handling of the Dundonald affair is a good case in point. Yet just or unjust, if the Crown's strength depended upon "the conviction that its neutrality is always beyond suspicion," Minto's administration can scarcely be counted a success.[5]

In the more prosaic realm of good works Minto had a much greater claim to satisfaction. His fearless intervention on behalf of Canada's Indian peoples and northern miners, his attempts to preserve the written and material records of its history were actions which clearly belong on the credit side of his ledger. The Patriotic Fund and the Tuberculosis Association owe their existence to his interest and determination, and in their time both worked to alleviate the distress of the less fortunate members of society.

Then, too, there was the nebulous area of viceregal influence exercised through tours and personal encounters. Disappointed social climbers might claim that Minto knew little of Canadian life outside Rideau Hall. However, Minto had been no wooden Governor insensitive to the claims and concerns of his constituency. During his administration he travelled over 113,000 miles to visit Canadians in mines, factories, and isolated farms. On tour he might forbid the formal banquet with its interminable toasts, but he rarely missed the opportunity to solicit the opinions of his audience. He was convinced that rulers and their deputies had an obligation to learn the minds of their people. He also went out of his way to meet and talk to those who possessed no official claim to recognition. Although in the presence of pompous politicians and bureaucrats, Minto seemed often to stand on his fragile sense of viceregal dignity; he never hesitated to espouse

[5] John T. Saywell, The Office of Lieutenant-Governor (Toronto, 1957), 27.

the cause of the small man or the neglected minority. He enjoyed breaking out of the suffocating confines of Rideau Hall and liked meeting people in less contrived circumstances. For example, during the great Ottawa-Hull fire of 1900 Minto joined the firefighters, worked all day, and rose early the next morning to help dig charred bodies from the rubble. On another occasion he left his viceregal train in Brandon, Manitoba, to perform a similar service on a wrecked train. Those who met him in these circumstances were convinced that they possessed an unusually sympathetic man as Governor-General. They saw him as a man who "would sooner grip rein over a good horse any day than twiddle his thumbs on that irksome throne in the Red Chamber."[6] They, not the politicians, detected the warm, affectionate character behind the stiff official mask. It mattered little to them that he had often stretched his constitutional position to the breaking point or that his precipitate interventions had frequently exacerbated rather than ameliorated a situation. But for all their goodwill his supporters could not mitigate his failings as a Governor-General.

A study of Minto's Canadian administration, however, is more than the creation of a balance sheet of viceregal vices and virtues. It also provides a perspective on an important period of Canadian political development, the high water mark of Canada's age of imperialism. As one form of English-Canadian nationalism, the Canadian imperial movement has been greatly maligned by its opponents. Only recently have Canadian historians begun to peel off the layers of distortion which have obscured our understanding of the imperial factor in Canadian history.[7] No misconception has possessed a hardier constitution than the imperial conspiracy theory, the notion that there existed a concerted turn-of-the-century plan to rob Canada of its political autonomy. Central to this theory is a basic confusion of Rideau Hall with Downing Street. Upon the assumption that Governors-General ought to possess severely restricted powers of discretion, historians have often written as though they possessed none. These writers have tended to see the viceregal incumbent as the puppet of two contending poles of authority represented by Ottawa and London. Their failure to appreciate the degree of viceregal discretion, their tendency to represent viceregal initiatives as evidence of extraneous influence, has distorted our perception of historical reality. An analysis of Minto's Canadian career provides ample evidence of the folly of this assumption. In other words, Rideau Hall and Downing Street did not work in tandem.

It is equally false to assume that the British government possessed a concerted imperial plan for the placid kingdom of Canada. Not only did it have more pressing concerns at this time, but an examination of Canadian-imperial relations suggests that its Canadian policy was the result of a pragmatic, ad hoc resolution of conflicting interdepartmental priorities, not the implementation of a pre-

---

[6] Toronto Star, May 8, 1900.

[7] Carl Berger, The Sense of Power (Toronto, 1970); S. E. D. Shortt, Conviction in an Age of Transition (Toronto, 1976).

arranged imperial blueprint. For example, the War Office tended to see Canada as an expensive liability which it attempted to liquidate through reform, recruitment, or repudiation. On the other hand, the Foreign Office, when it thought at all of Canada, viewed it as a troublesome pawn in a global power game. Although the Colonial Office frequently bore the brunt of criticism for unpopular imperial decisions as well as the blunders and stupidities of its agents, this traditional scapegoat of sensitive Canadian autonomists proved a loyal, determined defender of Canadian interests. In other words, British policy toward Canada depended upon the shifting balance of power within the British Cabinet, as the resolution of the Alaskan boundary dispute so clearly demonstrated. Far from the seat of power, the Viceroy was as impotent in these matters as his government. Yet a study of lost causes and failures can still dispel illusions and provide historical insight.

Bibliography

Primary Sources

1. Personal and Official Papers

BRITISH MUSEUM
H. O. Arnold-Forster Papers
Arthur Balfour Papers
E. T. H. Hutton Papers

CORPORATION OF HOVE LIBRARY, HOVE
Garnet Wolseley Papers

INDIA OFFICE LIBRARY, LONDON
George Curzon Papers

McGILL UNIVERSITY, MONTREAL
William Peterson Papers
Amy Roddick Diary

NATIONAL LIBRARY OF SCOTLAND, EDINBURGH
The Fourth Earl of Minto Papers

OXFORD UNIVERSITY, CHRIST CHURCH LIBRARY, OXFORD
The Third Marquis of Salisbury Papers

PUBLIC ARCHIVES OF CANADA, OTTAWA
Robert Borden Papers
Adolph Caron Papers
Raoul Dandurand Papers

George T. Denison Papers
Wilfrid Laurier Papers
Ernest Pacaud Papers
George Parkin Papers
Records of the Governor General's Office
Joseph Israël Tarte Papers
John S. Willison Papers

PUBLIC ARCHIVES OF NOVA SCOTIA, HALIFAX
F. W. Borden Papers

PUBLIC RECORD OFFICE, LONDON
Colonial Office 42 Series
Foreign Office 5 Series
War Office 32 Series
John Ardagh Papers

UNIVERSITY OF BIRMINGHAM, BIRMINGHAM
Austen Chamberlain Papers
Joseph Chamberlain Papers

UNIVERSITY OF WESTERN ONTARIO, LONDON, ONTARIO
David Mills Papers

2. Government Records

Canada, Committee on the Defences of Canada. *The Defences of Canada.*
    Ottawa, 1866.
Canada, House of Commons. *Debates.* 1898-1905.
Canada. *Sessional Papers.* 1898-1905.
Great Britain, House of Lords. *Debates.* 1898 and 1905.

3. Newspapers

Border Standard, January 1886-January 1887.
Halifax Chronicle, 1898-1905.
London *Daily Mail*, October 20-December 1, 1898.
Montreal *Gazette*, February 3-March 31, 1894; 1898-1905.
Glasgow *Herald*, 1909, 1911.
Hawick Express, January 2, 1886-January 1887.
Halifax Herald, 1898-1905.
Toronto *Monetary Times*, 1899-1905.
London *Morning Post*, 1874, 1877.
The Times, August 1898-December 1898.
La Presse, novembre et decembre 1924.
McGill Outlook, January-June 1900.
Manitoba *Free Press*, January 1900-March 1900.
Newspaper Scrapbook. 3 vols., Minto Papers.

4. Books

Aberdeen, Lord and Lady. *We Twa.* 2 vols. London, 1925.
Amery, L. S. *My Political Life.* Vol. 1. London, 1953.
Argyll, The Duke of. *Passages from the Past.* Vol. I. London, 1907.
Bernier, J. E. *Master Mariner.* Ottawa, 1939.
Borden, Henry, ed. *Robert Laird Borden: His Memoirs.* Toronto, 1938.

Boulton, C. A. Reminiscences of the North West Rebellion. Toronto, 1886.
Buckle, George Earle. The Letters of Queen Victoria. 3 vols. London, 1932.
Cartwright, Rt. Hon. Sir Richard. Reminiscences. Toronto, 1912.
Chamberlain, Rt. Hon. Joseph. Imperial Union and Tariff Reform: Speeches
    Delivered from May 15 to November 4, 1903. London, 1903.
Choquette, P.-A. Un demi-siècle de vie politique. Montreal, 1936.
Clark, William. Empire Club Speeches. Toronto, 1904.
Cory, William. Letters and Journals. London, 1897.
Decelles, A. D., ed. Sir Wilfrid Laurier: Discours à l'étranger et au Canada,
    1871-1901. Montreal, 1909.
Denison, Colonel George T. The Struggle for Imperial Unity: Recollections
    and Experiences. Toronto, 1909.
Dundonald, Earl of, Douglas M. B. H. Cochrane. My Army Life. London, 1926.
Forbes, Archibald. Memoirs and Studies of War and Peace. London, 1895.
Gilbert, Martin. Servant of India. London, 1966.
Gooch, G. P. and H. Temperley, eds. British Documents on the Origin of the
    War. Vol. 1. London, 1932.
Hamelin, Marcel, ed. Les Mémoires du Senateur Raoul Dandurand 1861-
    1904. Quebec, 1967.
Haultain, Arnold, ed. Goldwin Smith's Correspondence. Toronto, 1913.
Hopkins, Castell. The Canadian Annual Review for 1902. Toronto, 1903.
————. The Canadian Annual Review for 1903. Toronto, 1904.
————. The Canadian Annual Review of Public Affairs 1904. Toronto,
    1905.
Hutton, Colonel E. T. H. Five Lectures on Mounted Infantry. London, 1891.
Langelier, Charles. Souvenirs politiques. 2 vols. Quebec, 1912.
Macdonald, E. M. Recollections Political and Personal. Toronto, 1938.
Machray, Robert, ed. Life of Bishop Machray. Toronto, 1909.
Marindin, George Eden. Letters of Frederic Lord Blachford. London, 1896.
Martin, Gilbert. Servant of India. London, 1966.
Middleton, Earl of. Records and Reactions 1856-1939. London, 1939.
Minto, 4th Earl. Speeches by the Earl of Minto. Calcutta, 1911.
Morison, E. E. The Letters of Theodore Roosevelt. Vols 3, 4, 5, 6. Boston, 1952.
Morrison, E. W. B. With the Guns of South Africa. Hamilton, 1901.
Ollivier, Maurice. British North America Acts and Selected Statutes. Ottawa,
    1962.
————, ed., The Colonial and Imperial Conferences from 1887 to 1937.
    Vol. 1. Ottawa, 1954.
Oxford, Margot, ed. Myself when Young. London, 1938.
Pacaud, L., ed. Sir Wilfrid Laurier: Lettres à mon père et à ma mère. Ar-
    thabaska, 1935.
Ponsonby, Arthur. Decline of Aristocracy. London, 1908.
Pope, Maurice, ed. Public Servant the Memoirs of Sir Joseph Pope. Toronto,
    1960.
Russell, Benjamin. Autobiography. Halifax, 1932.
Russell, Bertrand. The Autobiography of Bertrand Russell, The Early Years:
    1872-World War I. Boston, 1969.
Saywell, John T., ed. The Canadian Journal of Lady Aberdeen, 1893-1898.
    Toronto, 1960.
Tupper, Rt. Hon. Sir Charles, Bart., G.C.M.G., C.B. Recollections of Sixty
    Years in Canada. London, 1914.
Willison, Sir J. S. Reminiscences, Political and Personal. Toronto, 1919.
The Anglo-Boer War 1899-1900. Cape Town, n.d.
The Dominion Annual Register for 1883. Toronto, 1884.

5. Articles

Archer, J. H. "North West Rebellion 1885." *Saskatchewan History* (Winter, 1962).
Borden, Sir Frederick W. "The Canadian Militia, Past, Present and Future." *Selected Papers of the Canadian Military Institute.* 1906.
Chamberlain, Joseph. "Anglo-American Alliance." *Scribner's Magazine* (December 1898).
Charlton, John. "The Commission's Work—Counter Influences." *Canadian Magazine* (May 1899).
Dundonald, Earl of, Douglas M. B. H. Cochrane. "Notes on a Citizen Army." *Fortnightly Review* (October 1905).
Elliot, Arthur, "Home Rule for Scotland." *Nineteenth Century* (March 1886).
Elliot, Gilbert [Minto, 4th Earl]. "War Correspondents." *Edinburgh Review* (January 1896).
Foster, John W. "The Alaska Boundary." *National Geographic Magazine* (November 1899).
Hutton, E. T. H. "A Co-operative System for the Defence of the Empire." *Proceedings of the Royal Colonial Institute* 29 (1898).
————. "The Evolution of Mounted Infantry." *Empire Review* (April 1901).
Kennedy, Howard Angus. "Memories of '85." *Canadian Geographical Journal* (May 1965).
Lodge, H. C. "Memoirs of Henry Cabot Lodge." *Proceedings of the Massachusetts Historical Society* (April 1925).
Minto, Lady. "The Great Dominion." *National Review* (March 1905).
McNeil, Alex. "British Trade and Imperial Reciprocity." *Canadian Magazine* (April 1903).
Melgund, Brig.-Gen. Viscount. "The Best Mounted Arm for the Volunteers, the Mounted Rifleman." *United Service Magazine* (September 1890).
————, Viscount. "The Recent Rebellion in North West Canada." *Nineteenth Century* (August 1885).
————. "Newspaper Correspondents in the Field." *Nineteenth Century* (March 1880).
Middleton, F. D. "Suppression of Rebellion in the North-West Territories of Canada, 1885." *United Service Magazine* (January 1894).
Stanley, G. F. G., ed. "The Campaign of 1885: A Contemporary Account." *Saskatchewan History* (Winter, 1960).
Underhill, F. H. "Lord Minto on his Governor Generalship." *Canadian Historical Review* (June 1959).

6. Pamphlets

Aitken, Samuel. *The Case of the Associated Board.* Toronto, March 29, 1899.
Asselin, Olivar. *Sir Wilfrid Laurier* (n.d., n.p.). First published in *L'Ame Française*, Paris, mars, 1919.
Bourassa, Henri. *Grand Bretagne et Canada.* Montreal, 1901.
Bryce, R. J. *Practical Suggestions for Reforming the Educational Institutions of Scotland.* Edinburgh, 1852.
Canadian Protest against the Introduction into Canada of Musical Examinations by Outside Musical Examining Bodies. Toronto, March 1899.
Churchman. *Lord Melgund and the Parish Schools.* Edinburgh, 1849.
Cook, John. *Remarks on Lord Melgund's Bill and the Means of Education in Scotland.* Edinburgh, 1851.

Ginsberg, Morris. Nationalism: A Reappraisal. Leeds University Press, 1963.
Jackson, Louis. Our Caughnawagas in Egypt. Montreal, 1885.
MacNaughton, John. Some Personal Impressions of the Late Earl Grey. Montreal, 1926.
Mason, James. The North-West Rebellion of 1885 (reprint, n.d., n.p.).
Minto [3rd Earl], William Hugh Elliot. Game Salmon, and Poachers. Edinburgh, 1863.
————. Remarks on the Government Scheme of National Education as Applied to Scotland. Edinburgh, 1848.
Palliser, Captain Edward (Late 7th Hussars). Report to Viscount Melgund Military Secretary on a Government Gun Factory at Quebec. Army and Navy Club, October, 1884.
Shortt, Adam. Imperial Preferential Trade from a Canadian Point of View. Toronto, 1904.
Smith, Goldwin. "Devant le Tribunal de l'histoire" (traduit de l'anglais par Henri Bourassa). Montreal, 1903.
The True Inwardness of the Canadian Northwest Rebellion of 1885 Exposed; or, Who is to Blame? (n.d., n.p.).
Todd, Alpheus. A Constitutional Governor. Ottawa, 1878.
Yarker, Margaret G. Echoes of Empire. Toronto, 1900.

Secondary Sources

1. Books

Adams, W. S. Edwardian Portraits. London, 1957.
Allen, H. C. and C. P. Hill, eds. British Essays in American History. London, 1957.
Amery, Julian. The Life of Joseph Chamberlain. Vol. IV. London, 1951.
Anderson, Major-General E. A. H. Pink & Scarlet or Hunting as a School for Soldiering. London, 1913.
Angers, F.-A., ed. La Pensée de Henri Bourassa. Montréal, 1954.
Annett, Douglas R. British Preference in Canadian Commercial Policy. Toronto, 1948.
Bailey, T. A Diplomatic History of the United States. New York, 1956.
Banks, M.A. Edward Blake, Irish Nationalist: A Canadian Statesman in Irish Politics, 1892-1907. Toronto, 1957.
Begbie, Harold. Albert Fourth Earl Grey: A Last Word. London, 1917.
Berger, Carl. The Sense of Power. Toronto, 1970.
Birch, James H. History of the War in South Africa. Toronto, 1899.
Bissell, C. T., ed. Our Living Tradition. Toronto, 1957.
Bond, C. C. Rideau Hall. Montreal, 1977.
Brebner, J. B. North Atlantic Triangle. Toronto, 1945.
Bridle, Augustus. Sons of Canada. Toronto, 1916.
Briggs, Asa. Victorian People. London, 1954.
Brown, Robert Craig and Ramsay Cook. Canada 1896-1921: A Nation Transformed. Toronto, 1974.
Brown, Robert Craig, and S. F. Wise. Canada Views the United States. Toronto, 1972.

Brown, Robert Craig. *Robert Laird Borden*. Vol. I. Toronto, 1975.
Buchan, John. *Lord Minto: A Memoir*. London, 1925.
Callahan, J. M. *American Foreign Policy in Canadian Relations*. New York, 1937.
Campbell, A. D. *Great Britain and the United States 1895-1903*. London, 1960.
Chadwick, St. John. *Newfoundland Island into Province*. Cambridge, 1967.
Charlesworth, Hector. *The Canadian Scene*. Toronto, 1927.
Colquhoun, A. H. U. *Press, Politics and People*. Toronto, 1935.
Commager, H.S. *The American Mind*. New York, 1950.
Cook, Ramsay. *French-Canadian Nationalism*. Toronto, 1969.
————. *The Politics of John W. Dafoe and the Free Press*. Toronto, 1963.
Cooper, John Irwin. *The History of the Montreal Hunt*. Montreal, 1953.
Cowan, J. *Canada's Governors-General, 1867-1952*. Toronto, 1952.
Creighton, Donald. *John A. Macdonald: The Old Chieftain*. Toronto, 1955.
Dafoe, John W. *Clifford Sifton in Relation to His Times*. Toronto, 1931.
————. *Laurier: A Study in Canadian Politics*. Toronto, 1963.
Dangerfield, George. *The Strange Death of Liberal England*. New York, 1935.
Das, M. N. *India Under Morley and Minto*. London, 1964.
David, Laurent Oliver. *Laurier: Sa vie, ses oeuvres*. Beauceville, 1919.
Davidson, W. McCartney. *Riel*. Calgary, 1942.
Dawson, R. MacGregor. *William Lyon Mackenzie King: A Political Biography, 1874-1923*. Toronto, 1958.
D'Egville, Howard. *Imperial Defence and Closer Union*. London, 1913.
Dennis, A. L. P. *Adventures in American Diplomacy, 1896-1906*. New York, 1928.
Duguid, Fortesque. *Official History of the Canadian Forces in the Great War 1914-1919*. Ottawa, 1938.
Duncan, Sara Jeannette. *The Imperialist*. Toronto, 1968.
Evans, Sanford W. *The Canadian Contingents and Canadian Imperialism*. Toronto, 1901.
Ewart, J. S. *The Kingdom of Canada*. Toronto, 1908.
Farr, David M. L. *The Colonial Office and Canada, 1867-1887*. Toronto, 1955.
Feiling, Keith. *A History of England*. London, 1952.
Fergusson, C. B. *Hon. W. S. Fielding*. 2 vols. Windsor, 1970.
Ferguson, John H. *American Diplomacy and the Boer War*. Philadelphia, 1939.
Fisher, Sydney. *Canada, Its History, Productions and Natural Resources*. Ottawa, 1905.
Forrest, D. W. and Dr. John Brown, eds. *Letters of Dr. John Brown*. London, 1907.
Gardiner, A. G. *The Life of Sir William Harcourt*. Vol. II. London, 1923.
Garraty, John A. *Henry Cabot Lodge*. New York, 1953.
Garvin, J. L. *The Life of Joseph Chamberlain*. London, 1934.
Glazebrook, G. P. de T. *A History of Canadian External Relations*. 2 vols. Toronto, 1966.
Goldman, Charles Sydney, ed. *The Empire and the Century*. London, 1905.
Gollin, Alfred. *Balfour's Burden*. London, 1965.
Goodwin, Michael. *Nineteenth Century Opinion*. London, 1951.
Gordon, Donald C. *The Dominion Partnership in Imperial Defense, 1870-1914*. Baltimore, 1965.
Gordon, Donald C. *The Moment of Power*. New Jersey, 1970.
Graham, Gerald S. *Empire of the North Atlantic*. Toronto, 1950.
Gravel, Jean-Yves. *Le Québec et la guerre*. Montreal, 1974.

Grierson, J. M. Records of the Scottish Volunteer Force, 1859-1908. Edinburgh, 1909.
Hamilton, Ian. The Happy Warrior (A Life of General Sir Ian Hamilton by his Nephew). London, 1967.
Hamilton, William B., ed. The Transfer of Institutions. Durham, North Carolina, 1964.
Hansen, M. L. and J. B. Brebner. The Mingling of the Canadian and American Peoples. Toronto, 1944.
Higham, John. Strangers in the Land. New Brunswick, New Jersey, 1955.
Hollis, Christopher. Eton: A History. London, 1960.
Howard, Joseph Kinsey. Strange Empire. Toronto, 1952.
Howard, Michael, ed. The Theory and Practice of War. London, 1965.
Howay, F. W., W. N. Sage, and H. F. Angus. British Columbia and the United States: The North Pacific Slope from Fur Trade to Aviation. Toronto, 1942.
Hubbard, R. H. Rideau Hall. Ottawa, 1967.
Hughes, T. Tom Brown's School Days. New York, 1885.
Jebb, Richard. Studies in Colonial Nationalism. London, 1905.
Johnston, Franklyn A. Defence by Committee. London, 1960.
Jones, W. D. Lord Derby and Victorian Conservatism. Oxford, 1956.
Keenleyside, H. L. Canada and the United States. New York, 1952.
Kendle, John. The Round Table Movement and Imperial Union. Toronto, 1975.
Kennedy, W. P. W. The Constitution of Canada 1534-1937. London, 1938.
Kruger, Rayne. Good-bye Dolly Gray. London, 1961.
Lee, Sidney. King Edward VII: A Biography. 2 vols. London, 1927.
Leggo, William. History of the Administration of the Earl of Dufferin. Montreal, 1878.
Lemieux, L. J. The Governors-General of Canada, 1608-1931. Ottawa, 1931.
Luvaas, Jay. The Military Legacy of the Civil War: The European Inheritance. Chicago, 1959.
MacDermot, H. E. Sir Thomas Roddick: His Work in Medicine and Public Life. Toronto, 1938.
Mack, Edward C. Public Schools and British Opinion. London, 1938.
MacKinnon, Frank. The Crown in Canada. Toronto, 1976.
MacMillan, Cyrus. McGill and Its Story 1821-1921. London, 1921.
McArthur, Peter. Sir Wilfrid Laurier. Toronto, 1919.
McDougall, Robert L. Canada's Past and Present: A Dialogue. Toronto, 1965.
Magnus, Philip. Kitchener: Portrait of an Imperialist. London, 1961.
Marshall, Herbert, F. A. Southard, and K. W. Taylor. Canadian American Industry. New Haven, 1936.
Miller, J. D. B. Richard Jebb and the Problem of Empire. London, 1956.
Minto, Mary. India, Minto and Morley 1905-1910. London, 1934.
Minto, Nina. Notes from Minto Manuscripts. Edinburgh, 1862.
Moore, R. J. Liberalism and Indian Politics 1872-1922. London, 1966.
Moreau, H. Sir Wilfrid Laurier. Paris, 1902.
Morrison, David. The Politics of the Yukon Territory, 1898-1909. Toronto, 1968.
Morton, Desmond. The Canadian General Sir William Otter. Toronto, 1974.
————. The Last War Drum: The North-West Campaign of 1885. Toronto, 1975.
————. Ministers and Generals: Politics and the Canadian Militia, 1865-1904. Toronto, 1970.
Morton, W. L. Achilles' Shield. Toronto, 1968.
Mowat, R. B. The Life of Lord Pauncefote. London, 1929.

Mulvaney, C. P. The History of the Northwest Rebellion. Toronto, 1885.
Nadel, George H. and Perry Curtis. Imperialism and Colonialism. New York, 1964.
Neale, R. G. Great Britain and United States Expansion: 1898-1900. East Lansing, 1966.
Needler, G. H. Louis Riel. Toronto, 1951.
Neuendorff, Gwen. Studies in the Evolution of Dominion Status: The Governor-Generalship of Canada and the Development of Canadian Nationalism. London, 1942.
Nevins, Allan. Henry White: Thirty Years of American Diplomacy. New York, 1930.
Newton, Lord. Lord Lansdowne: A Biography. London, 1929.
Norwood, Cyril, and Arthur H. Hope. The Higher Education of Boys in England. London, 1909.
Notman, W. The Governors-General and Their Wives. Montreal, 1907.
Penlington, Norman. The Alaska Boundary Dispute: A Critical Reappraisal. Toronto, 1972.
_____ . Canada and Imperialism 1896-1899. Toronto, 1965.
Pope, Joseph. The Tour of Their Royal Highnesses the Duke and Duchess of Cornwall and York. Ottawa, 1903.
Porter, McKenzie. To All Men. Toronto, 1960.
Pratt, Julius W. Expansionists of 1898. Chicago, 1964.
Price, Richard. An Imperial War and the British Working Class. Toronto, 1972.
Preston, Richard A. Canada and "Imperial Defense." Durham, 1967.
Preston, W. T. R. The Life and Times of Lord Strathcona. Toronto, n.d.
Rumilly, Robert. Histoire de la Province de Québec. Vol. IX. Montreal, 1942.
Ryan, William F. The Clergy and Economic Growth in Quebec 1896-1914. Quebec, 1966.
Saunders, E. M. The Life and Letters of the Rt. Hon. Sir Charles Tupper, Bart., K.C.M.G. 2 vols. London, 1916.
Saywell, John T. The Office of Lieutenant Governor. Toronto, 1957.
Schull, Joseph. Laurier: The First Canadian. Toronto, 1965.
Semmel, Bernard. Imperialism and Social Reform. London, 1960.
Shortt, S. E. D. Conviction in an Age of Transition. Toronto, 1976.
Siegfried, Andre. The Race Question in Canada. Toronto, 1966.
Skelton, Oscar Douglas. Life and Letters of Sir Wilfrid Laurier. 2 vols. Toronto, 1965.
Smith, Goldwin. Canada and the Canadian Question. Toronto, 1891.
Smith, Janet Adam. John Buchan. London, 1965.
Stacey, C. P. The Military Problems of Canada. Toronto, 1940.
_____ . The Nile Expedition. Toronto, 1959.
Stanley, George F. C. Canada's Soldiers, 1604-1959. Toronto, 1960.
_____ . Louis Riel. Toronto, 1965.
Strachey, Lytton. Eminent Victorians. London, 1948.
Tansill, Charles Callan. Canadian American Relations, 1875-1911. New Haven, 1943.
Tawney, R. H. The Radical Tradition. Harmondsworth, 1964.
Thayer, W. R. Theodore Roosevelt. Boston, 1919.
Thistlethwaite, Frank. The Great Experiment. Cambridge, 1955.
Thompson, F. M. L. English Landed Society in the Nineteenth Century. Toronto, 1963.
Thorburn, Hugh. Party Politics in Canada. Scarborough, 1967.
Thornton, A. P. Doctrines of Imperialism. New York, 1965.

_____ . The Habit of Authority. London, 1966.
Todd, Alpheus. Parliamentary Government in the British Colonies. Boston, 1880.
Venn, J. A., compiler. Alumni Cantabrigienses. Part II, Vol. IV. Cambridge, 1951.
Wade, Mason. The French Canadians, 1760-1945. Toronto, 1956.
Wallace, Stewart. The Growth of Canadian National Feeling. Toronto, 1927.
Warren, Arnold. Wait for the Wagon. Toronto, 1961.
Wasti, Syed Razi. Lord Minto and the Indian Nationalist Movement 1905-1910. Oxford, 1964.
Weens, George Tancred of. The Annals of a Border Club. Edinburgh, 1903.
Whitton, Lieut.-Col. Frederick Ernest, comp. and ed. The History of the Prince of Wales Leinster Regiment. Aldershot, 1924.
Willison, J. S. Sir George Parkin: A Biography. London, 1929.
_____ . Sir Wilfrid Laurier and the Liberal Party. 2 vols. London, 1903.
Willson, Beckles. The Life of Lord Strathcona and Mount Royal. 2 vols. Boston, 1915.
Winks, Robin W., ed. British Imperialism: Gold, God and Glory. New York, 1963.
Wrench, John Evelyn. Alfred Lord Milner: The Man of no Illusions, 1854-1925. London, 1958.

2. Articles

Allen, Richard. "The Social Gospel and the Reform Tradition in Canada, 1890-1928." Canadian Historical Review (December 1968).
Argyle, Duke of. "The Saskatchewan Scare." Fortnightly Review (July, 1886).
Bailey, Thomas A. "Theodore Roosevelt and the Alaskan Boundary Settlement." Canadian Historical Review (June 1937).
Baylen, Joseph O. "W. T. Stead and the Boer War: The Irony of Idealism." Canadian Historical Review (December 1959).
Bond, Brian. "The Territorial Army in Peace and War." History Today (March, 1966).
Brown, R. Craig. "Goldwin Smith and Anti-Imperialism." Canadian Historical Review (June 1962).
Buchan, John. "The Royal Scots (The Royal Regiment)." Journal of the Society for Army Historical Research (Summer, 1933).
Carlyle, Randolph. "Our National Arm." Canadian Magazine (September 1908).
Carmen, Francis A. "The Honourable Richard Cartwright." Canadian Magazine (July 1921).
Chevrier, Bernard. "Le Ministère de Félix-Gabriel Marchand 1897." Revue d'histoire de l'Amérique française (juin 1968).
Clippingdale, Richard T. "J. S. Willison and Canadian Nationalism." Canadian Historical Association Historical Papers (1969).
Cole, Douglas L. "John S. Ewart and Canadian Nationalism." Canadian Historical Association Historical Papers (1969).
Cooper, John A. "Editorial Comment." Canadian Magazine (December 1899).
_____ . "People and Affairs." Canadian Magazine (July 1900).
Corcoran, James I. W. "Henri Bourassa et la guerre sud-africaine." Revue d'histoire de l'Amérique française (janvier, juin, septembre et décembre 1965).
Cosmas, Graham A. "From Order to Chaos: The War Department, the National Guard, and Military Policy, 1898." Military Affairs (Fall, 1965).

Cox, H. "Canada During the Laurier Regime." *Edinburgh Review* (April 1912).

Cox, J. G. Snead. "French Canada and the Empire." *Nineteenth Century* (November 1900).

————. "The Outlook at Ottawa." *Nineteenth Century* (July 1899).

Cross, J. A. "The Colonial Office and the Dominions Before 1914." *Journal of Commonwealth Political Studies* (July 1966).

Drage, Geoffrey. "Imperial Organization from a Business Point of View." *Fortnightly Review* (December 1905).

Dreyer, Fred. "Three Years in the Toronto Garrison." *Ontario History* (March 1965).

Evans, Sanford W. "Empire Day." *Canadian Magazine* (July 1899).

Farr, David Morice. "Lord Dufferin: A Viceroy in Ottawa." *Culture* (March 1958).

Forsey, Eugene. "The Crown and the Constitution." *Dalhousie Review* (Spring, 1953).

Frewen, Moreton. "Memories of Melton Mowbray." *Nineteenth Century and After* (December 1915).

Gibson, F. W. "The Alaskan Boundary Dispute." *Canadian Historical Association Report* (1945).

Gilbey, Walter. "English Horse-Breeding and Army Remounts." *Nineteenth Century* (June 1904).

Gluek, Alvin C. Jr. "Pilgrimages to Ottawa: Canadian -American Diplomacy." *Canadian Historical Association Historical Papers* (1968).

————. "The Passamaquoddy Bay Treaty, 1910: A Diplomatic Sideshow in Canadian-American Relations." *Canadian Historical Review* (March 1966).

Gordon, Donald C. "The Colonial Defence Committee and Imperial Collaboration: 1885-1904." *Political Science Quarterly* (December 1962).

Gordon, Milton. "Assimilation in America: Theory and Reality." *Daedalus* (Spring, 1961).

Graham, G. S. "Imperial Finance, Trade and Communications, 1895-1914." *Cambridge History of the British Empire*. Vol. III. Cambridge, 1959.

Grant, W. L. "Sir Richard Cartwright." *Canadian Magazine* (January 1913).

Gundy, H. Pearson. "Sir Wilfrid Laurier and Lord Minto." *Canadian Historical Association Report* (1952).

Hamilton, C. F. "The Canadian Militia." *Canadian Magazine* (July 1908).

————. "The Canadian Militia: The Beginning of Reform." *Canadian Defence Quarterly* (April 1930).

————. "The Canadian Militia: The Dead Period." *Canadian Defence Quarterly* (October 1929).

————. "The Canadian Militia: The South African War." *Canadian Defence Quarterly* (July 1930).

Harnetty, Peter. "The Imperialism of Free Trade: Lancashire and the Indian Cotton Duties, 1859-1862." *Economic History Review* (August 1965).

Hart, H. McB. "Mid-Victorian Hawick." *Hawick Archaeological Society Transactions* (1960).

Heroux, Omer. "Lord Minto et M. Laurier." *Le Devoir*, 19 décembre, 1924.

————. "M. David, M. Laurier et Lord Minto." *Le Devoir*, décembre 1, 1924.

Horowitz, Gad. "Conservatism, Liberalism and Socialism in Canada: An Interpretation." *Canadian Journal of Economics and Political Science* (May 1966).

Hurd, Archibald S. "The Foreign Invasion of Canada." Fortnightly Review (November 1902).
Jebb, Richard. "Twelve Months of Imperial Evolution." Proceedings of the Royal Colonial Institute XXXIX (1907-08).
Koebner, Richard. "The Concept of Economic Imperialism." Economic History Review II/1 (1949).
Kubicek, Robert. "Joseph Chamberlain, the Treasury and Imperial Development 1895-1903." Canadian Historical Association Report (1965).
Landon, Fred. "A Canadian Cabinet Episode of 1897." Proceedings and Transactions of the Royal Society of Canada XXXII (1938).
LaPierre, Laurier L. "Joseph Israël Tarte and the McGreevy-Langevin Scandal." Canadian Historical Association Report (1961).
————. "Joseph Israël Tarte: Relations Between the French-Canadian Episcopacy and a French-Canadian Politician, 1874-1896." Canadian Catholic Historical Association Report (1958).
Lefroy, A. H. F. "British Hopes and British Dangers." Canadian Magazine (May 1893).
Levitt, Joseph. "La perspective nationaliste d'Henri Bourassa 1896-1914." Revue d'histoire de l'Amérique française (mars 1969).
Lewis, John. "The Future of Imperialism." Canadian Magazine (July 1900).
Lighthall, W. D. "The Governor-Generalship." Canadian Magazine (February 1907).
"Lord Minto's Viceroyalty." Edinburgh Review (October 1910).
Lyttleton, Edward. "Athletics in Public Schools." Nineteenth Century (January 1880).
MacDonald, Norbert. "Seattle, Vancouver and the Klondike." Canadian Historical Review (September 1968).
Machray, Robert. "The Granary of the Empire." Nineteenth Century (August 1903).
MacLean, Guy. "The Canadian Offer of Troops for Hong Kong." Canadian Historical Review (December 1957).
Madden, A. F. "Changing Attitudes and Widening Responsibilities, 1895-1914." Cambridge History of the British Empire. Vol. III. Cambridge, 1959.
Martin, G. E. D. "Was There a British Empire?" Historical Journal XV/3 (1972).
Matthews, C. A. "Canadian Celebrities Hon. Frederick William Borden, Minister of Militia." Canadian Magazine (March 1900).
"The Militia Council." Canadian Magazine (May 1905).
Miller, Carman. "Lord Melgund and the North-West Campaign of 1885." Saskatchewan History (Autumn, 1969).
————. "Sir Frederick William Borden and Military Reform, 1896-1911." Canadian Historical Review (September 1969).
————. "English-Canadian Opposition to the South African War." Canadian Historical Review (December 1974).
Mills, David, "The Nicaragua Canal and the Clayton-Bulwer Treaty." Canadian Magazine (March and April 1899).
Morrow, F. St. John. "The Marquis of Lansdowne." Fortnightly Review (July 1905).
Morton, W. L. "The Meaning of Monarchy in Confederation." Transactions of the Royal Society of Canada I, Section IV (June 1963).
Muller, Dorothea R. "Josiah Strong and American Nationalism: A Reevaluation." Journal of American History (December 1966).
Munro, John A. "Ontario's Response to the Alaska Boundary Decision, 1903." Ontario History (December 1965).

Neary, Peter. "Grey, Bryce, and the Settlement of Canadian-American Differences, 1905-1911." *Canadian Historical Review* (December 1968).
Neatby, H. Blair. "Laurier and Imperialism." *Canadian Historical Association Report* (1955).
"Our Food Supplies and Imperial Preference." *Edinburgh Review* (October 1910).
Page, Robert J. D. "Canada and the Imperial Idea in the Boer War Years." *Journal of Canadian Studies* (February 1970).
Patterson, Norman. "The Canadian Contingent." *Canadian Magazine* (December 1899).
Peacock, W. T. "Early Stocking-Makers and Their Industry." *Hawick Archaeological Society Transactions* (1960).
Pelletier, Jean-Guy. "La Presse Canadienne-Française et la Guerre des Boers." *Recherches Sociographiques* (décembre 1963).
Penlington, Norman. "General Hutton and the Problem of Military Imperialism in Canada, 1898-1900." *Canadian Historical Review* (1943).
Perry, Warren. "Military Reforms of General Sir Edward Hutton in New South Wales, 1893-96." *Australian Quarterly* (December 1956).
A Political Onlooker. "The Functions of a Governor-General." *Canadian Magazine* (June 1900).
A Political Onlooker. "The Issues of the General Election." *Canadian Magazine* (April 1900).
Pollock, Frederick. "Imperial Organization." *Proceedings of the Royal Colonial Institute* XXXVI (1904-05).
"Preferential Trade." *National Review* (April 1904).
"Preferential Trade and Empire." *National Review* (May 1904).
Pollock, Frederick. "Imperialism and Canadian Opinion." *Nineteenth Century* (December 1905).
Ranson, Edward. "Nelson A. Miles as Commanding General, 1895-1903." *Military Affairs* (Winter 1965-66).
"Reciprocity, Tariff Reform and Mr. Taft." *Edinburgh Review* (October 1911).
"A Regrettable Incident in Canada." *National Review* (July 1904).
Roberts, Paul Ernest. "Elliot, Gilbert John Murray Kynynmond." *The Dictionary of National Biography 1912-1921*. London, 1927.
Russell, B. "Recollections of W. S. Fielding." *Dalhousie Review* (Spring, 1929).
S. "Current Events." *Queen's Quarterly* (July 1902).
Savage, D. C. "Scottish Politics, 1885-6." *Scottish Historical Review* XL.
Schneider, Fred D. "Laurier and Canada's Two Nations." *South Atlantic Quarterly* (Autumn, 1962).
Scott, W. L. "Sir Richard Scott, 1825-1913." *Canadian Catholic Historical Association Report* (1936-37).
Shields, R. A. M. "Imperial Policy and the Ripon Circular of 1895." *Canadian Historical Review* (June 1966).
Stacey, C. P. "Defence." *Canadian Defence Quarterly* (April, 1931).
————. "Canada and the Nile Expedition of 1884-85." *Canadian Historical Review* (December 1952).
————. "John A. Macdonald on Raising Troops in Canada for Imperial Service, 1885." *Canadian Historical Review* (1957).
———— and E. Pye. "Canadian Voyageurs in the Sudan, 1884-1885." *Canadian Army Journal* (October-December 1951).
Stevens, P. D. "Laurier, Aylesworth, and the Decline of the Liberal Party in Ontario." *Canadian Historical Association Historical Papers* (1968).

Stewart, Alice R. "Sir John A. Macdonald and the Imperial Defence Commission of 1879." Canadian Historical Review (June 1954).
Tucker, Albert. "The Issue of Army Reform in the Unionist Government, 1903-05." Historical Journal (March 1966).
Vevier, C. "American Continentalism: An Idea of Expansion, 1845-1910." American Historical Review (January 1960).
Watt, F. W. "The Theme of 'Canada's Century,' 1896-1920." Dalhousie Review (Summer, 1958).
Wells, Samuel F. "British Strategic Withdrawal from the Western Hemisphere." Canadian Historical Review (December 1968).
White, James. "Henry Cabot Lodge and the Alaska Boundary Award." Canadian Historical Review (December 1925).
Wiebe, Robert H. "The House of Morgan and the Executive, 1905-1913." American Historical Review (October 1959).
Wilde, Richard H. "Joseph Chamberlain's Proposal of an Imperial Council in March, 1900." Canadian Historical Review (September 1956).
Wood, William. "In Case of War." Canadian Magazine (June 1898).
W.P.M.K. "The Office of Governor-General in Canada." University of Toronto Law Journal VII/2 (1948).

3. Theses

Barker, Aileen E. "Laurier, French Canada and the Boer War." M.A. thesis, University of British Columbia, 1959.
Brothman, Brien. "The Attitudes of the Quebec Press to American Imperialism: 1895-1903." M.A. thesis, Laval University, 1974.
Colvin, James A. "Sir Wilfrid Laurier and the Imperial Problem, 1896-1906." Ph.D. dissertation, University of London, 1954.
Donald, H. M. "Life of Lord Mound Stephen." Ph.D. dissertation, University of London, 1952.
Greening, W. E. "The Toronto Globe and Canadian Politics, 1890-1902." M.A. thesis, University of Toronto, 1939.
Hallett, Mary E. "The Fourth Earl of Grey as Governor-General of Canada." Ph.D. dissertation, University of London, 1969.
Hill, Robert Andrew. "Robert Sellar and the Huntington Gleaner: The Conscience of Rural Protestant Quebec, 1863-1919." Ph.D. dissertation, McGill University, 1970.
Hyatt, A. M. John. "Arthur Currie: A Military Biography." Ph.D. dissertation, Duke University, 1964.
Kendle, J. E. "The Colonial and Imperial Conferences 1887-1911." Ph.D. dissertation, University of London, 1965.
Neatby, Herbert Blair. "Laurier and a Liberal Quebec." Ph.D. dissertation, University of Toronto, 1955.
LaPierre, Laurier L. "Politics, Race and Religion in French Canada: Joseph Israël Tarte." Ph.D. dissertation, University of Toronto.
Miller, Carman. "The Public Life of Sir Frederick Borden." M.A. thesis, Dalhousie University, 1964.
————. "The Public Career of the Fourth Earl of Minto in Canada." Ph.D. dissertation, University of London, 1970.
MacLean, Guy Robertson. "The Imperial Federation Movement in Canada, 1884-1902." Ph.D. dissertation, Duke University, 1958.
Morton, Desmond. "Authority and Policy in the Canadian Militia 1874-1904." Ph.D. dissertation, University of London, 1968.
Penlington, Norman. "Canada's Entry into the Boer War." M.A. thesis, University of Toronto, 1937.

Stevens, Paul Douglas, "Laurier and the Liberal Party in Ontario." Ph.D. dissertation, University of Toronto, 1966.

Wasti, Syed Razi. "Lord Minto and the Indian Nationalist Movement, with Special Reference to the Political Activities of the Indian Muslims, 1905-1910." Ph.D. dissertation, University of London, 1962.

Index

Index

Aberdeen, John Campbell Gordon (Earl of), 47-48, 55-56, 59, 61, 81, 180, 184
Aberdeen, Ishbel Maria Majoribanks (Lady), 48, 55-56, 57, 59, 61, 88, 180, 184
Admiralty, 54, 81, 83-84, 145-46
Afghan War (2nd), 18
Afghanistan, 19, 30
aide-de-camp, 56
Aitkens, Samuel, 62-64
Alaska Boundary Dispute, 1, 87, 95, 161-67; Canadian protest, 167, 169; Canadian reaction, 129, 169; decision, 168, 169, 193; ratification of Herbert-Hay Treaty, 167; tribunal, 165-67
Allan, Montague, 181
Allan Steamship Line, 28
Alverstone, Richard E. W. (Baron), 168-70
American Embassy (London), 157, 159-60, 168
American presidential election (1904), 58

Anderson, John, 56, 104-106, 116, 138, 148, 163-64, 167
Andrews, C. A. (Capt.), 143
Anglican Cathedral (Quebec), 189
Anson, Henry, 36-37
Arabi-Pasha (Ahmed Arabi), 21
Archives (Dominion), 178
Arctic sovereignty, 190
Army (British), 13, 33, 44, 72, 74-75, 132-33, 135, 142-43, 145, 147-48. See also Regulars
Army Act (British), 72
Arnold-Forster, H. O., 65n, 145-46, 154
Associated Board of Musical Examiners, 62-64
Auditor-General, 67
Australia, 29, 46, 62, 65n, 70, 122, 184
Aylesworth, Allan, 168
Aylmer, Matthew (Col.), 137, 141, 180

Bagehot, Walter, 52
Baker, G. B. (Senator), 151-52

Balfour, Arthur (Earl), 128, 145, 146, 158, 166, 168
Balkans, 17
Banff Hot Springs Hotel, 59
Bank of Montreal, 179
Baptist, 187
Baring, Edward Charles (Baron), 21, 48
Basutoland, 21
Batoche, 32-35
Battleford, 32-33
Bay of Quinte Reserve, 176
Beith, Robert, 109
Bell, Arthur C., 58-59
Berger, Carl, 4
Berlin (Germany), 8
Bernier, Joseph Elzear, 190
Black Week, 107
Blair, Andrew, 162
Blake, Edward, 62
Bloemfontein Conference, 86
Boer War. *See* South African War
Bombay, 18
Bonaparte, Napoléon, 154
Borden, F. W., 65-69, 99, 102, 131, 187, 193; Canadian G.O.C., 140-41; civilian control, 140, 148ff.; and Domville, 66-69; and Dundonald, 148ff.; Esher Report, 148; honorary colonels, 140-41; honours, 182; and Hughes, 70-75; and Hutton, 108ff.; imperial commissions, 137; imperial tariff, 126; military autonomy, 135; Militia Act (Section 79), 82-83, (Amendment of), 143-48; Militia Council, 148ff.; Militia reform, 139ff.; and Minto, 120, 139ff.; Orders and Regulations (para. 68, 69), 142ff.; Queen's Memorial Service, 189; reorganization of Department, 140-41; and Seymour, 77-79; South African War, 92ff.
Borden, R. L., 129
Bourassa, Henri, 106, 122, 127
"Boutellier" incident, 112
Bow River, 173
Boyd, John A., 182
Brandon (Manitoba), 195
Brighton (England), 13
Britain: society, 7, 20, 88, 103-104; and U. S., 156-58, 161. *See also* Cabinet (British)
British Columbia, 92

British Empire Chambers of Commerce Congress (1903), 126
British Empire League, 50, 85
British Intelligence Corps, 73
British North America Act, 52-53, 144
British Museum, 179
Broderick, St. John William (Earl), 46, 48, 143, 145-46
Brown, John, 22
Bruce, Robert, 154
Bryce, Lloyd, 157
Buchan, John, 1-5, 8, 13-14, 46-47, 60, 66
Buchan, Lawrence, 182
Buller, Redvers (Gen.), 30, 65
Burma, 30

Cabinet (British), 97-98, 105, 122, 125, 139, 166, 196
Cabinet (Canadian), 38, 52-53, 62, 65; Alaskan Boundary, 164-65; Alaskan tribunal, 166; and Contingent crisis, 93-94, 98-103, 109; honours, 181; and Hutton crisis, 110-115; imperial preference, 126; Queen's Memorial Service, 187-88
Calcutta, 18
Calgary, 32
Cambridge University, 12-13
Campbell, Colin, 28-29
Canada: defences, 28-29, 131-55; in 1883-86, 24-25; North West, 30; people, 104; and U.S., 28, 156-71. *See also* English Canada and French Canada
Canadian-American Relations, 28, 64, 156-71, 194; Alaskan tribunal, 166-68; Canadian strategy, 161, 163; in 1898, 157-58; Herbert-Hay Treaty, 165-66; I.J.H.C., 161-62; pelagic sealing, 28, 162, 170; public pressures, 162; reciprocity, 128-29, 161. *See also* United States
Canadian Association for the Prevention of Tuberculosis, 190, 194
Canadian Club, 63
Canadian Commission of Defence, 76, 132, 136. *See also* Leach, E. P.
Canadian contingents, 30, 95, 193; debate on, 85-95; 1st contingent, 93, 95, 97-101, 107; 2nd contin-

gent, 103, 107-108; 3rd contingent, 110. See also South African War

Canadian Government, 29-32, 35, 37, 51, 96-97, 104, 107. See also Cabinet

Canadian Landmark Association, 177

Canadian Manufacturers' Association, 126

Canadian Military Gazette, 72

Canadian officers, 30-32, 35; and British Regulars, 75, 132, 137-38, 142-43, 146-48; General Officer Commanding, 140-41; South African veterans, 137, 139;

Canadian Pacific Railway, 180-82, 184

Canadian Pacific Railway strike, 184

Cape Town, 20, 87

Cardwell reforms, 13, 16

Caribbean, 146

Carling, John (Senator), 69

Carlist War, 17, 129

Carlos, Don (Carlos Maria De Los Dolores), 17

Carlyle, Thomas, 15

Caron, A.-P., 27-28, 31-32, 35

Cartwright, Francis Lennox (Capt.), 141

Cartwright, Richard, 62, 64, 129, 142, 162, 169, 170, 189

Catholic Basilica, 189

Catholic School rights, 187

Caughnawaga Reserve, 175

Cavagnari, Louis, 19

Central America, 162

Chamberlain, Austin, 125

Chamberlain, Joseph, 1, 2, 19, 54, 70-75, 80-81, 84, 87, 90-91, 93-94, 137-38, 146, 149, 155, 167-68, 170, 177; Alaska dispute, 163, 166-67; Duke of Cornwall's tour, 184-85; honours, 181, 182; Imperial commissions, 137; Imperial Conference, 124; Imperial Council, 122-23; Imperial preference, 1, 58, 129, 131, 155; Imperial Union, 97, 99, 102, 104-105; and Laurier, 125; Militia reform, 145; and Minto, 2, 48-50, 128-29, 158; October 3rd telegram, 90-91, 93-94; recall of Hutton, 109-17, 120; resignation, 125; and South African War, 86ff.

Charlton, John, 162

Chartered Company, 49, 85

Chatham (New Brunswick), 56

Chevalier, Napoléon, 65, 66

Chicago, 90, 91, 92, 160

Choate, Joseph, 164, 165

Christ Church Anglican Cathedral (Ottawa), 187-89

Churchill, Randolph, 21

Church of England, 187

Church of Scotland, 9, 188

Clan-na-Gael, 41, 184

Clark's Crossing (Saskatchewan), 32-33, 35

Clayton-Bulwer Treaty, 158, 161, 163

Clement, W. H. P., 175

Cleveland, S. Grover, 158

Clouston, Edward, 181

C.M.G., 37, 182

Colonial Conference (1897), 61, 132, 126, 129

Colonial Conference (1902), 124, 135

Colonial Office, 54, 56, 63, 64, 71, 74, 75, 96, 103, 180; Alaska boundary, 163, 165-67; on Alverstone, 169; amendment of Militia Act, 144, 148; Canadian G.O.C., 141; control of militia, 144, 145; Duke of Cornwall's tour, 185; firing of Dundonald, 154; honours, 180; imperial commissions, 137-38; military exchanges, 133; and Minto, 2, 138, 148, 160; para. 68, 69 (Orders and Regulations), 142ff.; ratification of Herbert-Hay Treaty, 167; recall of Hutton, 114-118; relative rank, 142ff.; rewards for Canadian veterans, 138-39; South African War, 84, 92, 104-106

Colonial Secretary. See Chamberlain and Lyttleton

Commander-in-Chief (Canadian Militia), 101, 136, 143, 147

Commercial Union Liberals, 162

Committee of Imperial Defence, 144-48

Committee on the Defences of Canada, 28-29

Connaught, Arthur William Patrick (Duke of), 49

Conservative Party (Canada), 62, 66, 67, 69, 74, 85, 101, 102, 121, 129, 151-52, 154; press, 101, 102, 183, 188

Conservative Party (Britain), 41, 42
Conservative-Unionist Party, 41, 42, 46, 48
Constantinople, 18
Cornwall and York (George V), Duke of, 56, 132, 160, 164, 181-86; tour: conflict, 184-86; criticism, 185-86; organization, 184-85; origin, 184; purpose, 183-84
Costain, Thomas (Capt.), 27, 47
Cotton, W. H. (Col.), 180
Crew, Robert Offlay Ashburton (Baron), 58
Cuba, 158
Curzon, George Nathaniel (Lord), 48, 183

Dafoe, J. W., 2, 80, 183
Daily Mail, 108
Danube, 18
David, L.-O., 2, 80, 84, 85
Davies, Louis, 64, 162-65
Davis-Allen, J., 87-89
Dawson (Yukon), 159
Dawson Citizens Committee, 174
Débats, Les, 186
De Blaquere, William (Baron), 183
Deering (Harvest Co.), 128
Denison, Frederick Charles (Col.), 27, 32
Denison, George T., 125
Denison, Septimus, 182
Detroit, 159
Devonshire, Spencer Compton Cavendish (Duke of), 48
De Winton, Francis (Col.), 25
Diamond Jubilee, 124, 159, 174, 184
Dilke, Charles W., 19
Dominion College of Music, 63
Domville, James W., 66-69, 79
Dorregaray, don Antonio, 17
Dresden (Germany), 8, 12
Drummond, George (Senator), 122, 123, 177, 181, 182
Drummond, Laurence, 57, 58, 64, 72
Dufferin, Frederick Temple Blackwood (Viscount), 51, 153, 192
Dufferin, Harriot Georgiana (Lady), 30
Dumont, Gabriel, 33
Dundonald, Douglas M. B. H. Cochrane (Earl), 120, 136, 144, 193, 194; appointment, 149; and Borden, 148ff.; firing of, 149ff.; and Militia Act, 144ff.; and Minto, 149ff.; personal quirks, 150, 153; and politics, 150-54
Dyea (Alaska), 165

Eastern Township, 151
Edgar, J. D., 87
Edinburgh Review, 45
Edmonton, 32
Edward VI, 58, 124, 128, 139, 158, 160, 164, 179, 185, 189, 190
Elgin, James Bruce (Earl of), 53
Elliot, Arthur, 7, 8, 10, 12, 18, 36, 42, 48, 85, 89, 126
Elliot, Eileen, 61
Elliot, Fitzwilliam, 10, 14, 16, 22, 30
Elliot, George, 9, 13
Elliot, Gilbert, John Kynynmound. *See* Minto, 4th Earl of
Elliot, Hugh, 16
Elliot, Larry, 60, 61, 64
Elliot, Nina, 9, 10, 11, 12, 15, 17, 19, 22
Elliots, 5. *See also* Minto, 5
Empress of India, 181
English Canada, 28, 106, 112; attitudes to South African War, 87, 89, 96; and Dundonald, 154; imperialism, 87, 89, 91, 121, 123, 182-87; values of, 173, 176-77
English Canadian Press, and British recruitment, 135; on South African War, 92-93, 95
Esher, Reginald Baliol (Viscount), 148-49
Esplanade (Quebec City), 100
Esquimault, 136, 139, 147
Estella (Navarre), 17
Eton, 7, 11, 12

Father Point, 73
farmers, 89
Farrer, Edward, 167
Fashoda, 81, 83
Fenian Raid medal, 142
Fenians, 25, 26, 30, 41, 113, 158
Fielding, W. S., 93, 95, 125, 126, 129, 153, 162, 165, 182, 185, 187, 189
fisheries, 28. *See also* pelagic sealing
Fisher, John (Sir), 81, 82
Fisher, Sydney, 151-54, 189
Fitzpatrick, Charles, 128, 165
Forbes, Archibald, 18

Foreign Office, 165-67, 196
Foster, George Eulas, 67, 68, 122
Foster, Hubert (Lt.-Col.), 64, 67, 114, 137, 140, 141
Foster, John W., 162
France, 81-83, 106
Franco-Prussian War, 16
Freeman, Edward, 15
Freeman, F. D., 179
French Canada, 28, 31, 83; British recruitment, 135; imperialism, 87; imperial preference, 126, 127; Minto's opinions of, 106, 120, 141, 177; and South African War, 92

Galloway, A. (Rev.), 44, 62
Gascoigne, N.Y. (Maj.-Gen.), 66, 67
General Officer Commanding (Militia), 1, 27, 110, 111, 117, 136, 193; a Canadian, 140-41; and Militia Council, 148, 149; re-definition of position, 117, 136, 137, 144, 145, 149
Gibbon, Edward, 15
Girouard, Percy, 141
Gladstone, William Ewart, 9, 19, 20, 25, 40, 41, 46
Gluek, Alvin, 157, 158
Gordon, Charles (Gen.), 27
Governor-General, 26; imperial agent, 104; military secretary, 26, 78; office, 3, 27, 78-79; powers, 52-53; salary and expenses, 55
Graham, Hugh, 92
Graham, J. H. C., 57
Grand National, 14
Grant, G. M. 122
Grassett, Henry James (Lt.-Col.), 32
Great Britain. See Britain
Great Dominion, The, 52, 64
Great Lakes, 30, 77
Grenville, George Leveson Gower (Viscount), 16
Grey, Albert (Earl), 48, 191
Grey, Charles (Gen.), 22
Grey Family, 8
Grey, Mary, 22. See also Lady Minto (4th Earl)
Guards Club, 21
Guise, Arthur, 58
Gundy, H. Pearson, 4, 81, 117

Haddo Club, 56
Haig, H. de H. (Capt.), 32

Halifax (Nova Scotia), 55, 81, 82, 83, 88, 132, 134, 136, 139, 147, 160, 184, 185
Halifax Chronicle, 187, 189
Hamilton (Ontario), 108
Hamilton Herald, 183
Hanover (Germany), 12
Harrington, Charles Augustus (Earl), 30
Hawaii, 158
Hay, John, 157, 158, 163
Hay-Pauncefote Convention, 163
Hendrie, William, 108
Herbert-Hay Treaty, 165-67
Herbert, Ivor (Gen.), 30, 178
Herbert, Michael, 158, 165-68
Herschell, F. H. (Baron), 161
Hexham (Northumberland), 40
Hexham Herald, 41
Hexham Liberal Association, 41
Hicks-Beach, Michael, 124-25
High Commissioner (British), 53
High Commissioner (Canadian), 38, 52, 87
Honours controversy, 179-83
Hopkins, J. Castell, 103, 104
Houghton, C. F. (Lt.-Col.), 34
House of Commons (Britain), 9
House of Commons (Canada), 67, 74, 87
House of Lords, 9, 41, 42, 45, 122
Howe, Joseph, 53
Howland, A. O., 182
Hudson Bay Company, 32
Hughes, James L., 63
Hughes, Sam, 65, 69, 79, 90; and Dundonald, 150-51, 154; and Hutton, 70-75, 117
Hutton, E. T. H. (Maj.-Gen.), 61, 64-67 and Borden, 65-66; civil-military authority, 140; Colonial Office, opinion of, 114, 116; dismissal, 108-17, 119, 120, 136, 153; and Domville, 66-69; French Canadians, 85, 117; and Hughes, 69-75; imperialism, 98, 99; and Minto, 2, 64-66, 85, 100, 102, 103, 106, 107; and Scott, 91-92; and Seymour, 75-79, 132; War Office, opinion of, 65n., 78

immigrants, 47, 158
Imperial Advisory Council, 3, 4, 122
Imperial Federation, 70, 100, 121

Imperial Federation (Defence) Committee, 3
Imperial Federation League, 2, 103
Imperial Government. See Cabinet (British)
Imperialism, 1, 97, 195; Canadian autonomy, 131-33, 156; debate on, 121, 122; decline of, 124; divisive nature of, 120; and English Canadians, 87, 89, 91, 121, 123, 182-87; and French Canadians, 87
Imperial Preferential Tariff, 1, 95, 123-29, 155, 170
India, 18, 19, 147, 161
Indian Advancement Act, 175
Indian Collection, 179
Indian Council, 122
Indian Mutiny, 134
Indians, Plains, 31
Indians, 31, 32, 33, 133, 158, 175-76, 194
Instructions. See Royal Instructions
International Joint High Commission (1898-99), 64, 83, 161-63
Irish Canadians, 25, 26, 89
Irish Catholic, 187
Irish Home Rule, 39, 40, 41, 58
Irwin, De la C. T., 180
Isle of Wight, 12

Jameson Raid, 49
Jersey, Victor Albert (Earl of), 183
Jervois Reports, 29
Jetté, Louis, 168, 182
Johnstone, Hope (Major), 14
Joly de Lotbinière, Henri-Gustave, 177

Kabul (Afghanistan), 19
K.C.M.G., 182
Keith, A. B., 144, 167
Khartoum, 27
Khayl, Ali, 19
Khedive, 21
Kimberley, 85
King-Byng Dispute, 103
Kings County (New Brunswick), 67
Kingsley, Charles, 15
Kings Regulations, 144
Kingston (Ontario), 188
Kitchener, H. H. K. (Viscount), 139
Kitson, Gerald, 64, 74, 108, 109, 119, 120, 137, 141, 164, 180
Klondike, 158

Klondike Nugget, 174
Klondike tour, 58. See also Yukon
Kruger, Paul, 88

Labouchère, Henry, 49, 158
labouring class, 41, 89
lacrosse, 191
Ladysmith, 120, 149
Laird, David, 176
Lake, Percy (Col.), 154
Lambert, J. T., 27
Lansdowne, Henry Charles Keith Petty-Fitzmaurice (Marquess of), 2, 22-28, 31, 35-37, 40, 46-48, 52, 78, 82, 107, 117, 143, 164-68, 176
Lansdowne, Maude Evelyn Hamilton (Lady), 48
Lascelles, W. F. L., 57, 58, 88
Laurie, John Wimburn (Lt.-Gen.), 32
Laurier, Wilfrid, 2-4, 61, 64, 72, 79, 80, 81, 141, 152, 161, 183; Advisory Council, 123; Alaskan boundary, 161, 162, 164, 165, 169; British recruitment, 133, 135; Canadian defence, 132, 151; contingent, 90-91, 97-107; dismissal of Dundonald, 153-54; dismissal of Hutton, 108-17; Duke of Cornwall's tour, 185ff.; English Canada, 95; Herbert-Hay Treaty, 165-66; honours controversy, 179-83; I.J.H.C., 161-62; imperial commissions, 138; imperial conference, 124, 125, 132; imperial preference, 124-29; imperial sentiment, 121, 122, 123; London Conference, 164-65; and Militia Act (Section 79), 83-84; and Minto, 2, 90-91, 94-95, 183; October 3rd telegram, 90-91; Ouitlanders, 87, 88; Plains of Abraham, 178; Queen's Memorial Service, 187-89; reciprocity, 161; repatriation of Royal Canadians, 134; secret agent, 166, 167; South African War, 84ff.; title, 95, 179; war crisis, 92-95
Laval University, 182
Lavergne, Louis, 177
Law Officers of the Crown, 142, 143
Layard, Henry, 18
Leach, E. P., 76, 132, 136
Legislative Council (Quebec), 61
Lennox, Wilbraham, 18

Letellier de Saint-Just, Luc, 112
Letters Patent, 52, 53
Liberal nationalist historians, 80, 96
Liberal Party (Britain), 9, 17
Liberal Party (Canada), 61, 65-67, 69, 89-90, 93, 127, 162, 182-84
Liberal Unionist Party, 40, 42, 48, 85
Lieutenant-Governors, 185
Ligue Nationaliste, La, 127
Limber Magna (Lincolnshire), 14, 15
Lincolnshire, 17
Liverpool (England), 17, 23
Lochgelly Collieries, 43
Lodge, H. C., 157, 158, 166, 167
London (England), 9, 21, 64, 65, 124, 146, 151, 163, 168, 169, 173
London (Ontario), 109
London Conference (1902), 164
London News, 186
Lonsdale, Hugh Cecil Lowther (Earl of), 48
Lorne, John Douglas Sutherland Campbell (Marquess of), 12, 25, 52
Louisburg, 178
Louise, Princess, 25, 49
Lynn Canal (Alaska), 159, 162, 164, 165
Lyons, Richard Bickerton Pemell (Earl of), 16
Lyttleton, Alfred, 145, 147, 148
Lytton, Edward Robert, 18

McCook, J. C., 159
Macdonald, John A., 24-25, 27, 29-32, 38, 47, 62, 82-84, 170, 188
McGee, D'Arcy, 25
McGill University, 120, 182
McGregor, J. D., 175
Machray, Robert, 187
McInnis, Miles, 41
McKinley, William, 157, 158, 160, 163, 184
MacMaster, Donald (Senator), 101
Madhi (Mohammed Ahmed), 27
Mahon, A. T., 158
Majuba Hill, 20
Manitoba, 187
Manitoba Free Press, 183, 187
Manitoba School Settlement, 95
Marconi, Guglielmo, 189, 190
Mariscal, Ignatio, 160
Maritime Provinces, 55
Markham, Alfred, 67-69

Martinique, 81-83
Maude, F. N. (Major), 57, 182, 184, 185
Maunsell, George J., 67-68
Melgund. See Minto (4th Earl)
Métis, 31-34, 37
Mexico, 160
Middleton, F. D. (Maj.-Gen.), 27, 31-35
Midlands Regiment, 32
Miles, Nelson (Gen.), 158
Militia (Canadian), 31, 33, 34, 131, 193; act, 131, 132, 141, 143ff.; British recruitment, 132, 135; and British regulars, 32-34, 75-79, 81, 132-33, 146-48; Canadian contingents, 91, 92, 107; exchanges, 132-33; French Canadians, 81, 83; functions of, 131; General Officer Commanding, 1, 110, 111, 117, 140; Governor-General, 101, 147; Halifax Command, 75-79, 132, 142-43, 147; linked battalions, 132; ministerial control, 140; protocol, 132, 148; reform, 139ff.; Regulations and Orders, 142, 148; relative rank, 147, 148; service in India, 147, War Office, 132, 133
Militia Act, 31, 72, 81, 111, 132, 136, 193; amendments, 141, 143-48; Commander-in-Chief, 110, 111, 117, 140; and Dundonald, 148-49; G.O.C., 140; Orders and Regulations, 142, 148; Section 79, 81-84
Militia Council, 148-49, 154
Militia Department, 27-29; imperial commissions, 137-41; patronage, corruption, 66, 69, 99, 108-17, 137, 145, 151-52; reorganization of, 140-41
Militia, Minister of. See Borden, F. W.
Military Institutes, 89
Military Secretary, 23, 25, 26, 35, 37, 64, 78, 79, 82, 124, 184, 188
Mills, David, 83, 111, 115, 117, 162
Milner, Alfred, 182
miners, 41, 194
Minto, Gilbert Elliot (1st Earl of), 8, 9, 10
Minto, Gilbert Murray (2nd Earl of), 8, 10, 11
Minto, William Hugh (3rd Earl of), 8-11, 22, 23, 35, 36, 42, 44

Minto, Gilbert John Murray-Kynynmound [4th Earl of]:
and Aberdeen, 55-57
Afghanistan, 18, 19
Alverstone, 168-69
Anglo-American rapprochement, 157-59, 170-71; Alaska boundary, 161-67; American society, 157-58; Anglo-Saxon kinship, 158; Herbert-Hay Treaty, 165-67; I.J.H.C., 161-62; pelagic sealing, 170-71; U.S. military, 159; U.S. visits, 158-61
archives, 178
arts and letters, 190
Bernier, 190
Board of Agriculture, 41
Borden, 120, 139ff.
Britain, 20, 158, 172, 179
Canada, 37, 47, 128, 155, 172-73, 179, 192
Canadian-American relations, 157-59, 170, 171
Canadian friends, 30
Canadian Government, 64, 97-99, 108-18, 119-20
Carlist Cause, 17
Chamberlain, 2, 48-50, 128, 129, 159
character, 10-11, 14, 15, 36-37, 44, 57, 59
clubs, 21, 22
Committee on Canadian Defences, 28-29
corruption, 66, 110, 111, 115, 116, 137, 145, 151-52, 174-75
Court, 48, 145
criticism of, 2, 80, 127, 183-88, 193
departure, 192
Deputy Lord Lieutenant, 42
Domville, 68
Dundonald, 149-54
Education, 9-12; Cambridge, 12; Eton, 10-11
Egypt, 21
elevation of, 193
English Canada, 87, 89, 121-22, 176-77
Esher Report, 149
estates, 8, 42-44
family, 8, 15
Fenians, 25, 26, 30, 40-41, 113, 158

Fisher, Sydney, 152
Franco-Prussian War, 16
French Canada, 87, 89, 106, 121, 177
Gladstone, 19, 20, 40, 46
Governor-General: appointment, 38, 39, 46-50; expenses, 55; position, 51-53, 174, 193; powers/duties, 53-57, 101, 136, 194; press comment, 61; staff, 57-59; term, 129
health, 17
history, 177, 178
Hughes, Sam, 71-75
Hutton, 2, 64-65, 92, 99-100, 107-18
Imperialism: Canadian imperial sentiment, 121, 125; Imperial Advisory Council, 122-24; imperial preference, 125-26; opinions of, 2-3, 49, 85, 86-87, 89, 135, 144; sentiment, 121, 125
income, 13, 18, 42-44, 55
India, 19
Indians, 158, 175, 176
Lansdowne, 2, 22-28, 31, 35, 36-37, 46-48
Laurier, 87, 90-91, 93-95
Liberal-Unionist candidate, 40-42
Louisburg, 178
Macdonald, John A., 32, 38, 81-84
Marconi, 189
marriage, 22
Military Secretary (Canada), 23-26, 36-37
Militia (Canada): British recruitment, 82, 130, 132, 135, 145;Canadian G.O.C., 141, 148; civil/military authority, 136, 140; Committee of Imperial Defence, 146-48; exchanges, 132-33; honorary colonels, 140-41; imperial commissions, 137, 138; linked battalions, 133, 134; Militia Act Amendment, 143ff.; Militia Council, 147ff.; Orders and Regulations (para. 68 and 69), 142ff.; redefinition of G.O.C. position, 117, 136-37, 144-49; reforms, 138, 139ff.; relative rank, 132; reorganization of, 139ff.;repatriation of Royal Canadians, 132, 134

on monarchy, 174, 183, 184, 189: Duke of Cornwall's tour, 183-86; honours, 179-83; precedence, 185
museums, 179
music controversy, 62-64
News correspondent and author, 17-18, 45, 47, 48
Nile Voyageurs, 27-28
North West campaign, 31-35
N.W.M.P. Commissionership, 38
physical appearance, 8, 62
Plains of Abraham, 178
Roberts, 19, 20, 21, 22, 40, 73, 74, 131, 138, 139, 141
Roosevelt, 157, 158, 159, 160, 163-67
Russo-Turkish War, 17-18
Scots Fusilier Guards, 13, 14, 15
Seymour, 75-79
Sifton, 174
social/political opinions, 1, 8-10, 13, 17, 19, 20, 46, 85, 158, 173, 174, 179
South Africa, 20-21
South African War: Cabinet crisis, 90-93, 94ff.; Canadian participation, 85; Contingents, 97-98, 104; October 3rd telegram, 90; Ouitlander resolution, 87-88; Section 79, Militia Act, 81-84
sports, 8, 11-13, 30, 190: racing, 12-15, 117
Tarte, 98-99, 104-105, 183
tours, 159, 174-76, 178
tuberculosis, 190
Volunteers, 15-16, 44-45
War Office, 139
Wolseley. See Wolseley
Yukon, 159, 174-75
Minto, Mary Grey (Lady), 25, 27, 30-31, 35, 48, 56, 57, 59, 88, 120, 125, 159, 177, 185
Minto Cup, 45, 191
Miquelon, 81-83
Mohawk Indians, 176
Monarchy, 174, 183, 184, 186, 191, 194
Montreal, 55, 61, 62, 81, 89, 105, 120, 126, 127, 177, 185, 186
Montreal Antiquarian and Numismatic Society, 177
Montreal Caledonian Society, 101
Montreal Hunt Club, 30

Montreal Riot (1900), 120
Montreal Star, 92, 101, 102
Montizambert, C. E. (Lt.-Col.), 32
Morlay, John, 30
Morning Post, 17, 18
Morton, Desmond, 4, 69
Mounted Infantry (Rifles), 16, 18, 21, 107
Mount Stephen, George Stephen (Baron), 30, 47, 48, 52
Mowat, Oliver, 186
Mulock, William, 93, 95, 122, 126, 141, 165, 182, 189
music controversy, 62-64

Nanaimo (B.C.), 56
Napier, William, 47
Nathan, M., 133, 134
National Council of Women, 56
National Patriotic Fund, 108, 194
National Policy, 25
New Brunswick, 66, 67, 68
New South Wales, 64, 73
New York, 36, 88, 90, 91, 159, 160, 173
New York Times, 58
New Zealand, 62, 122, 135
Niagara Falls, 184
Nicholson, William, 145
Nile Expedition, 26-28, 175
Nineteenth Century, 46, 47
Northcote, S. S., 32
North American Review, 157
North West. See Western Canada
North West Field Force, 32
North West Mounted Police, 38, 107, 117, 175, 176, 189
North West Rebellion, 31-35, 47
North West tour, 37
North Victoria, 69
Nova Scotia, 178

Ogilvie, William, 175
Olney, Richard, 157
Omdurman, 57
Ontario, 89, 95
Ophir, S. S., 185
Orton, George (Dr.), 33, 34
Ottawa, 23, 30, 31, 34, 35, 36, 37, 54, 55, 56, 58, 61, 62, 64, 76, 81, 82, 87, 88, 89, 90, 92, 93, 100, 149, 159, 161, 174, 176, 187, 188
Ottawa Citizen, 183
Ottawa-Hull fire (1900), 195

Ottawa *Journal*, 185
Otter, William (Lt.-Col.), 32, 139, 141
Ouitlanders, 85, 87, 88, 97
Oxford University, 19

Pacific Scandal, 153
Palmerston, Henry John Temple (Viscount), 9
Panama, 158
Panet, C. L., 29
Parent, S.-N., 177, 182, 189, 190
Paris, 16, 162
Parkin, George, 52, 64, 120, 122, 125, 139, 151, 186, 193
Parliamentary Government, 2, 52, 153
Parliament Hill, 189
Parsons, Charles (Gen.), 120, 149
Patronage, 66, 110, 111, 115, 116, 137, 145, 151-52, 174-75
Patteson, T. C., 30, 47
Pauncefote, Julian, 159, 161, 163
pelagic sealing, 28, 162, 170
Pelletier, Oscar, 141
Penlington, Norman, 4
Pemberton, Kit, 16
Peterson, William, 120, 177
Philippines, 158
Pickles, Wilfred, 151, 152
Pinault, L.-J., 90, 180
Place de la Concorde, 16
Plains of Abraham, 178
poaching laws, 9
Pope, Joseph, 182, 185, 187
Portland Canal, 164, 169, 170
Portland, William John Arthur Charles (Duke of), 48
Poundmaker, 37, 176
Préfontaine, Raymond, 182
Preston, Richard, 4
Princess Louise Hussars (8th), 66
Protestant clergy, 89
Puerto Rico, 158

Qu'Appelle (Saskatchewan), 31, 32
Quartermaster-General, 154
Quebec Citadel, 55, 99
Quebec (City), 23, 60, 62, 64, 73, 81, 88, 99, 100, 121, 160, 161, 171, 178, 184, 185, 189, 192
Quebec (Province), 95, 98, 99, 104, 106
Quebec Garrison Club, 99, 102
Quebec Literary and Historical Society, 177

Quebec Provincial Secretary, 151
Queen's Regulations, 142
Queen's University, 122

reciprocity, 128, 129, 161
Reconnaissance of the Eastern U.S. Frontier, 76
Recruitment (British), 82, 130, 135, 145
Red Cross, 108
Redmond, John, 58
Red River, 31
Red River Expedition, 27
Regulars (British), 33, 72, 74, 75, 132; and Canadian Militia, 75ff., 81, 132, 142-43, 146-48; exchange, 132; recruitment, 82, 130, 135, 145; reinforcements, 35; return to Canada, 145.
Reid, Whitelaw, 165
Rhodes, Cecil, 49, 50, 85
Rice, P., 27
Richardson, John (Cat), 12, 14, 18
Rideau Cottage, 25
Rideau Hall, 23, 25, 36, 37, 48, 54, 55, 56, 58, 95, 103, 108, 112, 150, 151, 161, 174, 183, 187, 189, 194, 193, 195
Riel, Louis, 31, 37
Rivière-du-Loup, 27
Rivoli, rue de, 16
Roberts, Frederick (Gen.), 19, 20, 21, 22, 40, 73, 74, 132, 138, 139, 141
Rockies, 173
Roosevelt, T. R. 157, 158, 159, 160, 163-167
Root, Elihu, 166
Rosebery, Archibald Philip Primrose (Earl), 11
Rosse, Donovan, 26
Rossland (British Columbia), 59
Rothschild, Nathan Mayer (Baron), 21, 49
Royal Academy of Music, 62
Royal Artillery Academy, 66
Royal Canadians (100th Regiment), 132-34
Royal College of Music, 62
Royal Colonial Institute, 3, 50
Royal Commission of Inquiry into the Militia, 116
Royal Instructions, 52
Royal Military College, 64, 114, 134, 137, 142

Royal Navy. See Admiralty, 29
Royal North West Mounted Police, 189
Royal Rifles (8th), 100
Royal Society of Canada, 190
Roxburgh Mounted Rifles, 16, 18
Roxburghshire, 8, 17, 42
Russell, John (Earl), 53
Russia, 19

Sabbatarians, 184
Salisbury, Robert Arthur Talbot Gascoyne-Cecil (3rd Marquis of), 46, 48
Sarmatian, S. S., 23
Saskatchewan River, 32
Saturday Night, 167
Scots Fusilier Guards, 13, 14, 15
Scotsman, 16, 60
Scott, F. G., 178
Scottish education, 9
Scottish Light Dragoons, 151
Scottish Lowland Brigade, 44
Scottish press, 57
Scott, Richard, 62, 64, 69, 73; and Hutton, 73, 92, 94, 109; and Minto, 91-94, 188-89; Queen's Memorial Service, 187-89; on war, 91, 93, 94
Selborne, William Waldegrave Palmer (Earl of), 146
Senate (Canada), 87
Senate (U.S.), 163, 165
Seymour, William (Gen.), 65, 75-79, 81-84, 90-91, 132, 136
Shaughnessey, Thomas, 181, 182
Sifton, Clifford, 126, 129, 153, 162, 165, 168, 169, 174, 175, 176, 183, 187
Sioux Indians, 176
Skagway (Alaska), 159, 164, 165
Skelton, O. D., 2, 80
Sladen, S. F., 57, 174, 188
Smart, Charles A., 151, 152
Smith, Goldwin, 30, 40, 46
Soldiers' Relief Fund, 108
Soldiers' Wives League, 108
South Africa, 46, 58, 62, 84, 134, 175, 184
South African League, 85, 87
South African War, 1, 3, 57, 65n, 81, 96, 103, 106, 108, 109, 110, 124, 127, 166, 173, 177, 178, 193; anti-war press, 89; Canadian criticism, 121; Canadian participa-tion, 70-75, 84, 86ff.; and Canadian press, 89, 91, 92, 93; Canadian recruitment, 135; Canadian veterans of, 138, 140, 141; effects on Canada, 121, 146; English Canada, 91
Southwell, H. (Rev.), 15, 22
sports, 11-17, 190-91
Stacey, C. P., 4
Standard Life Insurance Company, 18
Stanley, Frederick Arthur (Baron), 180, 189
Steele, S. B., 175
Stevenson, A. A., 101, 102
St. James (Court), 23
St. James' Gazette, 10
St. Jean, 65
Saint John Sun, 67
St. Lawrence River, 60, 192
St. Louis (Missouri), 59
St. Margaret's Church, 22
Stone, F. G., 141, 142, 180
St. Pierre, 81-83
Strange, T. Bland (Lt.-Col.), 32
Strathcona, Donald Smith (Baron), 52, 87, 116, 183, 190
Strathcona Horse, 110
Sudan, 30
Supreme Court of Canada, 160
Sutherland, Cromartie (Duke of), 49
Sutherland, James, 110
Swift Current (Saskatchewan), 32

Tarte, Israël, 91, 92, 93, 94, 98, 99, 103, 104, 105, 106, 109, 126, 128, 162, 183, 189
Tayler, Thomas, 41
Theâtre Nationale française, Le, 127
Thompson, John S. D., 188
Tel-el-Kebir, 21
Times, 16, 18, 47, 169, 186, 193
Todd, Alpheus, 2, 52, 153
Toronto, 55, 67, 89, 93, 134, 145
Toronto Club, 66
Toronto College of Music, 63
Toronto Conservatory of Music, 63
Toronto Globe, 92, 93, 104, 105, 122, 127
Toronto Hunt Club, 30
Toronto News, 126
Toronto Star, 186
Toronto Telegram, 183
Toronto World, 92, 186

Tory. *See* Conservative
Transvaal, 20, 70, 81, 85, 86, 87, 89
Travellers Club, 21
Trinity College, 18
Tunisian, S. S., 192
Tupper, Charles, 38, 62, 87, 121, 122
Turf Club, 21
Turkey, 18
Turner, George, 166, 167

Ultramontane, 99
United Service Magazine, 34, 45, 57
United States, 28, 82, 83, 160; Alaska, 1, 87, 95, 161-63, 166-68; and Balfour, 146; and Britain, 156; and Canada, 28, 128, 156-71; and Chamberlain, 146; Clayton-Bulwer Treaty, 158, 161, 163; Congress, 158; Hay-Pauncefote Convention, 163; Herbert-Hay Treaty, 165; I.J.H.C., 161-62; imperialism, 156-58; military, 159; pelagic sealing, 28, 162, 170
Upper Canada College, 64

Vancouver *World*, 186
Vanity Fair, 55
Van Straubenzie, Bowen (Lt.-Col.), 32
Venezuelan Scare, 158
Venice, 18
Viceroyalty of India, 1, 161
Victoria (British Columbia), 55
Victoria Cross, 74
Victoria, Queen, 37, 48, 49, 52, 121, 160, 174, 184, 186-88, 189
Vince, D. McLeod (Lt.-Col.), 114
Vogt, A. S., 63
volunteers, 15, 16, 44, 45

War Office, 21, 23, 27, 28, 30, 31, 44, 54, 75-79, 81, 90, 92, 95, 97, 98, 107, 111, 114, 196; Canadian

G.O.C., 141; and Canadian Militia, 132-33, 139, 144, 154; imperial commissions, 137; linked battalions, 133, 134; Militia Act amendment, 144; Minto's "two-master" plan, 136; Orders and Regulations (para. 68 and 69), 142ff.; recruitment, 133, 135, 145; Royal Canadian Regiment, 134; Section 79, Militia Act, 81-84
War Office (reconstruction) Committee, 148, 149
Warre, Edward, 11
Washington, 64, 83, 120, 159, 160, 161, 162, 164, 166, 167
Washington Treaty, 28
Wellington, Arthur Wellesley (Duke of), 154
Western Canada, 30, 100, 126, 128, 135, 145, 172, 173, 184
Westinghouse (Electric Corp.), 128
Westminster, 105
Whig, 9
White, Fred, 117
White, Harry, 157, 158, 159, 165, 167
White, William (Lt.-Col.), 69, 114
Williams, Arthur T. H., 32, 33
Willison, John S., 92, 93, 122, 126
Windsor (England), 22
Winnipeg, 30, 173
wireless communication, 189
Wise, Henry Ellison, 32
Wolseley, Garnet, 16, 18, 21, 22, 26, 36, 40, 45, 46, 47, 48, 49, 52, 64, 70, 98, 140
Wood, William, 178
Woolwich, 66

Yukon, 58, 159, 164, 174, 175
Yukon Council, 175

Zulu War, 19